RATIONAL GRIDLOCK

Patrick B. Edgar

University Press of America,® Inc.
Lanham · Boulder · New York · Toronto · Plymouth, UK

Copyright © 2011 by
University Press of America,® Inc.
4501 Forbes Boulevard
Suite 200
Lanham, Maryland 20706
UPA Acquisitions Department (301) 459-3366

Estover Road
Plymouth PL6 7PY
United Kingdom

All rights reserved
Printed in the United States of America
British Library Cataloging in Publication Information Available

Library of Congress Control Number: 2010929162
ISBN: 978-0-7618-5165-3 (paperback : alk. paper)
eISBN: 978-0-7618-5166-0

∞™ The paper used in this publication meets the minimum
requirements of American National Standard for Information
Sciences—Permanence of Paper for Printed Library Materials,
ANSI Z39.48-1992

Table of Contents

List of Figures and Tables	iv
Preface	v
Chapter 1: Public Disconnectedness	1
Chapter 2: Overview of the Rational Model and Its Influence on Administrative Strategies	15
Chapter 3: The Organizational Level	31
Chapter 4: Moving to Outcome-Based Strategies	49
Chapter 5: Locus of Control, Procedures, and Human Service Outcomes	69
Chapter 6: Outcome-Based Models and Public Administration	85
Chapter 7: The Human Sacrifices to Rationalism: The Decay of Community, Responsibility, and Reason	99
Chapter 8: Various Attempts at Reform Within Rationalism	119
Chapter 9: An Emerging Paradigm: Chaos Theory	133
Chapter 10: Applying the New Paradigm	149
Index	165
Biography	168

List of Figures and Tables

Figures

Figure 3.1 Perrow's Task Environment Matrix	39
Figure 3.2 Measure of Stakeholder Climate	42
Figure 3.3 Average Number of Hours of Contact per Day	43
Figure 5.1 Components of Outcome Measurement Management System (CARF)	73
Figure 6.1 Enactment Theology	91
Figure 9.1 The Bifurcation Model	135
Figure 9.2 Fractal	136

Tables

Table 7.1 Anomia Scale	107
Table 9.1 Comparison of Rational and Chaos Theory	137

Preface

Earlier this summer, while watching the confirmation hearings for Justice Sonja Sotomayor, I noted a rather profound discussion. The nominee and a senator appeared to be covering the same ground and were unable to find any common ground. Judge Sotomayor had stated that it was impossible for a judge to approach cases in an objective manner. Rather, the judge should be aware of their biases based on their collection of experiences and do their best to allow for such in reaching decisions. The senator was rather appalled by this position because he believed that a judge must always be objective. He contended that to think otherwise was a violation of the very essence of what it was to be a judge. No matter how many times the judge tried to explain what she was asserting, the senator became even more adamant in his response. What was happening in this instance was a clash of paradigms. The judge was presenting a post-rationalist perspective and the senator was arguing a rationalist one. Since they each operated out of their own paradigm, they were literally speaking two different languages.

This touches upon what I mean by Rational Gridlock. For the past 20 years, I have worked as a consultant for public and non-profit agencies. The projects I undertook ranged from confronting morale issues to measuring citizen satisfaction. Over those years, I became more and more convinced that there was something amiss. It appeared that reasonable people frequently engaged in what did not appear to be reasonable actions. The actors in these cases expressed varying degrees of frustration at trying to accomplish their mission but not being able to make the needed adjustments when they arose. On the one hand, the professionals knew what needed to be done and desired to be problem solvers. On the other hand, they were consistently concerned with not overstepping their bounds. What was it, I asked, that prevented them from taking the kinds of actions they knew they should take? Essentially, what I found was that there was a prevailing sense that maintaining a form of order was more important than solving problems. The structure of the organization was more important than the task itself.

We live in a world in transition. Many of the transitions are elusive to our understanding. On the economic front, the language centers around globalization, while desperately clinging to a belief that we should be able to live as we always had, with the wealthy nations remaining wealthy. On the political scene, we desire more freedoms but resist the idea that other should have similar freedoms or, even more importantly, we cannot abide the reality that greater freedom creates—one in which beliefs and practices beyond our understanding should be able to co-exist with our own. Benjamin Barber speaks of the collision of McWorld and Jihad—one which contradicts itself because there is no apparent way to resolve the competing values. In the sciences, we seem to be capable of more and more amazing feats at the same time we fear the loss of humanism and the rise of a world where our own technological achievements may result in our own demise. We want expanded horizons but not with the loss of traditions. It is this transitional period that overshadows the world of public administration and our very institutional base. In short, we seem disconnected from the future of possibility and the past of certitude.

I begin this discussion with a reflection on this disconnectedness. The difficulties surround the administrative state which interfere with our ability to accomplish the goals of policy at all levels involve the impediments to eliciting the most out of employees, citizens, and leaders. But the undercurrent of this phenomenon rests in the apparent inability of the general public to connect practices with outcomes; to grasp the relationship between the operation of governance and their own well being. This is readily observable in the vitriolic dialogue we can observe in popular media and public discourse itself. The very notion of cause and effect seems to have gone completely awry. This I attribute to our continued faith in Rationalism even though all indications are that this philosophy has really lost its merit. In the second chapter, I review the nature of the Rational Model and Its Influence on Administrative Strategies. I move from a set of models of administrative strategy in the current field to a basic understanding of how rationality is at the base of them all. The discussion then moves to how rationality is tied to our belief in using the bureaucratic ethos for problem solving. This leads to a further discussion of how at the level of organization we hold to a paradigm that is on shaky ground. Chapter 3 then, reflects on the organization level by analyzing administrative strategies within a particular context, with the idea of generalizing the findings. This chapter uses a variety of techniques for guiding us to assess our own task environment, suggesting that there are different ways that we should begin the assessment of management strategy.

In Chapter 4, I move to a preliminary proposal that we need to move to administrative strategies not driven by controlled procedures but those guided solely by desired outcomes. Then I proceed through a very brief history of the field of public administration to show how the rational model has tied everything to process and outcomes have gotten lost over the years. Using one of my own larger consulting projects, I trace out a particular case study in services to the developmentally disabled to demonstrate the relevant dynamics. Chapter 5 identifies what I call, Human Sacrifices to Rationalism – The Decay of Community, Responsibility, and Reason. Reliance on Rationalism has become so universal and unwavering that even when individuals and jurisdictions know what they want they are unable to have any observable impact on the mechanisms of their own governance. This is a matter of focusing on deficiencies, disintegrated interest groups, and an unwillingness to face up to unappealing decisions. Chapter 6 describes various attempts at reform within the rational paradigm. There have been many instances of attempting to overcome Rationalism through empowerment. However, these have also fallen short and resulted in "re-bureaucratization." Recent events have increased the need to move to something completely different. However, they still fail to reject the rational paradigm. This leads me to suggest that there is a need to develop a new paradigm altogether. I grant that this is problematic in itself because it is not certain that changing paradigms is necessarily something we accomplish intentionally. With that in mind, I describe what an emerging paradigm is: chaos or transformational theory. In this, I focus on attacking the very epistemological base of rationalism and then trace different sets of assumptions that lead to different logical development. The elements found in Chaos Theory stemming from the field of physics and other natural sciences are shown to have promise for postulating administrative strategies that will be more successful. Finally, I take the step that is both risky and exciting, applying the paradigm to the field of public administration. The replacement of the old paradigm will have to be carried out in a fashion that will allow disruption and risk. This will facilitate the resulting permutations that are likely to follow, including error. The key is replace a fear of "failure" and re-emphasize the value of learning. The conclusions proceed from the organization level to the individual manager and staff member levels. I then discuss some needed philosophical changes for agencies in general and finally indicate some needed elements at the community level. The true challenge is to unload the Rational security blanket. We have relied on this model to explain our world for some time now and it is not a comfortable thing to let it go. Just the same, it is this act of clinging that is causing greater disruption not the movement to a different manner of thinking. As the events of the current Obama administration seem to show, any effort to change is not going to be met with universal appreciation and the level of fear will surely increased as we proceed. As one adage goes, I never said it would be easy, just worth it.

I genuinely hope that this work will be received in the manner that it is given with a certain amount of humility and a great deal of hope. We can change our manner of operating in this field and, I submit, we must. I do not claim for one second to be any kind of higher authority. Rather, these are the observations of one who has struggled mightily with understanding the practice of public administration. I am one who, as a colleague once described it, considers public administration as a cause for celebration. I also accept the adage passed on to me by Chet Newland that public administration is "a search for reasonableness. I believe we can do better. Whether it is my ideas that make this happen or those of someone else, I am convinced that this is a time of opportunity.

    I remain grateful to those who have instructed me over the years, whether they are professional educators or practitioners. It is only through their willingness to share and impart their wisdom that I have gained anything at all. I am particularly grateful to those who have helped me over the years in my research and professional development. Some of those of particular note include Donald Spencer, former Dean of the Graduate School of the University of Montana, who inspired me to be excited about possibilities and inquiry, Jonathan Tompkins, also of the University of Montana, who patiently mentored me in becoming a professor and researcher, Chester Newland and John Kirlin of the University of Southern California who mentored me in ways they could not know, and Donald Kettner, President of Dawson Community College, who inspired me to take risks and always be willing to grow. I will always be grateful to those who care about me and permit me to keep exploring, especially my own children. They are a source of strength and inspiration, as they put up with me in so many ways.

Patrick Edgar
Magnolia, AR
September 2009

Chapter 1: Public Disconnectedness

At some point, it becomes necessary to announce that the emperor has no clothes. It takes little effort to find discontent in the general public here in the United States. Just take a walk anywhere and observe or sit in among a group of people in a restaurant or other public space and listen. It will not take long before someone is heard complaining about their government, their community, their place of employment, or how much they have to pay in taxes. In fact, it is very difficult to find anyone who is not unhappy about such things. One could argue that this is just a matter of the human condition. Such an argument is extremely difficult to refute or support since we can only compare social conditions within our own life span or rely on writings of earlier periods. We cannot walk among the people of those other times. Nevertheless, I suggest that there is more to it than that. I argue that this is a result of a culture that has placed itself in a very unnatural state. This is more than a matter of casual rumblings. There is a deeper restlessness at work here. I only need point to low voter turnout in our elections to indicate something much more fundamental. While people support the general ideal of democracy, they show little interest in being a part of it. Even though there is much media buzz about a growing sense of a call to public service as a result of the Obama election, the actual numbers are not all that reassuring.

Oddly enough, I am not talking about apathy. I do not believe for one second that the American people are apathetic. There is a passion in these conversations. People are truly interested in what is happening around them. However, they feel powerless to do anything about it. Allow me to offer some suggestions as to the underlying factors to this state of anomie or a sense of not belonging. I specifically speak of the U. S. culture because it stands in contrast to others in so many ways in this regard. Even in comparison to other western cultures, the conditions I describe in the U. S. differ. Europeans frequently express wonder at how Americans react to their own government.

The source of discontent and, in many cases, anomie is directly tied to the Rational administrative state alongside the dynamics of consumerism and juxtaposed with postmodernism. As Alasdair MacIntyre describes in his book, *After Virtue*, we have proceeded into the bureaucratic ethos, wherein our sense of right and wrong is filtered through this technocratic condition.[1] The bureaucratic ethos is not confined to the institutions of government. It goes far beyond that. This ethos has evolved within the culture and through it. This requires a much deeper examination of who we have become as a people. The difficulties surrounding the administrative state, which are interfering with our ability to distinguish right from wrong, exist at all levels of government as well as our lives in community. They involve impediments to eliciting the most out of citizens, employees, and leaders. It is no coincidence that we can only move from one contrived scandal to another. The instruments of government themselves have become helpless in the confines of this ethos. A brief review of some of the more specific conditions may shed some light on how this relates to discontent and anomie. The best way to describe this condition is disconnectedness. I define disconnectedness as the condition wherein the general public perceives itself as separate from its government in the sense that they generally fail to see the connection between themselves and public policy. The very instruments of government, especially the bureaucracy, act in ways seemingly independent of the citizenry. Disconnectedness also describes our relationship to our neighbors, families, and to some extent, ourselves.

The Challenge of Citizen Input—Disconnectedness

The best way to demonstrate disconnectedness is to examine a few examples of some common misconceptions. These show how individuals and groups can operate on a system of logic that defies reason. This is largely a matter of being so determined to advocate for a point of view, sometimes referred to as single issue politics, that the broader picture is often ignored. There is an increasing difficulty connecting choices to consequences. There is an even larger impediment to recognizing our interdependence.

Misconceptions

It is common for citizens to accept assumptions that defy logic. Allow me to provide a few examples. These are just a few of the misconceptions that I have encountered in my work as a consultant. They demonstrate how citizens have become so caught up in individualism and, I might add, wishful thinking that they actually believe ideas that with only a little examination can be seen as false.

Example 1—Renters Don't Pay Property Taxes. This statement is commonly made during public meetings involving the expenditure or increase of property taxes. The point being made typically is that property tax increases should not be put up for a public vote because the renters will automatically vote in favor at the expense of the property owners. It has also been used as an argument by residents in neighborhoods trying to prevent rental properties from being allowed in their area. The facts easily refute this argument. Unless property owners are now registered philanthropists, their tenants are paying the property tax as part of their rent. Landlords frequently use property tax increases to justify increases in rent. If the property tax was not a part of the rent, this would not be a reasonable justification. Certainly, if one understands that landlords rent out their property with the intent to make a profit then one must conclude that the rent includes the property tax. In fact, there is ample evidence that renters are paying the property tax and then some. Landlords tend to calculate the amount considered toward the tax higher than the actual amount they pay. This allows them to protect themselves against any increases in the taxes. It also allows them to increase their profit.

Even in cases of rental agencies, management companies, or housing projects, property tax is part of the calculation that sets the rent. Actually, in the instances of agencies or management companies, it is more likely that property taxes will be overestimated. Such agents seek whatever means they may identify to increase their profits. It is only reasonable to expect agents to behave in this way. The motivation for managing properties is for profit. With respect to housing projects, as a rule the tax is not excused for such properties. Even if the claim is that the tax is subsidized by the government, the truth is that the tax is paid by the renters because the government entity is funded to provide all the other services and space.

The significance of this myth is that it is being used as a point of division between landlords and tenants. By extension, this is a way of dividing the rich from the poor. If individuals accept this as being true then it creates a false set of differences between owners and renters. The likely outcome is that the landowners will attempt to co-opt all the power over the collection and distribution of property taxes. This will necessarily be to the detriment of the renters. If renters accept it as being true they may accept this loss of control and not participate in mill levy elections. There is evidence that this has already begun. Participation in mill levy elections by lower income voters is very low. Since so many public programs that benefit the poor and provide opportunities for their children are supported by property taxes, especially schools, this places a serious impediment on the low income families.

It is very important that this kind of myth not be allowed to go unchallenged. This promotes conflict between people unnecessarily. Since renters and owners both pay property taxes, this is a false division. The continuation of the myth distracts the people from the real issues involved in making local resource allocations. Understanding that everyone pays this tax emphasizes the common interests of the community. However, the argument continues to be used for campaigns and in public meetings. This demonstrates a lack of connection between the citizens and the actual impact of taxation.

Example 2—Not participating in electoral politics or voting means one is apolitical. On many occasions, I have heard people state with a certain degree of pride that they are apolitical. Essentially, they are suggesting that their unwillingness to join in the conduct of elections or other parts of the political process relieves them of any of the stain of politics. Their argument usually involves some declaration of the sorry state of politics. Since all of the politicians are ineffective or even corrupt there is no sense in participating in the process. No politician represents their interests or can measure up to their standards of behavior so they just will not vote for anyone or pay much attention to any of the nonsense associated with politics. By declaring themselves apolitical they absolve themselves of any responsibility for what happens in the public sector.

The fact is that through such inaction, people actually contribute to what they see as the unsatisfactory state of politics that they are so quick to decry. The very act of deciding not to participate is, in fact, *very political*. It actually suggests a latent acceptance of the current political system. This is indeed a very important statement regarding the state of affairs. Democracy as a viable system relies on the participation of the citizenry. When people choose not to participate, they are in effect endorsing a system other than democracy. Their nonparticipation insinuates that they are willing to defer to some other authority to make decisions for them. Even if that is not their intention, it is the outcome. Decisions will be made whether they participate or not.

Elected representatives are not likely to advocate for positions that will not influence their election. Political strategists are well aware of the interests that are represented at the polls. They tend to target groups that are likely to show up on election day. They are sensitive to the fact that certain people in their community do not vote on a regular basis. The more one participates in the system, the more attention they tend to receive from those who organize political campaigns. Furthermore, if campaigners do not hear certain perspectives, they cannot champion them. It is unreasonable to expect that a person who runs for elected office will automatically understand everyone's point of view. It is the responsibility of the voter to make that view known. This is generally carried out through the electoral process. It is relatively easy to dismiss the process as ineffective which is debatable. However, it is certain that the process will not be effective for the person who does not vote.

The general claim of many non-voters is that the political process is controlled by big money. This is in large part true, since it takes a great deal of money to run a political campaign, especially in this day of media politics. Candidates have to rely on those groups or individuals that have substantial resources. However, this works both ways. The groups that have the resources rely on the cooperation of the general public. They cannot expect to have their way if the majority is against their point of view *and willing to act on that opposition.* Most corporations, for example, still must rely on the people to purchase their product or to provide the labor. Thus, they really cannot force some policy upon the people. Of course, the problem has always been getting the people to believe this. On the occasions when the people have unified in opposition, the corporations or other minority interests have not been able to withstand the pressure. The relatively progressive labor laws are an excellent example of this truth. The only reason that we have a minimum wage at all, or child labor laws, or safety standards, is that the workers stood up for them. It is only when the heads of companies and governments convince the people that there is no hope that they prevail. Thus, inaction on the part of the general public is the most effective means for those at the top of the heap to have their way.

It is virtually impossible to be apolitical. The fact that one participates in the markets (shopping in stores), uses public facilities (drives on the streets), or complies with the laws (registering your car) makes them a part of the political system. In order to be apolitical, a person would have to remove themselves completely from society. Any interaction with other people in society is necessarily political. People either endorse the current system or reject it, actively or passively. Certainly, no one would suggest that the action of the Freemen in Montana in the 1990s or Timothy McVeigh was apolitical. While they may have laid claim to being outside the system and rejecting the political system, what they did was quite the contrary. They took very clearly political positions and acted upon them in a very dramatic fashion. Yet, they claimed that they were refusing to participate in the U. S. political process. It is fairly clear that their behaviors brought about quite a reaction. Thus, they actually stimulated the process to act. If their point of view had been a majority point of view and the majority acted on it then the result of their actions would have been very different.

The cold, hard truth is that declarations of being apolitical are nothing more than statements of either irresponsible or ill informed people. I would argue for the latter. The current education system is one that mostly ignores its primary function. The primary function of public education is not to prepare people for the workforce, although that is important. Its primary purpose is to promote civic virtue. The application of the knowledge, skills, and abilities acquired through education is for the betterment of society at large. This is what civic virtue is all about. If we only focus on the technical skills of reading, math, and science we miss the point altogether. Having said this, I do not excuse the non-participants completely. They make a choice that is based on an unwillingness to do otherwise as much as it is derived from ignorance. It is easier to excuse oneself from accepting the burden of learning about the issues, challenging leadership, and acting upon one's beliefs. However, such a choice precludes anyone from complaining about the system. It seems to be the most common thing in the world for the same people to be complainers.

Example 3—Term limits will increase the responsiveness of elected officials to the electorate. The imposition of term limits gained momentum all over the country during the 1980s and 1990s. The sponsors of term limit initiatives sold this strategy as a way of reasserting control over government. The core point of their argument is that incumbents have an unfair advantage over challengers and that the longer one remains in office the less accessible they are to the electorate. The focus of the incumbent becomes the maintenance of power for the sake of power. To correct this, the voters are called upon to limit the number of terms anyone may serve in office. This has been applied to governors, legislators, and mayors. (The courts have overturned term limits on Members of Congress requiring an amendment to the U. S. Constitution. The responses to this ruling have been attempts to have candidates voluntarily sign commitment to limit their own terms.) Once such term limits are imposed, then the elected official will be more responsive to the voters because the lure of increasing power is removed. Thus, reinstating the tradition of citizen government and eliminating professional politicians.

There are many reasons that these arguments are simply not true. The most significant one is that it is based on a false assumption; that the voters are somehow impotent in the face of incumbency. The truth is that the voters have always had the power to remove an incumbent. There has been no reason for voters to continue to re-elect representatives other than f or the voters own desire for an increase in power. Voters were consistently convinced that the more seniority their representative gained, the more influence they would acquire. This would serve the voters' interests very well since it increased the possibility of government programs in their district. Being reasonable themselves, the incumbents use this as a major aspect of their campaigns. They remind the voters of their various chair positions on subcommittees and committees or the value of their overall experience. The incumbent also has the advantage of providing ongoing constituent services. The campaigns also focus on the number of programs, especially those which provide jobs, which were brought into the district or state because of this higher level of influence. Naturally, the greater the influence, the greater is the size of the contributions by the interest groups. One should recall that interest groups are made up of people and have constituencies as well. Thus, the voters have two distinct means available to them to limit the terms of their representatives. They can simply choose to forego all of the advantages of having a senior member or they can encourage their own special interest group to contribute to the challenger's campaign. The imposition of term limits, then, is simply the voters crying "Stop me before I do it again!"

Another misconception involved in term limits is that it returns power to the voter. Actually, it is likely to result in just the opposite. As term limits have taken effect, the turnover in the legislative bodies increased. The high turnover in state legislatures will shift the amount of influence over to those that will necessarily have the greater seniority. This will include the bureaucracy and the lobbyists. The long tenures in state capitols of the non-elected, place them in a position of possessing most of the information needed to make decisions. The level of expertise of institutional memory is severely reduced in legislative bodies that are limited. Consequently, there is a likelihood that mistakes will be repeated and successes not retained. I recall a member of the legislature in one state who had been in the House for forty years. He was the chair of the Appropriations Committee for 26 of those years. Whenever agency personnel had to testify before the committee, they knew full well that they were not going to put one over on him. It was uncanny how he would be able to ask the very question that those testifying hoped he would not. That is the advantage of allowing legislators to be re-elected as many times as they choose to run. His expertise was highly regarded by legislators and bureaucrats alike. It makes no sense to push someone like that away from the legislature.

By way of comparison, under non-limited terms, senior members of Congress and state legislatures have been able to develop equally effective information bases to those of the bureaucrats and lobbyists. A perfect example of this was Senator Sam Nunn of Georgia. He had been on the Armed Services committees so long that he was well aware of the history of the Department of Defense; the previous testimony of defense experts; the personalities of those involved in Defense; and records of defense contractors. This kind of knowledge was not gained overnight. Since Senator Nunn was in the Senate for so long, he stood as a major defender of the general interest in defense policy. Without such seniority available, it would have been all too easy for the Department of Defense, or of even more concern, defense contractors to control the information used in making policy and appropriations decisions. It would also be much easier for those trying to sell armaments to manipulate the information surrounding their technology. The fact that almost all policy areas have increased in complexity like defense is a very compelling argument for not limiting terms.

Limiting terms through initiative or amendment will place an unnecessary constraint on the voters. The decision to remove the voters' ability to send a quality individual to represent them as many times as the voters wish will only serve to strengthen the non-elected. It is an incredible twist of the truth to suggest that the electorate benefits in any way by removing one of its options. Once again, this shows a lack of connection between the voter and government. If the majority did not believe they were not connected to the power of governance, they would not accept this argument.

Example 4—A candidate for office may claim that he or she is not a politician. This is one of my favorite oxymora. I have seen more campaign ads over the last 10 years or so in which the candidate or his/her spokesperson declares that they deserve votes because they are not politicians. This one is almost too easy to dispel. It is incredible that anyone accepts it as true. By the very act of running for office one becomes a politician. Perhaps, what they mean is that they have never held political office. That, however, is a different thing. I realize that by stating the truth in such a way, the candidate is admitting they have no experience. Instead, they want the voter to believe that they are not one of those politicians. The real problem is that it works. So people actually vote for a candidate because they are not politicians. Which either means that the voters do not know what a politician is, or they are willing to elect someone with no experience. No one in the private sector would presume to boast that they are inexperienced. Common sense dictates that there is value in experience, especially for those in leadership roles. This can only be explained by a lack of connection between the election of an individual and the task they are being selected to perform.

These are just a few examples of concepts accepted in the general public which run contrary to logic. More importantly, there is a consistent theme in each of these examples and, by extension, to the phenomenon of disconnectedness in general. In each of these examples, the citizens give away their power in some way. The renters are convinced that they have no say in local schools. Non-voters surrender their choice to others. Term limits take away the ability to have a competent representation before the more well-organized bureaucracies, special interest groups, and corporations. People are convinced that it is preferable to have an inexperienced non-politician in elected office.

As will be described in more detail in Chapter 4, it is not uncommon for the general public to expect the impossible. This is uniquely tied to the idea that there is no connection between policy and real effects. One example is the finding in some of my surveys that respondents both wanted improvements in their neighborhood or consistency (e.g., excluding multi-family housing) while at the same time being against zoning ordinances. Essentially, the two preferences are mutually exclusive. The only way to regulate types of housing or requiring minimum standards of upkeep is to have zoning ordinances. The open-ended comments of respondents clearly demonstrated that this connection was not being made. The respondents were convinced that they could expect the local government to keep things right without using ordinances. The larger concept was that citizens wanted less government but more control over their living conditions. So the connection between the role of government and their desires is not made. I wish I could say that this is rare, but that has not been my experience. The general public sentiment rests in a paradox that calls for reduction in their risk without government intervention.

The essence of the disconnection is that so many people assume that policies can be enacted that have no impact on them. In each of the examples described above, the general public envisions government as something quite separate from themselves. This is particularly demonstrated by the fact that so many people will use the term, the government as a very distinct entity. Since this is a democratic republic, the government is the people in the final analysis. This is more than just patriotic sentiment. There are innumerable examples where the general public has resisted the *status quo* to bring about real change. There are shifts in public policies that are the direct result of an active electorate. The real concern here is that the longer that this concept of the government is allowed to persist, the easier it becomes for those who are not interested in democracy to hold sway.

One of the more common observations in local governments is that most of the resistance to policies is an expression of not in my back yard (NIMBY). However, I suggest that it goes beyond NIMBY. First of all, NIMBY assumes a certain amount of conscious selfishness. It is a very real effort to keep anyone or anything away from their neighborhood. In my discussions with individuals in the communities where I have consulted, I have not found that to be their motivation. They are sincerely concerned about the change in their living environment. The interesting aspect of this is that they seem completely unaware of how their resistance adversely affects others. Their interests are completely separate from anyone else's. Of course, the easier argument would be to blame these reactions on "NIMBYism" and chalk it up to flaws in human character. There are certainly those who are selfish in their intent and some who resist government intervention out of racist or other discriminatory motives. However, I have not found a sufficient number with such motives to conclude that these are the primary explanations. It does not seem to matter what political perspectives people have. Liberal or conservative, there is a tendency to fail to connect preferences for policy to individuals. A far more convincing argument to me is that it is increasingly difficult to connect government actions with individual choice and vice versa. The underlying forces that contribute to this disconnection are many. The following are a few of what I find to be the more important contributing factors.

Excessive Rule-Making or Continuing Bureaucratization

An area of challenge that has been repeated by just about every American citizen is the problem of the bureaucracy. Recently, it seems that every difficulty that we now face or have ever encountered in the past is attributable to the bureaucracy. These problems are described in terms of the immense number of forms and "red tape" involved in dealing with any institution. Critics charge that the bureaucracy stands as a barrier to reasonable solutions. The interesting aspect of this is that "the bureaucracy" is seen as this huge, faceless monolith that consciously or unconsciously interferes with every aspect of our lives.

The vitality of bureaucracies is a source of frustration to so many. The best recent examples of perceived culpability on the part of bureaucracies are the current challenge to the performance of the intelligence agencies in light of the September 11 catastrophe or the failure to respond to Hurricane Katrina. Congressional hearings, cabinet level reforms, and even presidential attention, all seem to be focused on the inability of these bureaucracies to pass on information in a useful manner. The proposal to reorganize these agencies in a manner more conducive to problem solving is the usual response. It is highly unlikely these reforms will have the desired effect. The problem rests in the nature of the ethos and in the organizational cultures, which cannot be changed by reorganization. This will be discussed in further detail in later chapters. The persistence of bureaucracy is found in its processes. The main instrument of control within a bureaucracy is rule-making. If a problem is identified, then the organization must devise a rule that will correct the problem. A lengthy process ensues which, begins by identifying the problem as it has exhibited itself. Once the root cause of the problem is identified, a rule is made to prevent future problems. Once the rule is made, individuals or organizations (those being regulated) begin a process of working around the rules. The bureaucracy responds by making new rules to cover loop holes and the process repeats itself.

Accountability and Performance

There appears to be no sense of accountability on the part of anyone. Multiple levels of decision making are typically offered as a substitute for accountability. It does not matter what level of government one addresses, the same principles seem to take hold. Some call it the runaround others may refer to it as jumping through hoops. In any event, it is virtually the same thing. If there is a problem no one appears willing to claim it until a process has taken place to create a new set of rules or procedures to address it. In addition to the rule-making process, a larger process operates. As things continue to go wrong, more institutions are created to oversee, correct, or displace. This is clearly seen at the federal level. Departments, administrations, and bureaus continue to multiply as problems are addressed. So after rule making fails to yield the desired effect, a new institution is created to resolve the issue. Even recent efforts at privatization are really no more than creating new institutions to provide services. The private organizations still rely on rule-making and structure to carry out the work. This will be discussed in some detail in Chapter 2. In the end, it is rather rare for anyone, elected or appointed, to be held accountable for outcomes. Recent efforts at performance standards in budgeting and control are steps in the right direction. However, these are superimposed on an institutional paradigm that is not designed to focus on performance outcomes. Instead, it will redefine performance outcomes in terms of process and resume its past practice of rule-making. In fact, as will be presented later, the concept of accountability for outcomes is a huge part of the problem. Accountability is in the form of process, not outcomes.

The aggravation associated with the instruments of government (private organizations as well) also rests in the inability to make decisions. There is an apparent resistance to make decisions that matter. On a daily basis, individuals that have regular contact with any bureaucracy find that it is nearly impossible to get a definitive answer. Those within the organizations find themselves in constant meetings which typically result in little or no decision. In my experience, most of the time the only real decision that comes out of a meeting is when to have the next one. This inability to decide is found at all levels from the local office to the national. The decisions that we do see are cosmetic at best. Even when faced with obvious crisis, it seems impossible to make substantive change. I suggest that the current process associated with the creation of the Department of Homeland Security is an excellent example of this. The dramatic response that was suggested was a reorganization of agencies. The problem, as described in hearings associated with the reform, is that the organizational cultures of the agencies in question (FBI, CIA, NSA, etc.) are such that they cannot process information in a manner that gets it to the appropriate people. There is no case, of which I am aware, that reorganization has successfully altered organizational culture. There may be some early enthusiasm but in the long run, agencies tend to return to their bureaucratic practices that impede decision making. In his book, *Inside Bureaucracy,* Anthony Downs describes this process very well.[2] The dynamics of decision making are described in more detail in Chapter 2. At this point, suffice it to say that bureaucracies are not designed to make decisions.

Corruption or Incompetence

As outcomes continue to fall short of expectations, people seek a reason. The usual recourse is to claim corruption. Hardly a day goes by that I do not hear someone carrying on about corruption in government. The term is used rather loosely in most cases, to be truthful. What some consider corruption is nothing more than an office holder following through on campaign promises to donors. As a rule, this is not a matter of voting because of the donation. It is more a matter that the campaigner agrees with the donor's position from the start. Because the person running is willing to support that particular donor's position, they are willing to contribute to a campaign. There are very few instances where a candidate literally extorts the money from potential donors or accepts actual bribes. This is not to suggest that the campaign finance situation is without its troubles because it most certainly has them. The current campaign climate and laws have developed in such a way that money has become overly important. Nonetheless, most of the time campaigns and donors stay within the boundaries of the law. While some corruption does exist, it does not explain declining community identification or perceived failures in governance. When the voters choose to act on a particular issue, it is usual for them to have an impact. The fact is that ordinarily voters do not act and instead complain about a system in which they have chosen not to participate. Corruption is a claim that is mostly wishful thinking again. It is much more convenient to blame others than to take responsibility.

Efficiency, Effectiveness, and Equity

Another persistent complaint is that the public sector is rife with budgetary inefficiencies, or at least it is perceived that they exist. The common perception is that government is inefficient because it wastes resources, lacks common sense, and is not run like a business. A common demonstration of this belief in budgetary inefficiency occurs with local mill levy elections. Voters turn down school levies based on their perception of wasteful spending. Frequently, there may be many reasonable explanations for what they see as wasteful. For example, one common outcome is for the district to have money left at the end of the year, which they either spend or lose. The balance is a result of some good fortune, such as a milder than usual winter. Usually, the money is used for projects or purchases that had been put off. Unfortunately, the voter sees this as wasteful. Even worse, if the local administration decides to return the money to the community, the voters may punish them by voting down the next levy. The logic of the voter is that the initial budget was inflated, having said that it is not unusual for the administration to be its own worst enemy. For example, some jurisdictions will warn the citizens over and over that if their budgets are cut, there will be dire consequences. However, after the cuts are made the administrators manage to make do and use creative measures to maintain services. After repeating this several times, the administration is believed to be crying wolf and then the cuts really do have the detrimental impacts predicted.

There is an almost idolatrous fixation on efficiency. From jurisdiction to jurisdiction, I have observed the same trend. Politicians and voters alike emphasize efficiency in a way that makes it sacred. It becomes the most inviolable value of all. If anyone wants to carry the day in a debate of public programs, they merely have to tie their point to efficiency. There seems to be almost no recognition of any other values that may be relevant. For example, a particular way of delivering services may be more efficient than any other but is totally lacking in effectiveness. The best example of this in recent times is that of welfare reform. The entire premise of the reform was efficiency. It is true that the changes were able to cut the number of cases by more than half. However, it is also true that it had no positive impact on the occasion of poverty. So even though the process was improved dramatically, the intended outcome of public assistance was completely lost.

Government is also perceived as ineffective at all levels, regardless of successes. Many of these criticisms I have found to be gross exaggerations of the truth or bordering on nonsense. Recently, as I was walking in the neighborhood, I noticed a street sweeper at work. A person standing in his driveway greeted me and then said, "there are our tax dollars at work! Look at that waste." I reflected on that for a moment and then pointed out that the sweeper was removing considerable debris from the gutter, this prevents the storm drains from backing up, which in turn, prevents flooding of the basements. This is typical of complaints of waste in government. Time after time, I hear similar criticisms only to observe that the critic fails to see the benefit of the action or even to notice that it is the most efficient way to do something. Of course, there are examples of inefficiency. There are also many cases where things could be done better. That is part of the human experience. However, the constant drumbeat of government waste is a bit exaggerated.

Part of the source of such complaints of inefficiency, waste, and fiduciary irresponsibility is tied to the fact that these are what are more frequently reported. It is extremely unusual for the press to report on bureaucratic successes. Ironically, the reports that come out of the agencies themselves frequently emphasize problems over successes. It is extremely rare for any report to focus on success. This is another symptom of a disconnected society. The media is expected to report on problems. It is believed that the role of the press is to expose the weaknesses of government. That being the case, it sets up a vicious circle. The more publicity problems receive, the more it is believed that there are greater problems to be reported. Journalists work harder to seek out these flaws and report them, which confirms the previous beliefs. Part of this is also related to the non-deferential nature of Americans who constantly criticize their government. It is extremely difficult to pick out where shortcomings end and nitpicking begins. Bureaucracy has come to be a derogatory term in spite of the fact that critics are typically unfamiliar with what the term means. In fact, the concept of bureaucracy is a reflection of modern culture. It is fairly normal for a person to assume a negative connotation when the word bureaucracy is spoken. Most political campaigns feed on this by associating the opponent with bureaucracy or claiming that they will stand up for the citizens against it. As noted above in the budgetary discussion, administrators can frequently be their own worst enemies. The bureaucrats turn to complex justifications which foster technocracy. Technocracy is government by experts which has resulted in convoluted language, procedures, and concepts. This tends to result in citizens and bureaucratic workers alike throwing up their hands in disgust and futility. To defend themselves, government agencies develop more procedures and explanations. As the complexity of structure increases so does the language used. Most importantly, the language used to describe government by its citizens is us versus them. This is most unfortunate in a democracy.

The question, then, is how did we get this way? For a nation which claims the mantle of leading democracy, it should be of great concern. The vision of the founders was of a nation wherein the people were empowered. Throughout our history, we have emphasized the expansion of democracy. While we are still a democratic government, it does not appear that the average citizen feels empowered. Whether real or imagined, there is clear evidence that decisions are made which impact citizens over which they feel little control. People do not connect their choices with outcomes. Citizens vote against their own interests. More and more citizens are not even familiar with the instruments of government. And yet, ironically, we continue to ask for more and more of the same. I offer an explanation for these behaviors and the frustration associated with them. I suggest that the problem lies in the fact that the Rational model has played itself out. Our devotion to linearity is now to our detriment.

In the chapters that follow, I will present what I have found to be the contributing factors to this disconnectedness and related issues. The way I have chosen to support the arguments is to use case studies. Case studies are most effective because they provide an opportunity to analyze many sides of an issue. I have contended for many years that one effective way to reach a genuine understanding of the dynamics of public administration is to use case studies because they keep all the variables within a real context. At the same time, some aggregate data is important to supplement the case studies, or at least the findings of the cases. The cases I use are the results of studies I have personally conducted. This also allows me to retain the context and avoids having to make assumptions regarding someone else's work. As actual cases, they will not necessarily fit precisely within the dimension of disconnectedness being discussed within a specific chapter. Consequently, I will be referring to cases that are developed in other chapters. I have chosen to keep the entire case together because of my preference for leaving variables within their context. The important point is that these are real events and persons. So the conclusions derived allow me to venture outside the larger body of work while remaining within the field of public administrations and the development of ideas over the years. Some of my findings could only have been derived from my personal interaction with key individuals. This is one way that I can both apply some principles of Rationality and refute them. It is in the actual context that it becomes possible to deconstruct the language games and hyper-realities that contribute to our disconnectedness.

---

1. MacIntyre, Alasdair, *After Virtue*, 2nd ed. (Notre Dame: Univ. of Notre Dame, 1984), 86.
2. Downs, Anthony, *Inside Bureaucracy.* (Boston: Little, Brown, 1967), 52-59.

Chapter 2: Overview of the Rational Model and Its Influence on Administrative Strategies

While not an exclusive explanation, I believe that a significant part of the problem of disconnectedness is related to how we organize our public (and to a large degree private) organizations. These organizations represent our value system in terms of how we address public concerns. Administration is not just something that is a concern to those who manage public organizations. Rather, it is the very nature of how we relate to one another in the *civitas* that part of our communities which is ordered in an official capacity. In order to understand what has brought us to the point of disconnectedness and to anticipate some solutions, we must first understand the underlying principles of administration that operate in present day governance. The essential elements of our structure of governance are based in the Rational paradigm. The term paradigm may perhaps be overused in popular literature but it is an important concept. By paradigm, I am referring to the epistemological root to our understanding of everything around us. Sometimes, the term has been used to indicate a model or even an organizational culture. The concept I prefer is the one presented by Thomas Kuhn.[1] The Rational paradigm fits this definition in that it is drawn from the linear way of explaining systems, most notably developed by Isaac Newton.

It is extremely difficult to avoid rationality to support any argument. However, I will do my best through the use of actual cases. This is a way to avoid proffering ideas that are based on linear thinking. By linear thinking, I mean that which relies on direct cause-effect relationships. Many studies rely on this when they show the relationship between two variables, which is easily recognized in the presentation of line graphs. I prefer to use a case study to demonstrate general ideas. By so doing, I believe it makes them easier to grasp. This is not to suggest that I rely exclusively on case studies but that I use them as a tool to "put flesh on the bones." Aggregate data, including that gathered by methods of surveys and public record, are also vital elements to increased understanding. The problem with such empirical methods is that they frequently prevent a clear understanding of the innumerable variables or relationships that come into play. The case study then is a qualitative tool to place the issues into a context. Rationally derived quantitative models are less able to provide this function.

Throughout this book, I draw from the consulting work I have done over the years. These cases have a particular elegance to them in that I entered as a participant-observer while developing models or data collection instruments for the client. I believe that such consulting work is of immense value in the field of public administration. They place the researcher in particular situations that elaborate the many possibilities of interaction. The consultant, if he/she approaches the project appropriately, is able to offer a perspective that is mostly outside the history of the group/organization in question. I approached every consulting project as unique and refused to offer a one-size-fits-all process to my clients. Consequently, I spent many hours researching the situation and interviewing stakeholders prior to ever developing a product in terms of either a research agenda or strategic plans. Most importantly, every single project was a learning experience.

One particular case I use here is the research I did for the Montana Institute on disAbilities to which I will refer frequently in this chapter. The institute had requested an analysis of administrative strategies for services to the developmentally disabled in the state. Their concern was that there were many proposals being bandied about for administering these services. Yet, there seemed to be little research available on the subject. Thus, they requested that a broad study be conducted to assess what strategies would be most appropriate. As this project proceeded, it became clear that the information required was related to the current state of administrative strategies in general. It became evident that something was going on that placed considerable strain on administrative bodies. That something, I suggest, is the building pressure for a paradigmatic shift.

Models of Administrative Strategy/Design

The first order of business is to establish a framework under which we can understand some of the more common administrative strategies/designs. While administrative forms may seem rather straightforward and matters of common knowledge, there are important principles at work that offer very important insights. Before we can attempt to analyze what formats are appropriate, we must understand these basic models as we find them in the country today. These forms are, by no means, exhaustive. Rather these are very general models. There are a great many variations in use today that combine elements of each of these.

Bureaucratic

This is perhaps the most misunderstood form of all. Typically, an incongruity occurs whenever the word bureaucracy is mentioned, people will show immediate recognition of what one is especially with respect to all of its drawbacks. The bureaucratic form has become somewhat demonized in recent years. Yet, on further examination, it becomes apparent that people do not know what a bureaucracy is or its fundamental principles. They will tend to automatically equate it to large government organizations that are inefficient and elusive to control. The fact is that bureaucracy is neither unique to government nor is it necessarily large. Its primary value is efficiency and it is very much under control because it is entirely rule-driven. The most thorough description of bureaucracy was developed by the German sociologist, Max Weber.[2] He correctly describes it as a rational system. Bureaucracies are designed to remove the human element from the administrative process. The emphasis on structure is no accident. In order to be rational, it must draw its dynamics from direct cause-effect relationships. In other words, every time there is a problem, a rule must be created to correct it. It is designed for efficiency because it constantly seeks the one best way to do anything. Once that way is

---

Weber's Characteristics of Bureaucracy

- *The principle of office hierarchy and of level of graded authority mean a firmly ordered system of super- and subordination in which there is a supervision of the lower offices by the higher ones.*

- *The management of the modern office is based upon written documents (the files), which are preserved in their original or draft form.*

- *Office management, at all specialized office management and such management is distinctly modern usually presupposes thorough and expert training.*

- *When the office is fully developed, official activity demands the full working capacity, irrespective of the fact that his obligatory time in the bureau may be firmly delimited.*

- *The management of the office follows general rules, which are more or less stable, more or less exhaustive, and which can be learned.*

---

found it is applied throughout the organization. Bureaucracy is *the industrial organization*. It is designed to behave like a machine of sorts because it emulates rational principles, which is the core of rationality, i.e., a mechanistic view of the world. The idea of hierarchy is not unique to a bureaucracy but finds its purest form in it. A hierarchy is not viewed as necessary by an administrative body because it serves some ruling class or exerts control over citizens. It is viewed as necessary because it reduces uncertainty. This is what Jacob Bronowski asserts is the purpose of science, therefore tying it directly to rationality.[3] There is no doubt about who is in charge. There are clear lines of responsibility as shown by the icon of bureaucracy -- the pyramid organization chart. To be certain that the human element is minimized, everything must be operated by rules and must be in writing. Theoretically, if a person in the organization should be removed by dismissal, resignation, or even death the organization will continue to function without a hitch because it is made up of positions not people. Another person merely steps in and follows the written rules and answers to the person occupying the position immediately above theirs and supervises those below. (Incidentally, that is why all reports and forms are in triplicateSone for the level above, one for the level below, and one for the files.)

Bearing the concept of rationality in mind helps us to understand a bureaucracy a bit better. The strength of a bureaucracy turns out also to be its weakness. Its strength is primarily in the fact that it is stable. No matter what occurs, the organization will likely remain intact. It also draws its strength from the fact that it is designed to minimize the impact of human non-rationality. The fact that it is slow to change keeps it from making drastic changes as a result of some popular movement. Say what one might, the bureaucracy is consistent and strong. Its stability is also what allows it to search for efficiency. Efficiency is merely performing functions with the least expenditure of energy and the bureaucracy is certainly adept at not expending energy unnecessarily, other than the excessive use of energy to preserve itself. The challenge to efficiency is not the bureaucratic structure but the people who occupy it. If the provisions of the model are followed, it will find efficiency.

These strengths are also glaring weaknesses. The inability to be flexible because it must preserve itself prevents the organization from responding well to crises or to identify policies or procedures that might be completely outside its present understanding of the world or *paradigm*. Ironically, its own efficiency drive causes it to spend way too much effort preserving itself and its procedures. Consequently, rules build upon rules as it seeks to correct every error that is discovered. Thus, bureaucracies seek safety and predictability above all other things. This, we will see later, is part of what drives government institutions. Finally, as bureaucracies seek to cover every eventuality with rules it also creates bureaus to implement the rules (hence the term bureaucracy). This results in burgeoning institutions about which we hear so much. This is specifically a result of trying to be safe. Consequently, the more these organizations are attacked, the more they build bureaus to protect themselves. Thus, it is more typical for bureaucracies facing budget-cutting environments or other attempts at reform, to increase its support staff while reducing its line staff. The members of the support staff are specifically intended to preserve the organization.

The important thing to remember about bureaucracies is that they are rational not irrational as many are so quick to assume. The problem is that they are trying to operate in a non-rational world. This causes them to lose sight of relevant issues because they must preserve their rationality. For example, the more attempts are made to reform the institutions, the more the rational elements are given power. This is particularly problematic in the human services field because it is more elusive to rationality than any other field. People just do not behave in the manner they are supposed to nor do they fall into the needed neat categories. Ralph Hummel describes many of the somewhat dysfunctional behaviors of bureaucracies that result from the need to preserve, not only the organization but the personal integrity of its members.[4]

Private enterprise

Starting in the late 1970s and certainly in the 1980s, the concept of privatization gathered considerable popularity. This was viewed as the most appropriate response to the inefficiencies of bureaucracy. The premise rested on the belief that we just need to move all of the government services to private enterprises and all will be well with the world. This may oversimplify the concept but it does not contradict its basic tenet. A private enterprise may or may not be bureaucratic. That is probably the greatest irony of all. Some of the world's largest and longest standing bureaucracies are private industrial giants such as Ford Motor Co. and International Business Machines (IBM). The true private enterprise is much more likely to be found in small businesses. The main features of the private organization that separate it from the public organization are that it is driven by profits and encourages risk-taking not that it is or is not bureaucratic. Of course, there is already a contradiction here. Once a private organization takes on the dynamics of a bureaucracy, it reduces its willingness to take risks. The very act of trying to preserve itself drives it into a different organizational form.

The early enterprises were found among the bourgeoisie of the 16th and 17th Centuries. The success of these enterprises was in the fact that they were focused on one outcome: make a profit. There is no getting around this as an underpinning of a private enterprise. In order to make the greatest profits, they took the greatest risks in some cases. For example, they funded explorations with almost no guarantee that the explorers would find anything at all (and sometimes they did not.) The private entities of the Industrial Age also focused on profits but over time took fewer and fewer risks. The unwillingness of large private entities to take risks resulted in the trend toward monopolies and sizable support staffs. I mention these historical examples because they really lend insight into the privatization push of the 1980s. The truth of the matter was that risk-taking was not a common feature of most of the organizations that were willing to take the contracts. One clear example is the defense industry. Defense contractors have become thoroughly intertwined with the bureaucracy of the Department of Defense. Additionally, they rely on bureaucratic principles to preserve themselves, along with rigging the market so that there is no other possible provider for the particular weapons system. Thus, risk is removed and it is difficult to move away from an existing military policy as much due to the defense industry as it is any bureaucratic resistance within the department itself. This is just one of many examples where so-called private industry is more public and bureaucratic than entrepreneurial. Consequently, they begin to quickly behave more like bureaucracies than enterprises.

The profit-making focus of an enterprise stands as both a strength and a weakness as well. The strength of this value, as so vigorously stated by its proponents, was that it seeks more innovative ways to carry out its functions. However, this may or may not be the most efficient; sometimes it is just the least expensive. One way this profit-seeking is accomplished through basing decisions on expected value.[5] Expected value is a calculation premised on profitability and probability which assumes an error rate. The organization can calculate a rate of error that is acceptable within its anticipated outcomes and perform in a manner that is cheapest while achieving an acceptable outcome. In the end, this macro-economic view will provide a service more cheaply than a bureaucracy because it can tolerate error. However, this too is its weakness. In the general area of public programs, it is likely that some of the services will exhibit the traits of true public goods. Public goods are properly defined as being non-diminishable [never used up], non-excludable [cannot limit beneficiaries], and non-appropriable [cannot control boundaries or product]. These diseconomies cause a private organization to malfunction because it cannot legitimately count on making a profit since these features are inclined make it impossible to calculate expected value. This is particularly problematic in the human services arena. How does one legitimately control the market or the beneficiaries in providing a basic human service like caring for the disabled? The truth of the matter is one cannot unless they are willing to make some hard decisions. This has been frequently accomplished by simply opting for a first-come; first-served strategy. In other cases, the clients most likely to receive services are those who incur the least expense sometimes referred to as creaming. One could easily argue that this does not adequately serve the public's interest.

A point to be made here is that the term Private enterprise has been largely misused in the privatization environment. A non-profit or not-for-profit organization cannot, by definition, be a private enterprise because they actually define themselves in terms of not making a profit. This suggests that the most common form of private organization that provides public services are not enterprises at all but some mutated form of that organization. Generally, these organizations attempt to identify some other measure of profit than monetary. This may be a process-based measure or it may be a longevity measure. These are the most common forms of profit in these types of organizations. The process-based measure typically takes the form of numbers served or some similar strictly quantitative unit of analysis which says little of the impact on a given problem or population. The longevity measure, which is equally common, relies on the ability to secure funding through grant programs or other mechanism as a measure of success. The longer the organization continues to function, the greater the evidence of its success. There are certainly examples of this across a broad spectrum of services. A provider of counseling service to youth may measure success based on the number of individuals who have received counsel. However, this says little about an actual outcome, i.e., a well-adjusted person. At the same time, success could be measured in terms of how long the counseling agency has existed and their ability to retain clients. It would be rather odd for an agency of this type to claim success based on the amount of money they made off the state. A raw truth is that these are artificial profits at best and do not lend themselves to actual private enterprise. The next two organizational forms are essentially attempts to resolve this problem of privatization without relying strictly on the private enterprise.

Public Cooperatives

These organizational arrangements were an early attempt to provide public services without compromising the public interest. Such organizations were created by the state or by an interest group in order to provide the services desired which did not technically become a part of the state system. However, the only thing that separates them from the state government is that the employees were not on the public payroll. While they are not entirely under the jurisdiction of the state, they tend to behave like state organizations because they have not fallen far away from their origins. Initially, they must follow all of the procedural guidelines of the state. The state does not need to regulate these frequently because they already behave like an agency and so regulate themselves by co-opting. The state will easily enter into arrangements with these firms because they so closely resemble public agencies. Examples of these are mental health services and animal control. Consequently, these organizations typically fall into bureaucratic behaviors. The problems that instigated the movement to the private sector persist because the organizational behaviors remain mostly the sameSrisk averse and based on process.

It is very typical for the members of these organizations to be former bureaucrats. Thus they easily behave in ways more like a bureaucracy than a private enterprise. For example, they may spend more energy protecting the structure of the organization than actually providing services. In other cases, they may dedicate themselves to preserving the state's bureaucracy itself as a self-preservation mechanism. The procedures of the cooperative will also center on rule-making rather than problem-solving through risk-taking. There are extensive written policies and most of the energy is spent on developing them. In other words, the nature of the cooperative is to be more rational than venturesome. They will most likely also base their profit on longevity rather than outcomes. Since they value survival, they are co-opted into the state's bureaucracy while maintaining an image of being independent.

The strength of this model is that it allows the provider to be more independent than a state agency. The contract is the only governing document in a technical sense. However, the provider is given little opportunity to be the creative party in the relationship. Rather the state spells out rigorous expectations, most of which have to do with process. From that, the provider takes the initiative of designing the plan of action. This, of course, is also its weakness. Once the provider allows itself so little license in designing the plan, it becomes all too easy to manipulate the definitions of success. The provider organization designs its evaluating devices to fit into the state's plan and adjusts functions to fall into the definitions mandated. The state is left with considerable leeway in controlling the procedures of the provider. This actually favors the cooperative moving more toward bureaucratic behavior. Since their primary measure of success is longevity, they will focus on procedure and structure. This makes them behave more like the agency that granted the funds because if their practices are more like those of the state they tend to ingratiate themselves more to the granting agency.

Contracted Services

The other most commonly used device for privatizing while attempting to avoid the pitfalls of a private enterprise is to contract out. This is somewhat similar to a cooperative but has some rather significant differences. First, the contractor is usually more independent than the cooperative from its inception. Interestingly, it is not unusual for the contractor to be in an almost adversarial relationship with the state. The contractor will assert its authority to control its own procedures. Second, the outcome expectations of the state are more specifically identified in advance. Unlike the grant-making process, the state will expend considerable effort up front to lay out the terms of the contract. In the granting process, the guidelines are loose, leaving the description of specifics up to the applicant (cooperative.) The contractor however, must respond to a "request for proposals" that is very extensive in its parameters and work around those as well as it can. Then there is a contract negotiation process that is undertaken (which actually establishes the adversary relationship in many cases.) The association with the state after that point is primarily found in contract monitoring. However, the nature of this contract monitoring can take as many forms as there are contracts. The monitoring may be intense and frequent or superficial and rare and all variations in between. Since it is extremely difficult for bureaucracies to change their behaviors, the regulating agency is more likely to engage in rigorous monitoring as a means of continuing rule enforcement and risk avoidance while the contractor is pushing to set its own agenda. This adversary relationship can use up a great deal of energy for both parties.

The strength of this model is that it lays out expectations in terms of outcomes quite explicitly. The hope is that the public's interest will be better served because it is defined so clearly. The procedures for achieving this are less specific. The contract removes much of the ambiguities of the cooperative or the strictly private enterprise. Thus, while the contractor is free to seek a profit in whatever form it takes, it must do so within some firm parameters. The state is able to use its rule-making abilities to correct for any deviations from the public policy intent. This is a more effective relationship between the state and the provider than the cooperative. This is rather ironic since initial examination of the cooperative relationship would seem to engender more control by the state. It does not turn out that way because the process of control is basically completed once the money is handed over. In the case of contracted services, the provider must continue to operate under the terms of the contract or risk losing the funding or some other sanction.

One would think that the basic objective of all of the models is to achieve some established outcome. However, this is generally not the case. Rational models are process centered. This means that most attention is devoted to the process or procedures. Outcomes are generally, a hoped for accomplishment. The experiences of the states have taught us that the implementation of outcome-based strategies is rift with substantial challenges. In fact, the general pattern is that any attempt to move to outcome or quality assurance models commonly ends up with a reversal to a bureaucratic, process-centered strategy. This pattern suggests that there is a basic incongruence between the underlying philosophies of the systems the outcome-based and the bureaucratic. I propose that the efforts to move to outcome-based values are contrary to the existing paradigm upon which the bureaucratic model is built. Briefly examining the relationship between an outcome-based value and administrative strategy; along with the nature of the Rational Model as a guiding force; leads to the need for a paradigmatic shift. The question is whether or not moving toward such a system as a subset of debureaucratization is possible.

Relationship Between Administrative Strategy and Problem-Systems

It should be clear at this point that there is some relationship between the use of rational problem-solving models and administrative strategies. The bureaucratic administrative strategy and its surrogates, the cooperative, and the contracted services, rely heavily on process and rule enforcement. The question is whether or not such an administrative setting can accommodate a problem-solving model of operation. This is not just a matter of some esoteric discussion of administrative theory. It goes well beyond that. The key concern is whether or not the current structures and belief systems can carry out what has been described as their goals. In order to address this question, we must first examine what the goals are and how they can be pursued.

The goals of problem solving in the public sector are fairly straightforward. As a result of the political process, it is determined that a current circumstance warrants attention. For example, it was decided early on in history that violent crimes and property crimes were unacceptable. The public process, usually found in the form of an authority figure was charged with deterring such acts. The government agencies (in whatever form they took) then established methods to stop crime. The citizens paid for these services through taxation. This basic Hobbesian situation presents a circumstance that, at first glance, is broadly conceded as a proper role of government. I would offer, however, it is still elusive to a universal outcome of success. While the public may agree in principle that crime should be reduced, it is not necessarily the case that either the definition of crime or the means of reduction are able to achieve such broad consensus. Not all people agree, for example, that illicit drugs are crimes per se. Many argue today that the list of such substances should not include marijuana. Still others might take a more libertarian view and argue that there should be no illicit drugs. At the same time, many argue that the profitability of drugs provides the underpinning of criminal acts, including theft and murder. There is also a lack of broad agreement on whether or not the procedures involved in abatement of crime are effective or that they are worth the trade-offs associated with them. There are many who are concerned that efforts to diminish violent crimes are achieving that result. So even in a basic area like criminal justice the outcomes are not easily derived or appreciated.

Now when one considers the increased complexity of societies, the ideal of the *civitas* is much more difficult to reach. As time passed, more deficiencies in the commons (general public) were identified along with the steps taken to correct them. Eventually, a point was reached where problems traditionally handled privately became identified as public interest. For example, it became a public process to care for orphans or the mentally ill. These continue to be viewed as problems or deficiencies with the desire to make them go away. Services to the developmentally disabled also fit in this scenario. In choosing to provide services for the developmentally disabled, communities acknowledged that this had become a public issue. The rationale was that this required intense effort and was better accomplished collectively. The earliest models subsequent to the choice to treat it as a public good were to provide institutions. At first, these were little more than human warehouses. Over time, the public became aware of horrific conditions in these institutions and demanded improvements. The response was the development of standards for the institutions. The state regulated the agencies and in most cases, took direct control of them. An infrastructure developed that sought to protect the mentally impaired from harm. The problem being addressed, then, was the need for safety for a vulnerable population. In more recent decades, the problem was redefined as a need for a quality of life that goes beyond simple safety issues. This resulted in a trend to deinstitutionalize the developmentally disabled and move them to more independent living arrangements. This example shows how problems are rarely solved as such. Rather they are re-defined and the responses altered to address this new definition. This is another essential element of rational thinking.

Continuing with the example of services provided for the developmentally disabled, we reflect on how the policy models evolved within the bureaucratic ethos. The goals of the bureaucratic ethos are preservation of the institutional structure, avoidance of risk, and predictability of organizational relationships. This has been described in some detail already, so I will not undertake to explain the elements of bureaucracy again. However, it is useful to juxtapose this ethos with the underlying principles associated with a human service like providing for the developmentally disabled. One of the basic premises of such human service is to solve problems that interfere with the well-being of the clients. Problem-solving models rely on flexibility, the ability of the organizations to learn, and dynamic relationships, i.e., those that encourage interaction. There is a strong relationship between the strategy and the norms of the organization or system. Examining each of these principles individually, it becomes clear that it is unlikely these two systems can exist simultaneously.

The primary model of service delivery in this context has been the bureaucratic. The drive to preserve the organization is essential to bureaucracy because the structure is designed to outlast human frailty. We should recall that the development of bureaucracy came as a result of frustrations with rather arbitrary systems of the past. Organizations came and went rather rapidly mostly because they depended heavily on the personality of the leadership. Knowledge was preserved as the privilege of the nobility or bourgeois. As the means of production became more and more centralized and relied more on stable organizations, it became important to craft an organizational model that by-passed the need to depend on personalities. In terms of the institutions that provided services to the developmentally disabled, this was a particularly acute issue. It was clear that much of the maltreatment of clients was directly associated with the leadership of the institutions themselves. It was viewed as desirable to remove as much of the arbitrary and capricious nature of institutional administration as possible. The bureaucratic model satisfied this requirement quite well.

However, it later became clear that the organization must be able to respond to changing conditions. The institutions proved highly resistant to any form of change. This proved to be harmful to the clients. Evidence mounted that continuing to rely on institutions would fail to achieve an appropriate goal for the clients, i.e., a reasonably productive and fulfilling life. The reliance on rule making and standard operating procedures were far too constraining for developing such a quality of life circumstance. This is similar to what O'Brien described as cooked map zones.[6] In order to change goals along with the changing preferences, the organization must have the flexibility to do so.

The bureaucratic mentality is extremely averse to risk. Its very existence is a result of trying to reduce risk which is not particularly conducive to flexibility. These organizations have been created to respond to deficiencies. This is a way to control the world around us. By identifying each problem area that must be addressed, deciding upon a response, and standardizing those responses, each source of trouble is eliminated long enough to encounter the next problem. Over time there is a rule for everything so that there is less risk of human imperfection found in *ad hoc* responses. However, a genuine problem solving system relies on some risk taking. The only way that it can learn about any problem is through encountering risk. When something goes wrong, the answer is not to put in place a permanent rule to avoid a recurrence. Rather, the problems that arise teach the participants more and more about their world. Sometimes, it becomes a matter of recognizing that what was perceived to be a problem is not one at all but merely a reality that calls us to a higher tolerance or a different appreciation. This can be especially true in working with the human services.

The most recognizable aspect of the bureaucratic world is its expectation of predictable relationships. That is the primary purpose of the hierarchical structure. By having established positions that are specifically accountable to other positions, there is little doubt about who works with whom. The adulation of the chain of command honors this very essential aspect of this organizational and societal value. A problem-solving system, on the other hand, requires less formal relationships and the ability to exchange knowledge across disciplines. The focus moves from the positions to the tasks. Consequently, it is not only unessential to have established formal relationships of subordinate and superordinate; it is an impediment to successful strategies. This is one of the major barriers to success to this point. Quality assurance methods emphasize team-building but the organizational culture continues to emphasize structure.

In light of these rather explicit contradictions, one might think that it should be a relatively simple matter to convert provider organizations over to the consumer-driven, flexible, systems that are more suitable to problem-solving. However, it is much more complicated than one might appreciate. The bureaucratic mentality does not exist in a vacuum, it arises from the culture. To this point, administrative strategies have made adjustments and attempted many kinds of reforms while clinging to the basic bureaucratic model. Part of the problem, as stated earlier, is that we generally do not understand what the bureaucratic model is and we are in considerable denial. The more basic problem though is that we persist in our belief in the prevailing paradigm: the Rational Model.

The Rational Model as a Guiding Force

The Rational Model evolved out of the Age of Reason, wherein we came to understand that in our world there are causes and effects. This was contrary to the sets of superstitions that had guided so many decisions in the earlier periods. One underlying principle is that we are in opposition to the chaotic forces of nature and must use rationality to counteract the negative consequences of this chaos. Value is found in order; order as we understand it. The world around us came to be viewed in a largely mechanistic metaphor. If a certain thing happens, particular results will occur. We applied this metaphor to economics, history, and human behavior itself as well as the physical sciences. As the deficiencies of our industrialized world presented themselves, we designed ways to respond to bring it back under control. If transportation was a problem, we built railroads. If a shortage of labor was a problem we built cities. If high unemployment resulted from economic turmoil stimulated by fear, we built the Welfare State.

In all of these responses we also crafted rational organizations to handle the need. We came to rely on the wisdom of our sciences to reduce the risk found in our lives. Every time something went wrong, priority was given to correcting it. A response is developed to identify the cause and rectify it. Now, we live in a society where we expect that everything we need has an institution that addresses it. As John McKnight correctly states, we have become a society of clients.[7] The rational belief system is so strong that it is now self generating. As further described by McKnight:

> The professional co-optation of community efforts to invent appropriate techniques for citizens to care in the community has been pervasive. We need to identify the characteristics of those social forms that are resistant to colonization by service technologies while enabling communities to cultivate care. These authentic social forms are characterized by three basic dimensions: They tend to be *uncommodified, unmanaged,* and *uncurricularized.*[8]

What McKnight refers to as colonization, I am attributing rationalization. The service technologies are the application of rational thinking to community problems. His description of commodification, management, and curricularizing are all elements of this rationality. To be commodified is to be made into an object which can then be manipulated rationally. So a service for the developmentally disabled became an object that is bounded by rules and applied equally to all clients. The idea of management in the rational paradigm is directly associated with identifying a cause for the effect and then regulating it to fit a preconceived notion of desirable behaviors. Thus, the clients are managed through rigid schedules and a set of routine procedures. When services are curricularized they are an object of study in order to apply empirical methodology leading to an analytical explanation of the various causes and effects. The professionals who administer services for the developmentally disabled are then able to consult the manuals to determine how clients should be handled. This process of rationalization is actually quite de-humanizing in its encounters with clients. Institutions now can actually identify the problem and then seek out its cause and design a response that reduces its impact. This is what McKnight describes as the development of "need maps."[9]

In addition to a perceived need to eliminate risk, we also feel compelled to be accountable. This requires accountability in very specific terms. We must measure everything. We become slaves to the numbers. An occasion that was described in one of the interviews of providers of services to the developmentally disabled demonstrates this practice. A staff team had determined that the consumer found value in swimming. They determined that this contributed to the individual's physical and emotional health (cause: lack of exercise; effect: lackluster attitude; correction: swimming). They decided then that the individual should swim once a week. So they put into the plan Swimming - 52 times of the year. As the year proceeded, schedules changed and the consumer became interested in other activities. In November the team noticed that he had been swimming only 21 times that year. So an immediate priority was placed on being certain that this person went swimming 31 times in the next six weeks! This may seem obviously ludicrous at first glance. However, it makes perfect sense if the idea of a plan is that it must be met. The Rational Model establishes such a mindset.

There is little doubt that the Rational Model continues to be the operating paradigm. A paradigm, as defined by Thomas Kuhn, is an underlying belief that guides the basic thought process. Earlier paradigms combined beliefs in divine intent with some scientific knowledge to arrive at conclusions. The Rational Model went to pure empiricism to arrive at conclusions. It is not likely that anyone will be shocked to learn that we believe that in order for something to be considered true it must be observable. We have developed rather elaborate methods of observation in order to accommodate this feature of the Rational Model. The paradigm also insists that we identify causes to effects. This is done through observation of single variables. One of the problems with this is that these single variables may behave differently in isolation than they do in concert with the other variables in their natural environment. Many of the physical sciences are discovering that even their laws are not as irrefutable as they once thought.

The Rational Model is the paradigm that keeps leading us back to the bureaucratic ethos. Bureaucracy, like it or not, is one of the major icons of rationalism. It is the logical outcome of holding to faith in the Rational Model. The demand for bureaucratic responses comes from the general public and not necessarily from the institutions themselves. However, there are occasions when a need is created in the minds of citizens by bureaucratic campaigns. For example, many of the problems that were described in my interviews regarding the experiences of the states' efforts at providing services to the developmentally disabled were directly related to maintaining this belief. They were only problems because they did not fit the mold of the rational system. If numbers were difficult to manage because the system was individualized it was because individualized systems are not rational. Many times reforms were reversed because there were a few instances of negligence which is indicative of a commitment to the emphasis on deficiencies. The Rational Model must focus on deficiency in order to find a cause for something not under our control. The discussion presented by John O'Brien of crooked map zones is directly tied to our continued fixation with the rational paradigm. Our rational systems cannot cope with changing desires because they are not sufficiently predictable.

It should be clear, then, that what is needed is not more reorganizations. The pressure to make essential change is much too great for that. We have shifted things around long enough. We cannot make change at the margins any longer. The evidence is rather compelling that there is a need for a genuine paradigm shift. The new paradigm must be prepared to accept risk. It must recognize that there is value in allowing for an acceptable level of perceived failure. The new paradigm must recognize that we are not in conflict with nature but part of it. Events will occur outside of our control. Our organizational systems must be able to be responsive without being rigid. In order to move to an effective outcome-based system, we must accept a premise that things change. Otherwise, instead of striving for outcomes that satisfy us, we find ourselves satisfying the outcomes. This will be a matter of encouraging every member of the agencies, providers, advocates, families, and individuals to re-think their belief system. The new paradigm must stress capacity over deficiency it must be able to celebrate the 95% success rate and not dwell on the other 5%!

The underlying principles of this new paradigm will be described in some detail in Chapter 8. Nevertheless, I can state at this point, it is clear that the paradigm must be crafted around people and how they actually move forward rather than its opposite. To make this a bit clearer, I return to the case of services to the developmentally disabled. This allows us to observe the interactions of various forces.

The Case of the Montana Institute on disAbilities

The Montana Institute on disAbilities had requested this analysis of administrative strategies to encourage the Montana system of services for the developmentally disabled to use an objective data base for developing long term strategies. The problem, as described by the Institute in its request for proposals was that:

> Gaining access to unbiased information regarding current issues in human services has been difficult and time consuming for human service professionals. . . Even more difficult is the task of objective assessment and analysis of information which is required to make recommendations for system wide or even individual agency change. Individual program staff and state officials lack the time required to research, summarize and disseminate information re: current trends.

Thus, my final report attempted to describe existing administrative alternatives for the delivery of services using the provision of services to the developmentally disabled as an example. This turned out to be a challenging project for many reasons. The process of gathering relevant information involved an examination of the prevailing models that exist in the field and comparing those with procedures and relationships in administration. One area of difficulty in carrying out such a task is that it is not always clear what issues in the current system may come to stand out prior to examination. My responsibility was to separate the primary issues from the more tangential and to ascertain what information would be most useful for all of the parties involved. Without such a preliminary examination, I stood the risk of presenting information that may not have been particularly useful or, even worse, would only contribute further to the confusion.

In order to accomplish this, the first stage of this analysis was to first, conduct discussions with representatives of the various parties in the field; second, to review the literature that deals specifically with the provision of these services; and, finally to compare this information with the predominant concepts in public administration regarding the larger administrative issues. The results of this phase of the analysis offered some rather compelling hints to the underlying problems. Following this part of the process, information was requested from six states that had been identified as relevant to the Montana case regarding their own systems Colorado, Wyoming, North Dakota, Utah, Idaho, and Oregon. With that information gathered, an analysis pulled together the larger understandings with the specific experiences which indicated generally successful strategies. Drawing from these and the information collected in interviews and examination of the literature, recommendations were designed relative to the issues identified in the initial request for proposals. It is vital that it be clear up front that the best strategy would have to be the one that could be agreed upon by the providers, clients, and administrators themselves. This was not small challenge as I discovered that the parties involved were equally immersed in the Rational paradigm such that it would be extremely difficult to convince them that substantial paradigmatic shift would be necessary to carry out what they had in mind. When cultures and subcultures are totally constructed under a broad belief system it is unlikely that they will be able to see beyond its borders. I was placed in a position in which I was trying to describe something outside of Rationality by using rational language. This is what Wittgenstein and others called "language games" wherein the language itself has established the ground rules.[10] Those charged with decision-making or even those who are the subject of the decisions are caught in the web of the language game. They have a set of terms which are associated with conclusions already drawn. The process of explaining to those within the language environment who are literally unable to see beyond it becomes paradoxical. Even beyond this, there is the challenge of what many choose to call "hyperreality." The idea most essential to hyperreality is the simulation and the simulacrum. The simulation is characterized by a blending of 'reality' and some form of representation, where there is no clear indication of where the former stops and the latter begins. The simulacrum goes one step further and may be defined as a copy with no original, or as Gilles Deleuze describes it, "the simulacrum is an image without resemblance." Nicholas Oberly expands on this notion in his description of the works of Baudrillard and Deleuze:

> Jean Baudrillard (1994) maps the transformation from representation to simulacrum in four 'successive phases of the image' in which the last is that "it has no relation to any reality whatsoever: it is its own pure simulacrum" (SS p.6). (see mimesis, representation.) Deleuze, Baudrillard, and several other theorists trace the proliferation and succession of simulacra to the rise of hyperreality and the advent of a world that is either partially, or entirely simulated. Frederic Jameson (1990) contends that one of the conditions of late capitalism is the mass reproduction of simulacra, creating a "world with an unreality and a free floating absence of "the referent"' (p. 17) One of the fundamental qualities of hyperreality is the implosion of Ferdinand Saussure's (1959) model for the sign (see semiotics) (pg. 67). The mass simulacrum of signs become meaningless, functioning as groundless, hollow indicators that self-replicate in endless reproduction. Saussure outlines the nature of the sign as the signified (a concept of the real) and the signifier (a sound-image). Baudrillard (1981) claims the Saussurian model is made arbitrary by the advent of hyperreality wherein the two poles of the signified and signifier implode in upon each other destroying meaning, causing all signs to be unhinged and point back to a non-existing reality (180). Another basic characteristic of the hyperreal is the dislocation of object materiality and concrete spatial relations.[11]

The relevance of the ideas of hyperreality and simulacrum here is that the bureaucratic and its related ethos has become the hyperreality. Those in power, as well as those who are subjected to it, operate within this hyperreality, believing that there are such things as objective knowledge. It was not unusual for me to hear from respondents in this study that things were a certain way because there were no alternatives "you have to have order."

---

1. Kuhn, Thomas S., *The Structure of Scientific Revolutions,* 3rd ed. (Chicago: University of Chicago Press, 1996).
2. Gerth, Hans and C. Wright Mills, *Max Weber: Essays in Sociology.* (Oxford: Oxford University Press, 1946).
3. Bronowski, Jacob, *The Common Sense of Science.* (Cambridge: Harvard University Press, 1978).
4. Hummel, Ralph P., *The Bureaucratic Experience*, 4th ed. (Bedford: St. Martins, 1994).
5. O'Brien, J., Poole, C. & Galloway, C., *Accomplishments in Residential Services.* (Olympia: Governors Council on Developmental Disabilities, 1981).
6. Ibid.,
7. McKnight, John, *The Careless Society: Community and Its Counterfeits.* (New York: Basic Books, 1996).
8. Ibid., 12
9. Ibid., 92
10. Wittgenstein, Luwig, *Philosophical Investigations.* (Malden: Blackwell, 2004).
11. Oberly, Nicholas, *Theories of Media: Keywords Glossary: Reality, Hyperreality,* (Chicago: The University of Chicago, 2004).

Chapter 3: The Organizational Level

To this point, I have focused on a macro-societal perspective in my examination of the field of public administration. From this perspective I argued that the paradigm within we operate, the Rational, is under considerable pressure to change. Continuing in this vein, I now move to examine the field from more of an organizational level of analysis. In so doing, I will draw again from the case of the services to the developmentally disabled but will also draw from other cases. The reason that I have elected to continue my focus on the student of services to the developmentally disabled is because it is a rather comprehensive review of an entire system. As such, it provides a working framework from which to draw some conclusions. While it is problematic to generalize from a particular subfield in human services to the larger field of public administration, it remains a useful instrument to clarify the complexities involved.

Moving to an organizational level of analysis, it is necessary to assess the philosophical climate of the field of services to the developmentally disabled. By this, I mean that it is fairly well known that shifts that take place within a field which have direct impacts on the language and expectations within each organization. While it remains true that the most successful way to design an organization is from the ground up i.e., through the task environment, this does not take place within a vacuum. Whatever is going on philosophically in the enterprise or system is relevant. After only a brief examination of the system of services to the developmentally disabled and discussions with some of the participants of the system it became readily apparent that the philosophical climate was in flux. This was also supported in the literature of the field. Most authors were quick to point out that much has changed in the field and much yet needs to be changed. Clarence J. Sundram, for example notes:

> There currently is a profound shift in thinking about the abilities, needs, and aspirations of people with disabilities, and in the process administrators are making significant changes in policy and practice away from the heavy reliance on rigid, highly structured residential and day programs to adopting more flexible methods of supports tailored to the needs of individuals.[1]

These shifts, as described by Sundram, are no small matter. They go directly to the root of the field. Any time there are basic shifts of this nature they challenge the organizations and persons within them in extraordinarily profound ways. This shift is having a serious impact on:
- providers, who used to be primarily government employees;
- administrators, who must operate through negotiation more than ever before; and
- consumer/clients, who must now be prepared to participate in making choices for their own growth and development.

These areas of philosophical shift deserve some particular attention. Appreciating the profound nature of these shifts is crucial to developing an administrative strategy. While the following discussion focuses specifically on services to developmentally disabled, it should be easy to see how philosophical shifts can have an impact on any organization.

Elements of Public Organizations

Deinstitutionalization

What may have been a political concept or mostly a slogan in the 1970s and 1980s has become an operating principle. In most states, the movement to deinstitutionalize became a legal matter decreed by the courts. [2] This was not just a matter of getting the developmentally disabled out of the institutions but of changing the very essence of the services provided for the clients. It also dramatically altered the organizational structures involved because it removed much of the attractiveness of acting in a bureaucratic manner. The statement of the desired outcomes by the Interagency Task Force on Developmental Disabilities lends some critical insight into the nature of this shift from institutions:

> Effective services are characterized by a balance of several living, training, and support elements that allow each individual the opportunity to exercise his or her fundamental rights. Training is one aspect of service delivery. Other aspects include a safe, homelike environment; supervision when necessary; recreation and leisure activities; nutritious and good tasting food; clean, appropriate clothing that fits; *the dignity of risk; freedom to make choices; community integration, social support, friends, and opportunities for happiness.* [emphasis added] [3]

This challenge to the states' provision of services went beyond merely closing institutions. It requires a completely different approach to the day-to-day activities, relationships of authority, and considerations of options. The system was being challenged to allow risk, something a bureaucracy is not equipped to do.

Emphasis on Quality

Throughout the public sector there has been a virtual stampede to incorporate Total Quality Management (TQM) into the practices and procedures of government. This has been occurring at all levels of government. From President Clinton's National Performance Review Team which was headed by Vice President Al Gore, to states' efforts at quality enhancement, to various commissions and teams in local governments, the theme is the same: it is time to bring quality to public services. The field of services to the developmentally disabled was certainly no exception. Heinlen points out that [a]s much as *continuum of care* was the watchword for human services in the 1970s, *quality* is the Shibboleth for the 1990s.[4] As noted by Sundram: For the last couple of decades, we have been engaged in borrowing from manufacturing industries methods of assuring quality and force-fitting them into a human service system.[5] His use of the term, force-fitting is indeed, accurate. Government has, in fact, been attempting to carry over *in toto* the TQM ideas promoted by W. Edwards Deming.[6]

The problem is that these methods are not entirely suited to government, partially due to the diseconomies which are tied to public goods, described earlier in the section on private enterprise. Another factor that makes this a challenging endeavor is that it is difficult to establish just who *the customer* is in government. Is the customer the client? That might not seem to be a problem except that the client does not pay for the service so it is hard to measure satisfaction through market success. Is the customer the citizen who pays the taxes? This would run counter to the idea that quality stands in opposition to strict budget accountability or that quality is a matter of outcome. The quality movement in government has stimulated more complex questions than those found in the private sector regarding how to improve the quality throughout the operation. The questions go right to the basic concern of how one actually defines and then measures quality. In order to pursue TQM in its entirety we must assume that there is a high level of agreement on what quality is and who is being served. That level of agreement does not exist and, in light of the cynicism found in the general public, does not seem likely to occur anytime soon. As effectively argued by Terry, the quality movement presents some serious problems in public administration.[7] The entrepreneurial model associated with the quality movement is rife with problems with respect to public administration. First, it requires that public administrators, including those in non-government organizations (NGOs) providing a public service, apply some form of raw power in order to carry out innovations. Second, the entrepreneurial model relies on the ability to make radical changes to find new efficiencies. Such changes are too likely to run contrary to the policy development process in a democratic society. Finally, public entrepreneurship is prone to disregard the role of tradition in public administration.

Assuming for a moment that quality in the system of services to the developmentally disabled (or other human services) is tied to the quality of life experienced by the clients, as suggested by Heinlen, there are still problems: Quality of life is subjective, idiosyncratic, culturally specific, and transient (Blatt, 1987; Edgerton, 1990, Goode, 1990). These very traits imply that quality of life cannot be assured through prescriptive regulation.[8] This suggests further that the implications for the system are indeed profound. More than that, it means that it must make considerable adjustments in order to incorporate quality of life as a measure of success. The consequences for the organizations are dramatic:

> [I]n the process of implementing profound changes in the service system, we have paid insufficient attention to the changing management and professional responsibilities that should accompany the new role of consumers. Today, the necessary preparation is more complex than learning the regulatory requirements and black letter laws. Instead, we are entering a new world that *will necessarily rely more heavily on the judgment of workers*. [emphasis added] [9]

This is a substantial shift in behaviors and relationships in such a system as human services. The arrangement must move from a highly regulatory one to a decentralized one based on trust. This, as will be noted a bit later, was a particular problem in many states.

Movement to quality is not without risk. In fact, that is at least in part, the main point. The systems must be able to accept a certain degree of risk. This is particularly the case in the provision of the human services, given the vulnerable nature of the clientele. It is possible for clients to be placed in situations where they make a choice that is inappropriate for them. The real problem here is the genuine temptation to return to strict forms of monitoring and regulation whenever there are problems. In such a response, the cure is worse than the disease:

> The state cannot expect community programs to respect and encourage consumer choice while it imposes standardized solutions upon them... consumer choice and least restrictive environment must be the driving forces of the system, not simply stated and not acted upon. [10]

So the conclusion must be that even though there are risks, the net gain overall is very much worth it. An administrative strategy had to be developed that encouraged the individual responsibility of the provider and established a supportive environment for such a process at the local level.

Consumer-Centered/Empowerment

Another trend throughout the public sector is to move toward systems of empowerment. This is an actually an alternative to the quality movement that specifically focuses its attention on allowing individual clients to make more of the choices rather than having them imposed by a rule-driven bureaucracy. The empowerment of citizens and clients alike is a core value of the New Public Service strategy as very clearly defined by the Denhardts.[11] This movement is particularly amenable to a more creative philosophy since it actually attempts to redefine the role of government to an extent. The difficulty in most cases is that the structures of many of the agencies have remained the same while trying to incorporate empowerment strategies. This means that bureaucracies attempt to administer an empowerment program which is antithetical to their very existence. I recall clearly an experience where I was lectured by a superior about the importance of empowerment. Lecturing is antithetical to empowerment. This demonstrates how difficult it can be to move to this kind of strategy.

In the system of services to at-risk clients including the developmentally disabled, there had been similar attempts to move toward client-centered programs. The clients and/or their family or guardians were actually given choices of which programs they wanted to have in their individual plans. Most such programs involved Individual Service Plans (ISPs). This is closely associated with the practice of utilizing case managers as opposed to care-givers. The case manager works with the individual and/or family or guardian to arrive at an ISP that will satisfy the objectives of quality of life and not impose programs on the individual. The ideal is for some form of growth and development for the individual that does not standardize the measures of success. Such a movement toward empowerment strategies really does cry for changed relationships not only at the client level but at the administrative level. Again, this requires that the regulatory agencies find ways to encourage the professionalism of the providers rather than impose rules:

> I have yet to encounter a safety net of laws, rules, regulations, and policies that was any stronger or more effective than a single concerned and engaged professional, standing shoulder to shoulder with an individual with mental retardation navigating the daily challenges of life in the community. [12]

It turned out to be a profound challenge for regulatory agencies to come up with strategies that shifted the control over to the individual providers. It continues to be essential, however, that they direct their attentions to just such an effort. The state cannot expect community programs to respect and encourage consumer choice while it imposes standardized solutions upon them. [13]

The movement to consumer-centered strategies carries a certain amount of risk as well. In fact, the need to minimize risk as a normal bureaucratic behavior has been rather problematic. All too frequently, for example, incident reporting and investigation procedures associated with consumer-centered strategies were viewed by program administrators as instruments of risk exposure rather than viable tools for risk management and quality improvement. Program administrators had to be more willing to yield control of their incident-reporting systems by transforming them into viable consumer-centered quality assurance tools to meet their needs, rather than resisting the movement to empowerment or public service. In the end, the movement to consumer-centered strategies is more likely to create more effective incident reporting systems and risk management than they are to increase risk. [14]

Virtual Agreement On the Need to Provide Services

This philosophical attribute is included because it is rather unique in the case of services to the developmentally disabled. This is especially true during the current political environment. Unlike the human service areas of welfare, health care, or education, there is somewhat universal acceptance of the state's responsibility to care for the developmentally disabled. The most rigid fiscal conservatives do not even dispute this conclusion. They may not agree on what it takes to provide the service but at least the matter of whether or not it is provided is not on the table. This is a very positive attribute to build upon. The very first step in developing consensus is to find areas of agreement. In the case of the system of services to the developmentally disabled, this turned out to be fairly simple. It all started with the agreement that the service should be provided. The administrators in welfare and health care probably wish they had it so good. While education at the elementary and secondary levels also enjoys universal support, there is enough volatility to the range of desired outcomes to prevent the same kind of support for education as a service.

To have universal agreement on the government's role to provide a service is, indeed, very rare. Thus, we should consider carefully the manner in which we do determine whether or not a service should be a part of government. On many occasions, I have asked students or other audiences to identify for me the proper role of government. Invariably, the responses tend to center around the idea the role is to provide services. This, however, is not the proper role of government in a democracy. Rather, the proper role of government is to provide for the public forum. Through this public forum, the type, extent, and form of services are determined. It is an on-going dynamic process and it is vital that public administrators be acutely aware of this as their role. This reinforces the idea of the New Public Service in reminding and urging public administrators to focus on stimulating the public forum not avoiding it. This may not be the most convenient part of the profession but it remains central.

Managed Care Options

Managed Care had been championed by some as a way of curbing costs in the system of services to the developmentally disabled as well as other similar human services. Some of the managed care corporations from the health care field made entreaties to states to handle the health care provision for the developmentally disabled in some cases and even the other array of services in others. Managed care mechanisms were devised nearly two decades ago as a way of reducing costs in acute medical care. The strengths of managed care corporations rest in their sophisticated management systems, negotiating power, and investment capital. [15] These attributes count for little, however, in the developmental disabilities long-term care field. In fact, they would probably be liabilities in the system. This also reveals some weaknesses in more purely privatized solutions to human service problems.

The sophisticated management systems may work well in fairly predictable environments of long-term care but the clients of human services are in and out of the system frequently and require a wide array of services. The need for tight record-keeping to protect the managed-care corporation particularly in a market sensitive to liability issues would likely result in a quasi-bureaucratic system, removed from public control by at least one level:

> [T]hese systems would represent a return to the centralized, rule-bound (regulated) systems of governance that turn front-line workers into passive actors and that needlessly override consumer and family choice.[16]

There is relatively little room for negotiation in the services to the developmentally disabled population, either in community-based programs or Intermediate Care Facilities for the Mentally Retarded (ICF/MR) which are protected through law and regulation. Rate negotiations need to be sensitive to local conditions, including contributions, programs, and clients.[17] There is not much opportunity for investment capital in the long-term care of the developmentally disabled. The primary use of Medicaid funds in the field limits the amount that is available to draw on for investment. There is no growth in technology similar to the medical field to use for investment gains either. The danger is that the managed-care corporations could actually drain more resources than they would bring into the long-term care arena.[18] Overall, then the evidence is rather substantial that managed care is not a viable option for long-term care of the developmentally disabled or, by extension, human services in general:

> The most serious concern is that the managed care organization's profit drive will do more harm than good for consumers, families, and taxpayers. A central part of a managed-care organization's function in the care field is the allocation of limited resources. The fear is that a for-profit managed-care organization will be more likely to allocate fewer rather than more resources because of the profit motive, as has been the pattern observed in health care (Families USA, 1995).[19]

This further supports the evidence that private enterprises are not necessarily ideal in providing human services. This was especially the case in dealing with a clientele as vulnerable as the developmentally disabled. It also suggests that privatization schemes have glaring weaknesses in dealing with some of the more complex issues of public service. I suggest that this is a matter of attempting to use simplistic strategies to solve complex problems. The need is to work at ways that communities, states, and even the national government employ methods that allow growth, learning, and ownership of human service issues.

The Task Environment

Before moving on to the overall administrative strategy issues of DD Services, human services, or agencies in general, it is necessary to discuss the role played by the task environment. All too frequently, organizational theories are developed which fail to take this element into consideration. Once can no more design a generic administrative strategy than they can offer parenting strategies that apply to all families. The task environment may be defined as the combination of objectives, purposes, procedures, knowledge, skills, abilities, and relationships that are needed to carry out the overall mission of the organization. Essentially it simply describes the uniqueness of the organizations and the individuals within them. After all, tasks are carried out by individual persons with unique abilities and developed patterns of accomplishing their objectives. This measurement of task environment is best carried out on the individual level of analysis and then extrapolated out to the entire organization. Bearing in mind these variables, the nature of task environment with some suggested measurement strategies offers some hints of any desired adjustments. The brief discussion of the philosophical climate of the current systems, above combined with that of task environment and values, completes the framework within which administrative strategy should be designed.

First, it is imperative that we direct attention away from setting organizational structure and more toward understanding search procedures that reflect what an organization does. Then it is possible to propose various structural and behavioral relationships that will be best suited to accomplishing that task. This is considerably different from what has been suggested by most management and organizational experts to this point. Even though the management theorists from the Classical/Scientific Management to the Human Resources schools of thought set out to discover the most efficient ways of doing things they spent all of their time on structures and generalized strategies. Consequently, what resulted were typically recommendations for the generic organization. Since generalized structure was the primary emphasis, the match between what any organization did and how it was managed was not as sound as one might hope. In the absence of any compatibility between structure and function, organizations would gravitate back to the one form that is actually designed to emphasize structure bureaucracy.

This inability to match function to structure is the heart of the problem being faced by government agencies that attempt to reinvent or move toward outcome-based strategies. In large part, they are basically not equipped to do so. Even though the intentions are noble and probably sincere, they attempt to reform by modifying the organization *first*, then move to reconfiguring tasks. That is backwards thinking if outcome-based strategies are the desired goals. The task environment must be understood first, then each organization *and suborganization* may be adjusted to suit that task environment.

There are many methods of assessing task environment. I usually suggest that more than one be used for my clients. For example, in the case of human services, the interactions are so complex that no one analytical tool is sufficient. It is wiser to examine the task environment on at least three dimensions because it more closely reflects reality. Failure to move beyond two-dimensional thinking will result in a probable return to the status quo because that is the basis of rationality. The first method I may use is borrowed from a model offered by Charles Perrow which bases its measurement on the processes through which the organization and its functionaries (people who actually do the work) learn. This is useful in that it stays away from structure altogether. The second method of analysis relates to the composition of stakeholders in and around the organization, which I borrow from Ian Mitroff. A third method of analysis is to measure the level of involvement between individuals and the consistency of their individual duties, which was proposed by Fred Fiedler.[20] These three methods will be employed here to provide a rather unsophisticated analysis of the task environment. A proper analysis should be conducted within each organization and move upwards to the larger system. Nonetheless, this brief analysis will offer some key insights into any needed administrative strategy.

In his book, *Complex Organizations*, Charles Perrow asserts that the best way to design a management strategy is to focus on what the organization does.[21] More specifically, the process through which functionaries learn how to do what they do must be evaluated. This will lead to a management strategy and ultimately a structure that makes more sense within the actual context of what is being performed. After all, the most important thing that management does is to facilitate the process through which the actual tasks may be successfully conducted. This is best understood in terms of how the individuals and the organization learn. An organization that does not learn ceases to function and reverts to structure preservation only. The term he uses to analyze the organization's capacity to learn is search procedures. A search procedure is the manner in which an individual becomes more competent in performing his/her job. Search procedures are either analyzable or unanalyzable. If it is analyzable, it is possible for the needed activities in performing a task to be laid out in definable steps or principles. For example, an assembly line worker performs through search procedures that are very analyzable. The actions for performing the operations associated with the particular part of the assembly that is taking place at a work station are readily put into steps. Another worker can easily fill in for that worker and follow the steps and perform quite well. A teacher, on the other hand, operates under search procedures that are very elusive to analysis. While one may attempt to describe what a teacher does in terms of steps, the ability to be effective as a teacher has almost nothing to do with the steps. Try teaching a group of middle school students with only a lesson plan and no other training. It will not take long to realize that how the task is performed involves knowledge, skills and abilities that are best gained through experience and some intuitive capability.

Perrow's Task Environment Matrix

Search Procedures	Analyzable	Unanalyzable
Few Exceptions	*Routine*	*Craft*
Many Exceptions	*Engineering*	*Non-routine*

Figure 3.1

The other dimension to Perrow's model is whether or not there are few exceptions or many exceptions to the search procedures. In other words, whether the tasks are performed pretty much in line with some firm set of principles or are they more likely to be ambiguous and the principles are only remotely related to what actually takes place. Again examples of occupations can help to clarify this idea. In the case of an architect, while the search procedures are largely analyzable because they are drawn from principles of physics, there may be quite a bit of variation in how the principles are applied. The craft of architecture is to honor the search procedures but to be able to apply them in variation. The assembly worker again, has search procedures that are analyzable but there are few exceptions to how to go about doing the job. The last thing a factory manager wants is someone to get creative on the assembly line. The teacher, again, has unanalyzable search procedures and there are many exceptions. What works one time in teaching a sixth grade class will not necessarily work with the next class. A carpenter is an example of a job with unanalyzable search procedures with few exceptions. To endeavor to describe in steps what the carpenter does would be a daunting task at best, if even possible. However, once the carpenter develops those skills, the way in which a house is built or furniture constructed is pretty much the same. The procedures are not varied very much. The illustration shown in Figure 1 helps to clarify this model. The matrix is useful in that it gives some universal concepts to be applied to the task environment. It is also particularly useful because it stays away from structure until the task environment is understood.

The second model for organizational analysis assesses the dynamics and influence of various stakeholders. Ian Mitroff cautions that the consideration of stakeholders in the task environment can be highly complex.

> There are no definite limits to the number of techniques that one could use to generate a set of stakeholders relevant to any given organizational problem. It must be kept in mind that we are dealing with complex, messy systems. As a result we do not obtain the kind of closure and definitiveness that one does in simple, closed systems.[22]

Having said this, Mitroff offers seven methods of observing stakeholders in and around an organization: imperative, positional, reputational, social participation, opinion-leadership, demographic, and organizational. These are means to discovering the types of stakeholders and the probable influence they may have on the organizational culture. This is clearly a part of task environment. In order to assess the impact of the stakeholders, it is necessary to identify two sets of dimensions. First, there are the differences between explicit and implicit stakeholders. While Mitroff argues that these are defined in terms of whether or not they are interdependent, I would argue that this is not the best means of defining the two. It is nearly impossible to establish whether or not one group is having an influence on another. In fact, it is very likely that interdependency is nearly universal. Instead, I would view these two variables as whether or not the organization *recognizes* the influence of the stakeholders. The more a group or individual is recognized as a stakeholder, the more an organization will need to consider them in the design of their operations. An organization that is well aware of having many stakeholders will operate differently than one that views itself as being relatively independent of them. The other dimension considers the type of stake that is involved and can be divided into four (1) Change and Creativity, (2)Business Political and Economic Functions, (3)Information and Communica-

tion, and (4)Ethical, Moral, Cooperative. These dimensions are defined by Mitroff as follows:
I. Change and Creativity
  a. The leaders of the organization must have the inspiration and creativity necessary to reevaluate the organization's current missions, purposes, objectives, and goals and to conceptualize new purposes.
  b. The managers must have the capability for translating new concepts, ideas, and purposes into concrete, visualizable programs of action.
  c. All stakeholders must have the spirit dedication, and commitment necessary to secure new purposes.
II. Business Political and Economic Functions
  a. The total resources held by the collection of stakeholders must be adequate to accomplish their purposes.
  b. The managers must reallocate the resources from stakeholder to stakeholders so that each stakeholder possesses the amount of resources necessary to carry out its tasks at the right time and place.
  c. The stakeholders must employ the resources they have effectively and efficiently when executing their tasks to ensure that maximally useful output is produced.
  d. The managers must distribute the output effectively to all relevant stakeholders.
III. Information and Communication
  a. The collection of stakeholders must have the capacity to acquire or produce basic knowledge scientific, industrial, and operations about the organization's products, technology, operations, finances, markets, and customers.
  b. The managers must ensure that the right information is transmitted to the right stakeholder at the right time.
  c. Each stakeholder must have the capacity to use the knowledge and information he or she receives to make effective decisions.
IV. Ethical, Moral, Cooperative
  a. Stakeholders must have the necessary peace of mind within themselves to be effective in their organizational life and the other aspects of their life.
  b. There must be a minimum of conflict between the internal stakeholders, individuals, groups, and departments that function within the organization.
  c. There must be a minimum of conflict between the organization and its external stakeholders such as governments, public interest groups, social activists, unions, and competitors.

These dimensions are useful in that they provide another way of measuring task environment. Using the table above, an organization can measure the degree to which they are influenced by stakeholders; the manner in which that occurs; and how the stakeholders interact

| Measure of Stakeholder Climate |||
	Explicit	Implicit
Change & Creativity		
Business-Political & Economic Functions		
Information & Communication		
Ethical, Moral, Cooperative		

Figure 3.2

Using a scale of 1 - 10, organizational analysts assess the degree to which each factor is happening. At first glance, this seems overly subjective but need not be. One method of assigning value is to ask those who are identified as stakeholders to rate each dimension. This will prove to be very useful data in ascertaining the task environment in terms of how open the system is and how it is influenced by external and internal stakeholders. It becomes even more useful when joined with the other two measurements of task environment.

The third model to be applied here focuses attention on relationships. Fred E. Feidler suggests that the development of effective leadership strategies depends on the ability to understand the relationship between the members of the group. [23] This also gives us some insight into appropriate leadership relationships within human services provider organizations and between them and the state agencies. This method is not as adept at staying away from structure while examining task environment. Since structure does involve relationships, it is fairly easy to drift into issues of structure while looking at task environment. If honored, however, the analysis of relationships is very useful in examining the task environment because it properly assesses how much control is needed for particular positions. The first element examined is the actual percentage of time spent in contact with other employees. This is particularly important because it alerts the management analyst to the need for social relations methods. If one is in contact with other employees most of the time, the structure may include elements of human relations programs, such as retreats and counseling. If there is not a great deal of contact these elements would actually be counterproductive. One of the laughable management undertakings in the 1970s was to institute retreats and T-sessions among teachers or even in some manufacturing operations. The employees could not see why they needed to be taught how to get along with people with whom they hardly came into contact.

Another relational measure is how often employees come into contact with clients. If there is considerable contact with clients or customers, there must be some emphasis placed on human resources types of strategies. In the case of services to the developmentally disabled, for example, there is considerable contact on the part of many of the employees with clients, perhaps much more than most organizations. Thus, there is a need to have a management style that encourages personal growth in the employee so that these relationships are more rewarding. Relationships with clients or customers may be stressful in the absence of personal growth. A factory worker, on the other hand will have almost no need to develop such growth. It is rather difficult to convince someone that they need to set goals if what they do cannot lead to much personal growth. The typical response of such a line worker to suggestions they should set goals is that their goal is to make it to the weekend. Their personal growth will have to be satisfied through other means. Thus reward systems for this kind of task environment are more typically compensatory or involve off-duty opportunities.

Average Number of Hours of Contact Per Day (8 hours)*			
	Employee	*Manager*	*Client*
Employee			
Manager			
Client			
Citizen			

Figure 3.3

*Contact is measured by actual time of cooperation or dialogue in a formal relationship.

Employee - a person actually carrying out specific tasks of the organization. (Some will have a mixture of management and employee hours.)
Manager - a person conducting administrative oversight of others.
Client - those actually benefitting from the service.
Citizens - those outside of the organization who receive no direct benefits.

The chart is applied by inserting the observed formal contact hours for each category. This measures both the level of contact and the level of formality. Generally, the higher the resulting numbers, the more highly structured the management strategy would need to be.

The final relational measure is the ratio of formal to informal contact between employees. Formal contact is defined as that which is almost exclusively vested in the office or position of the individuals. This is closely related to the amount of contact that employees have but adds another dimension as far as quality is concerned. In some work environments the relationship is mostly formal. For example, a receptionist in a doctor's office necessarily conducts most transactions with the doctor in a formal sense (i.e., notifying them of appointment arrivals or processing the records.) The doctor and the receptionist may be cordial to one another but rarely collegial. In a university on the other hand, the contact between faculty would more ideally be informal most of the time. This is because they view one another as equals and have little to do with the performance of the others in the conduct of their work. In the typical human service system, the degree of contact is largely less formal than most organizations. This is primarily due to the fact that the work with clients is unique and the need for direct supervision of staff is rare. The analysis of relationships is demonstrated by Figure 2 above.

By applying an analysis of search procedures, stakeholders, and relationships in the organization, the task environment may be more accurately assessed. Such assessment will prove very useful in arriving at appropriate structural arrangements. It should be recognized at this point that the task environment is probably not universal throughout any organization. This was found to be the case in provider organizations for the developmentally disabled. Some of the organizations had environments that involved analyzable search procedures with few exceptions. A smaller provider who dealt with clients whose needs were consistent mostly fell into this classification. An institution dealing with severely disabled clients with poor communication skills commonly fell into this category as well. However, an Intermediate Care Facility for the Mentally Retarded (ICF/MR) which dealt with clients with a variety of skill levels, was more likely to have a task environment with unanalyzable search procedures with many exceptions. The relationship levels varied significantly as well. The main point here is that task environment analysis should be performed at the local level and then some assessment of the structural arrangements may take place. That being said, in the case of human services, it is safe to say that generally the providers operate in an environment with unanalyzable search procedures with many exceptions, a relatively high level of stakeholders operating on the ethical, moral, and cooperative dimension, and relational contact largely frequent and informal. This task environment calls for a very hands off approach to management with human resources methods such as individualized growth plans (for employees) and mutually constructed measurements of success.

Value Selection as a Guide to Administrative Strategy

While the discussion to this point has focused on the need to evaluate task environment and general philosophical climate, these are not necessarily the first steps that need to be taken in determining administrative strategy. The most important process that must be undertaken is the development of agreement on the values to be served. Much more often than not, this process is not actually carried out. In fact, most organizations assume that there is general agreement on values when there is not. This is typically the case because the parties are not aware that there are other options in value selection than the ones they hold themselves. For example, in the welfare arena the administrative branch of the agencies typically held that the highest value was the efficient distribution of resources, including keeping fraud to a minimum. However, the front line staff considered the highest value to be effective distribution of resources so that beneficiaries are more likely to have a reasonable quality of life. This undisclosed conflict was probably more responsible for the failures of the welfare system than anything else.

The broad values that may be pursued in public administration are fairly universal. The device I have found useful is to present them as the six E's of public administration: efficiency, effectiveness, equality, economy, excellence, and education. A brief description of these, particularly in terms of human services, should clarify the process that must be conducted and how profound the choice of values may be.

Efficiency

This is probably the most misused of the values because it is constantly invoked without an understanding of what it entails. It is properly defined as the greatest outcome with the least expenditure of energy. Most of the time, this energy is measured in money. Thus the most important variable is the amount of energy/money expended per case.

Effectiveness

Effectiveness is sometimes confused with efficiency but is actually frequently in conflict with it. Effectiveness is the greatest outcome relative to the starting point. So the most important variable is the progress of the population being served.

Equality/equity

Equality/equity is the priority of ensuring that all parties being served are reaping equal results. There is some variation in how this may be accomplished. Thus, equality may be understood as having the goal that all persons receive equal processes or services. Equity on the other hand, relates more to the desire that all persons being served achieve an equal outcome .

Economy

Economy is also confused with efficiency at times. However, economy focuses on the most beneficial outcome to the budget or to the larger economy. When this is given priority, the focus is on spending money where it will have the greatest financial benefit. For example, education funds are directed to the school district which will yield the greatest economic growth.

Excellence

This is the value being served by the quality movements, at least for the most part. The focus is on quality in terms of client/customer satisfaction. This is much more flexible than the other values in that the others can easily be subordinate to it without being contradictory.

Education

Education is usually not considered a value in public programs explicitly. However, it is not unusual for systems to value it over all other outcomes. The priority is placed on the various stakeholders, including persons being served and employees gaining the greatest knowledge. For example, this may be a matter of learning how to move to self-sufficiency as with the stated goals of welfare reform programs.

The choice of a value for an organization is ideally set system-wide. However, it is not always practicable. The more important matter is to be reasonably certain that there is value agreement vertically rather than horizontally. For example, in the system of services to the developmentally disabled it was important for the agreement to occur from departments of human services, to the regional offices, to the providers. Where there were other values in the other parts of the system (e.g., Intermediate Care Facilities or small group homes) the part of the state administrative system that worked with such groups should have been in agreement with their values. It should be clear that it is all right for different groups of providers to have differing goals. That being said, it is probably not necessary in most cases to achieve any kind of unanimity. The more appropriate outcome is one of consensus. There is a clear distinction between these two concepts. Unanimity is a point at which all have agreed to some value or statement of purpose. Consensus, on the other hand, is a point at which all parties can live with the stated values. The former is virtually unachievable and the latter is possible with considerable effort. Again using the services to the developmentally disabled as an example, while there had been indications that the smaller rural providers had a different point of view (i.e., degree of control) it was in the state's best interest to move toward more universal agreement on values. To be direct, even though the small providers stated that they prefer to be more integrated in the state regulatory system, it was preferable for the parent of state government to encourage them to move on their own.

An excellent example of a state system that has truly attempted the principle of moving on agreement on values first and then designed systems to support it was in Oregon:

> By 1990, personnel in Oregon's Office of Developmental Disability Services had completed a process that provided an explicit, public clarification of the values, principles, and outcomes that the state's service system is expected to produce for individuals with mental retardation and their families. This new vision is described in a document Toward Quality Lifestyles (Toews, 1990), which delineates how the Oregon service system is shifting away from the traditional continuum of services which often forces individuals with disabilities to adapt to preexisting buildings, facilities, or service models and toward a service system that adapts to the unique support needs of individuals. [24]

The fact that the first step in this process was to come to agreement on the values to be served was largely responsible for the fact that the system has been shown to be quite effective in the beginning. However, as we shall see later this system also runs into some more profound challenges. From the point of value agreement, a system was designed that altered the levels of responsibility for successful outcomes. The system was designed to serve the values of excellence which are evidenced in improvements for clients in achievements of independence, productivity, and integration. This was to be measured in observable outcomes which are assessed by the providers themselves. The program of continuous quality improvement was implemented by including a two-pronged approach. Providers were taught how to gather timely and accurate information about the quality of their service processes and then were taught how to use this information in team meetings. Thus, the individual providers had direct responsibility for tracking and improving quality. They were able to use the information gathered to steadily improve what they did and were motivated further by the experience of self-actualization that is derived from observing one's own accomplishments. The reliability of their measurements has been tested and shown to be quite high. [25] These are impressive results of a system improvement that began with value clarification. While this program is specific to Intermediate Care Facilities for Mentally Retarded (ICF/MRs), its outcomes are generalizable to other systems. The crucial point is to work on value clarification first, and then proceed to administrative strategy to satisfy the agreed-upon values.

Summary and Conclusion

The elements of successful administrative strategy are indeed complex. This Chapter suggests a broad-based plan of action for undertaking strategy selection. The discussion of the relevant organizational types, task environment and philosophy specific to systems led to the need to agree upon values first. The purpose of this conceptual discussion is to explain the logic behind the current administrative paradigm. By proceeding from the larger context of various types of organizational approaches to analysis of the task environment in the organization to the dominant philosophies that are pushing those task environments and finally to the base point of values that incorporate the philosophies, it should be clear that there is a direct link between values and administrative strategy. The interrelationship between values and structure is such that the only way to design effective strategies is to seriously undertake value clarification. This brings us to a point of understanding the relationship between administration and society. From this end, it is fairly easy to see the Rational model at work. The next chapter deals with the relationship of the general public discourse and resulting actions to the Rational model and how this has brought us to the point of disconnectedness.

---

1. Sundram, Clarence J., "Quality Assurance in an Era of Consumer Empowerment and Choice," *Mental Retardation* 32, no. 5 (1994): 371-375
2. Interagency Task Force on Developmental Disabilities Action Plan for Modification of the Montana Developmental Disabilities Service System (November 28, 1989).

3. Ibid., p. 5
4. Heinlen, "Quality of Care, Quality of Life: A Rural Perspective," *Mental Retardation* 32, no. 5 (1994): 374-376.
5. Sundram, "Quality Assurance in an Era of Consumer Empowerment and Choice," 371.
6. Swiss, James W., "Adapting Total Quality Management (TQM) to Government," *Public Administration Review* 52, no. 4 (1992): 356-361.
7. Terry, Larry D., "Why We Should Abandon the Misconceived Quest to Reconcile Public Entrepreneurship with Democracy," *Public Administration Review,* 53, no. 4 (1993): 393-395.
8. Heinlen, "Quality of Care, Quality of Life: A Rural Perspective," 374.
9. Sundram, "Quality Assurance in an Era of Consumer Empowerment and Choice," 373.
10. Heinlen, "Quality of Care, Quality of Life: A Rural Perspective," 375-376
11. Denhardt, Janet V. and Robert B., *The New Public Service: Serving Not Steering*, (Armonk: M.E. Sharpe, 2002).
12. Sundram, "Quality Assurance in an Era of Consumer Empowerment and Choice," 374.
13. Henlein, "Quality of Care, Quality of Life: A Rural Perspective," 375.
14. Ray, N. K., "From Paper Tigers to Consumer-Centered Quality Assurance Tools: Reforming Incident Reporting Systems," *Mental Retardation*, 33, no. 4 (1995): 239-247.
15. Ashbaugh, John and Gary Smith, "Beware the Managed Health-Care Companies," *Mental Retardation*, 34, no. 3 (1996): 189-193.
16. Ibid., p. 191
17. Ibid., p. 191
18. Ibid.
19. Ibid, p. 193.
20. Fiedler, Fred E., *A Theory of Leadership Effectiveness* (New York: McGraw-Hill, 1967), 307-311.
21. Perrow, Charles, *Complex Organizations: A Critical Essay,* 3rd ed. (New Haven: Random House, 1986).
22. Mitroff, Ian I., *Stakeholders of the Organizational Mind,* (San Francisco: Jossey-Bass Inc., 1983), 32.
23. Fiedler, Fred E., "The Contingency Model: A Theory of Leadership Effectiveness, " *Problems in Social Psychology*, ed. Carl W. Backman and Paul F. Secord (New York: McGraw-Hill, 1970), 279-289.
24. Newton, J. Stephen, William R. Ard, Jr., Robert H. Horner, and James D. Toews, "Focusing on Values and Lifestyle Outcomes in an Effort to Improve the Quality of Residential Services in Oregon," *Mental Retardation*, 34, no. 1 (1996): 1-12.
25. Ibid. 5-6.

Chapter 4: Moving to Outcome-Based Strategies

Now that we have examined some of the attributes of current public organizations and some of the more common administrative strategies, we turn to consider efforts made to develop designs based more on outcome than process. This, it would seem, is the nature of any attempt at problem solving. However, as noted in the previous chapter, bureaucracies are not particularly successful at problem solving. Much of this has to do with what I like to call, the victory of process over outcome. As a response to this, the development of outcome based strategies has been advocated for several decades now. For example, we have seen a variety of attempts to move the public sector to more performance-based budgeting practices. There have also been several commissions which sought to reform the public agencies so that they could be more responsive to the political system and to accomplish stated goals. These have had some short term successes and a few longer term ones. Overall, however, the need for outcome based strategies persists. This was the premise of the National Performance Review of the late 1990s, continuing with the Bush Administration's Management Reform initiatives.[1] There have been several attempts in the state and local systems of government for outcome based strategies as well. Some have been more successful than others. Nevertheless, I suggest that none have achieved the level of focus on outcomes or performance that has been sought. There are many explanations for this failure. I argue that the problem rests in the underlying paradigm that has formed these organizations.

To understand this, we must first recognize that bureaucracy is just one organizational form and it is not the only one. It is not the same as "large" and it is not a synonym for any kind of public administration. A bureaucracy is an intentional way of designing an organization that was generally formulated during the Industrial era. We have used the term to refer to other administrative practices in earlier eras and organizations incorrectly. A bureaucracy is a rational organization that emphasizes "fixed and official jurisdictions" as so clearly defined by Max Weber. This approach was viewed as the most sensible way of solving society's problems during the height of the Industrial era. It employs the underlying belief that there are more or less direct cause-effect relationships and they are discoverable. Such a belief is at the very core of rationality which is the premise of bureaucracy. Therefore, organizations divide tasks into specialties and utilize hierarchical structure to maintain control in order to treat the individual cause-effect relationships.

The second recognition must be that bureaucracy is not inherently evil. Bureaucracy, as an organizational form, has been largely responsible for many of the "successes" in American history. It was largely responsible for the victory of World War II.. It contributed to the incredible period of economic growth in the 1950s and 1960s. It is merely a means to certain kinds of ends. If all of the principles of bureaucracy were to be honored it would likely result in a very efficient and controlled system of task accomplishment. It was vastly better than the arbitrary approaches to administration carried out prior to the 19th Century. By focusing on procedures and rules rather than the power of individuals, bureaucracy was able to move government and industry forward. The real problem lies in the fact that bureaucracy is no longer necessary in order to control organizations, partially because we now have information technologies that can exchange ideas without a need for structural control.

Bureaucracies are intentionally designed to enforce rules and procedures *first*. The structure is supposed to maintain itself and to be certain that it does so it deals in positions not people. This may sound a bit callous but the value of a rational system was that it was reasonably predictable. In order to accomplish this goal of predictability it was necessary to base everything on rationality. As soon as people were added to the picture, rationality went out. So in order to avoid such an outcome, every attempt was made to remove people from the dynamics of the structure itself. Consequently, in order to preserve positions, rules were created so that no matter who is in the position the same rules will be the governing force. Therefore, it is no accident that the administration of programs, like Aid to Families with Dependent Children (AFDC) were based on rule enforcement rather than problem solving. In order to be problem solvers, the administrators must be able to face each problem uniquely since that is the nature of problems. Such allowance would be antithetical to the principles of bureaucracy.

There are basic sociological contributors to bureaucracy, as well. As society came to accept rationality more, we assumed that all problems could be solved by finding the root cause and correcting it. Essentially, then we only needed to eliminate all root causes to create a reasonable society. The instrument at the disposal of government institutions, as noted above, is rule making. In modern governance, the strategy became one of creating rules that corrected problems. So if the problem was that people were not keeping their sidewalks clear of snow, a local government would simply pass a rule (ordinance) that required them to do so. The agencies could then use their rule enforcement abilities to bring about the desired effect. Needless to say, this became a rather universal means of confronting problems. If people did not have adequate housing, a rule was passed by Congress that programs should be implemented that provided adequate housing. This brings us to the point of recognizing the historical as well as the organizational forces behind the bureaucratic ethos. Once we understand a bit of where we have been, then we can look at attempts to adopt problem solving or outcome based methods of organizing and governing.

A Thumbnail Sketch of the History of Public Administration in the U. S.

We begin first by looking briefly at the history of public administration in the U.S. From the beginning, shortly after Woodrow Wilson's landmark article in 1887, the focus has been to develop rational guidelines for conducting the public's affairs.[2] This is presented in terms of general schools of thought or models. Some authors have presented these movements in terms of paradigms. I have not opted to do so because it is inconsistent with the definition I offered in Chapter 1. The various reforms have been attempted within the same Rational paradigm. Included in the brief history of the field itself, I will offer a synopsis of the developments in public personnel administration, budgetary theory/practice and program evaluation. The intersections of these events in public administration are not precise. So what is presented is a general overview, grouping the ideas within loosely defined periods of time. What I intend to demonstrate is the collective ideas of the field during this history.

Phases of Public Administration

I have chosen to draw heavily from the historical development presented by Nicholas Henry. I have found this to be the best portrayal of the evolution of public administration in the United States.[3] The chart which follows depicts the significant periods in public administration. This, I find is a very useful way to examine the history of the field. The point here is not to provide a comprehensive study of the field but to place ourselves in time, understanding what has brought us to this point. This also contributes some evidence of the challenges of outcome-based strategies. The chart also shows the general movements in other aspects of the field: public administration theory, public personnel administration, budgetary principles, and organizational theory. I have chosen to break these out in this manner because it shows how the various ideas were integrated and a little of how each influences the other. It also shows the prevailing ideas of the periods.

Phase 1: The Reform Period

This period was marked by the beginnings of real reform in government at the process point. Government involvement had grown to the point that it was no longer appropriate to allow strictly patronage systems to carry out the tasks. The projects were getting much too complex and more people were being directly affected. The field itself was focusing its attention on the need to separate politics from administration. This was directly tied to the development of a civil service system that places a demarcation between elected officials and those conducting the day-to-day business of governance. The budgetary system retained the elements of the spoils system, however. Thus, funds were still allocated based more on political power than on programmatic needs. The prevailing theory of organizations continued to be based on personal power. Very little was considered as far as any scientific study of management was concerned. The model assumed that leadership was a matter of charisma and personal ability.

Phase 2: The Principles of Administration Period

During this time, the scholars in the field promoted the need to develop some principles by which the leaders in the public sector should be governed. The belief was that if these principles were standardized there was a better chance of consistency and accountability. The best known examples of this were W. F. Willoughby's, *Principles of Public Administration* and Frederick W. Taylor's *Principles of Scientific Management*. Another model that attracted considerable attention was Luther Gulick and Lyndall Urwick's, *Papers on the Science of Administration*, which presented the seven principles of administration in the acronym, POSDCORB (Planning, Organizing, Staffing, Directing, Coordinating, Reporting, Budgeting). The emphasis in personnel strategies was an extension of Taylor's Scientific Management, which emphasized standard operating procedures and identification of the one best way to perform duties. The budgetary practices had moved to a more rational system of line item budgeting, which required that agencies submit requests for funds based on identified expenditures rather than being based purely on political strength. The major organizational theories were also those that came from Scientific or Classical management models. These stressed the need to organize in a standard and predictable manner.

Phase 3: The Administrative Management Period

This period is marked by a further move to rational methods of organizing in the public sector. A notable contributor to this model was Chester Barnard in *Function of the Executive* and Herbert Simon in *Administrative Behavior*. The emphasis here was the counterbalance to the principles, rejecting this method as a reasonable way to govern because there was no way to know all of the choices available. This period also showed serious challenges to the ideal of the separation of politics and administration. Those in the political science discipline saw this as an unreasonable alternative since the administrative structures still needed to be responsive to the political forces. The Brownlow Committee of 1937 endorsed this wave of thought by asserting the need for centralizing control in the political bodies rather than allowing the administrative agencies to have their own locus of control. Budgeting practices were focused on performance as a means of allocating resources. This was mostly a matter of trying to tie funds to responsiveness to the political process rather than on actual outcomes. The main organizational theories were the Human Relations School which emphasized the need to acknowledge the social aspects of the organization. It instituted ideas like suggestion boxes and company gatherings outside of the work place. This was a direct outcome of the Hawthorne Studies which identified the impact of personal recognition as a motivator.

Phase 4: Professional Career System Period

The field of public administration itself was rather weak during this period as it had come to be dominated by political science. The values here were that administration was reintegrated with politics as a way of reining in the power of the bureaucrats. Thus, public administration was viewed as merely a subset of political science in that it brought management theories to the politicians. At the same time, there was a steady rise in the number of professionals entering the civil service system. This brought some need to recognize the highly skilled nature of these civil servants. The personnel administrative thrust was on the need for using the civil service regulations to exercise management control by the political leadership. This was also a time of heightened government intervention in many areas of citizens' lives. The budgetary process emphasized experimentation in controlling the budgets more on the political end through Planning, Programming, Budgeting, Systems (PPBS). This again stressed the need to control where funds were going based on specific program intents. Specifically, budget proposals from the administrators were drafted in terms to alternative policies and the cost of each. However, most of the energy was focused on funding processes rather than actual outcomes.

Phase 5: The Management Science Period

During this period, the need to acknowledge the importance of the public administrator was again identified. The public sector had grown immensely and there was a compelling need to identify appropriate management methods. The complexity of programs also dictated this need for professional skills and the management methods associated with them. The notable works in the field during this time included James G. March and Herbert Simons, *Organizations*, and James D. Thompson's, *Organizations in Action*. A significant contribution to the field was by H. George Frederickson in his, *New Public Administration*. This work called upon the professionals in the field to recognize how much they are responsible for contributing to the decision making process, not just as underlings carrying out the mandates of political leaders. These contributions emphasized the need to focus the attention of the field of public administration on methods of management. This was particularly carried over into the public personnel field as the human resource programs centered on their use as management tools. The budgetary theories that were employed were Management by Objectives and Zero-Based Budgeting. These were viewed as more scientific (i.e., rational) ways of distributing resources. The concentration was decidedly on process. The political leadership asserted that by requiring the administrators to follow the specific procedures within these budgeting methods then more rational choices would be made and wasteful programs discarded. The organizational theories reflected this fascination with method in the Systems and Organizational Culture theories. These emphasized focusing on the internal workings of the organization in order to apply their efforts to the task more effectively.

Phase 6: Performance Management Period

This period has been dominated by the need to improve performance. The field itself focused more and more on the unique nature of public administration. More professional development is emphasized along with advances in education. Personnel administration is marked by procedural devices for adjudication and the specific identification of the Senior Executive Service (SES) which is a level of administration acting as a go-between for the political leadership and the civil service. The budgetary practices emphasize more top-down management as the priority became reducing the deficit. The tradition of promoting a new budgeting system fell from favor. Rather, the previous systems continued to be used under a broader umbrella of budgeting as political management. The first reflection of this trend was Target Based Budgeting Agency spending limits or "targets" are set by the elected officials. Agency heads are to achieve their targets in whatever way they deem appropriate. Agencies are frequently given incentives to achieve the targets. This results in the demise of bottom-up budgeting since it grants all the power to the chief executive to set the targets. The budget became more of a separate concern in the political sphere. The main organizational theories are Quality enhancement (which are also referred to as Excellence approaches) and Contingency or Transformational theories. These emphasize the empowerment of individuals throughout the organization.

The emphasis in this chapter is to examine recent efforts to move toward outcome-based strategies and self monitoring procedures in light of the historical and sociological roots. These can be seen in the light of the larger evolution of the field as natural outgrowths of its overall direction. The study of services for the developmentally disabled will again serve as a case. The second phase of the study was an examination of outcome based strategies for these services. As the study proceeded, it became clear that the major considerations were implementation strategies, in general. The fact was that there were numerous outcome-based models in existence at the time of the study. Both of the major certifying associations had developed rather extensive models that could be used by any provider. Much of what was being done within the human services field in many states was outcome based. However, the fact remained that these systems did not govern how programs were administered in the states. In fact, it became clear that, in spite of years of efforts to implement outcome-based systems, the rule centered bureaucracies persisted. Other states in the region were experiencing the same difficulties. Even though they had attempted to implement outcome-based systems they seemed to gravitate back to the bureaucratic model. This suggests one of two possibilities: (1) outcome-based systems are ineffective, leading us back to the bureaucratic approach as the only reasonable means to administer human service systems or (2) there is a fundamental flaw in the underlying philosophy which drives these systems. In other words, we must either work within the bureaucratic ethos or we must make change that alters our very thought processes. After considerable review of the history of similar reforms in other states, examination of the data, and review of the literature related to delivery of human services, I have concluded the latter.

The challenges are great indeed. However, the payoff to moving to a more appropriate paradigm should be enormous. I acknowledge that I am suggesting that a large number of people must face a rather dramatic shift in thinking. That, as it turns out, will be the greatest challenge of all. I urge the reader to approach this with an open mind and a commitment to discovering the possibility of forging a system of services that will be truly driven by the consumers' best interests. I also believe that this environment presents us with an opportunity to demonstrate a better way of encountering a wide array of human service problems and moving to a philosophy that is more effective as well as more human friendly.

Literature/Documents

In order to gain a better understanding of outcome-based models, I immediately began the research process by gathering information from a variety of sources. These materials included extensive descriptions of outcome-based models from accreditation associations and private firms, as well as state agencies. It was clear that many organizations were committed to adopting this approach to improve services to the disabled. The Rehabilitation Accreditation Commission (CARF) provided extensive materials which included Survey Guides for Individual Service Plans and for Consumer and Family Quality Measures. They also provided a variety of source books and accreditation guidelines. The Accreditation Council (AC) sent Guidelines for Outcome Measures for Early Childhood and for Families and Children. The Research and Training Center on Residential Services and Community Living of the University of Minnesota provided materials on innovative programs from around the nation. Their publication, *Reinventing Quality* (while employing a tired phrase) was most useful in focusing the conceptual development. The Neighborhood Living Project of the University of Oregon provided materials on Outcome Measurement and an Outcomes Measurement Operations Manual. The DD Services Bureau of the State of Oregon provided a Core Competencies Resource Guide and other materials related to the implementation of quality assurance models. The Department of Developmental Services of the State of California provided interview guides for developing an Individual Program Plan, a Providers' Handbook for Quality, and a visitor's guide for observing quality. The State of Montana provided materials related to the organizational plans and data. Paradigm Systems® of Salem, Oregon provided extensive materials on "Advocates Involved in Monitoring" (AIM), a program designed to employ self monitoring to improve outcome assessments, survey guides for developing Individual Plans, and Guides for Continuous Quality Improvement. This description only highlights the material made available and barely covers how much is available with respect to outcome-based models. This intense interest in outcome-based plans is not confined to services to the developmentally disabled or just to human service, for that matter. Agencies across the spectrum of services, from the U. S. Forest Service to the Department of Defense, have published and promulgated many such programs. For purposes of this discussion, I will continue to focus on the process I employed to examine the possibility of outcome-based strategies within the context of services to the developmentally disabled (or DD Services). Just the same, I am convinced that these findings are generalizable to other sectors.

Interviews

While collecting the written materials, I also conducted interviews of an array of interested parties and authorities. Most of these interviews were in person which is a preferred means of information gathering since it allows for the visual exchange of data as well as voice. The interviews were open-ended, permitting the greatest opportunity for exploration of some rather complex concepts. Telephone interviews were conducted with CARF and AC as well as the Research and Training Center of the University of Minnesota. The conversation with Mr. Dale Dutton of CARF was quite informative not only in the sense that it revealed the association's commitment to outcome-based models. It also became clear that it has been extremely difficult to arrive at satisfactory results with these models. The expressed concerns centered on the resistance of most providers to allow the outcome systems to determine compensation for services. It was also clear that the states had been having difficulty administering these systems because they were not necessarily compatible with the agencies' data collection strategies. A telephone conversation with Dr. Barbara Pollister of the University of Minnesota, reinforced the strong commitment in the field to move to outcome-based models. However, it was also apparent that the implementation of these strategies had not been altogether satisfactory. In fact, after reviewing some of their literature on innovative strategies, it was clear that the model had been administered almost exclusively on a local basis and that the tendency was to revert to more bureaucratic approaches as soon as any difficulties arose.

The first face-to-face interviews were conducted in Montana. These included discussions with several of the providers around the state. These conversations further clarified the nature of the problems being confronted by the system. Many of these difficulties have already been described in the previous chapter. However, the information pointed to some even more profound challenges facing the system. It was becoming clear that the perspectives even within the group of providers varied considerably. It was also evident that the ongoing planning process (Strategic Planning Across Montana (SPAM)) was receiving very mixed reviews. This alerted me to the possibility that the process, even though it was being effectively facilitated, was not getting at the underlying impediments. There was genuine confusion throughout the system when it came to future direction as well as the current state of affairs. This provided an indication of either some fundamental tension taking place that prevented the participants from communicating their visions effectively or a more rudimentary conflict of interests or philosophy.

The Montana interviews included some direct care staff members and family members as well. These discussions also revealed considerable tension within the system. The direct care staff was generally committed to the concept of outcome-based assessment. However, they felt that they were receiving conflicting messages from the management of the system itself. If they focused on outcomes and consumer desires, they would not be able to comply with all of the expectations of reports and procedures. The family members revealed a basic level of conflict and confusion from the perspective of those who relied on the services. There were very dramatic differences with respect to expectations and values. While some of the families were advocating for more independence on the part of the consumer and for much more integration, others were concerned more with receiving what they perceived as an entitlement. The former group was mostly interested in promoting change and more supported living while the latter was more guided by the need to be a client. This kind of essential difference in understanding also indicated a very profound tension throughout the system. Finally, discussions with the Montana Department of Public Health and Human Services (DPHHS) indicated that there were also striking differences in perception within the agency itself. The basic conflict related to the degree of control exercised by the agency and the values that should be emphasized. An interview with the Developmental Disabilities Planning and Advisory Council (DDPAC) also demonstrated some rather fascinating conceptual turmoil within the system. It had become rather obvious to me that the overall picture is very complex and that the nature of the tension within the system is multi-dimensional. This is no bipolar conflict where there are two clearly defined points of view. Rather, there are multiple differences of perception occurring both horizontally and vertically.

After I had gathered so much information from the documents and the Montana interviews, I went on the road to learn more about what other states had experienced. I chose to go to Oregon and California because they had both gone through the implementation of outcome-based strategies and because they are western states. It is preferable to examine states with similar cultures in order to derive any findings that are germane to human services overall. The literature had shown that other states had embarked on ambitious outcome-based systems as well. Systems of particular note were identified in Pennsylvania and Massachusetts. Many of their programs had taken a somewhat different approach to administration of DD Services, especially as they related to locus of control. The Oregon experience was particularly attractive for this study because they had drawn upon some of the same resources as Montana for their reforms. Their experience was also useful in that it had a relatively long history which would provide some very important longitudinal information.

The first interview was with Paradigm Systems, Inc., a firm which had been contracted by the State of Oregon to develop and implement an outcome-based system in 1994. Paradigm developed and delivered to several providers in the state a system called Advocates Involved in Monitoring (AIM) that emphasized surveying the consumer and developing a plan that met those needs. The program also included an interesting approach to self monitoring. The monitoring was performed by advocates. Paradigm conducted training for these auditors so that they properly gathered the desired information. The basic premise was that the observers should trust their senses in evaluating whether or not the provider met the needs of the consumers. As a follow-up project, Paradigm also developed a Continuous Quality Improvement (CQI) program for state providers. This was a direct carryover of W. Edwards Deming's Total Quality Management (TQM) strategies that have attracted so much attention. The CQI program emphasized the development of a commitment to quality throughout the organizations. This was accomplished by training management personnel to become facilitators of a quality driven program. Paradigm was very enthusiastic about these programs. They certainly appeared to be exactly what was needed to implement an outcome-based system. However, I soon discovered that they had been discontinued, which suggested that there was something amiss.

This brought me to the meeting with the agency director of DD Services for the State of Oregon. The discussion was most informative in that it presented a different perspective regarding attempts at outcome-based systems. The history of all the reforms in the state was most intriguing. The Legislature had mandated that the Oregon system move to outcome-based strategies back in 1984. Consequently, the state experience presents quite a revealing story related to how such strategies fare. The chart in Figure 3 on the following page summarizes how the Director described their current programs. What is significant about this description is that it demonstrates that there have been many approaches incorporated as means to get to a more effective system. The variations are indicators of the multidimensional character of human service systems, especially as they result from mandates by the Legislature to be outcome-based. It is rather apparent that this effort has proven to be problematic. The conversation began with the Director stating that he found that quality assurance systems in general are suspect. Their experience lends considerable insight with respect to implementing programs which center on outcomes. Specifically, Oregon tried these innovations but they never got much farther than pilot programs. In the end, the need for accountability superseded the attraction to more purely outcome-based strategies. This will be discussed more later.

The next interview was conducted with the Neighborhood Living Project of the University of Oregon. This project is something of the equivalent of the Rural Institute at the University of Montana and similar efforts found in most states, except they are also responsible for gathering data for the state agency. The most recent development to come from the project is the Residential Outcomes System (ROS), which is a revision of an earlier version called the Valued Outcomes Information System (VOIS). The update was a result of a collaborative effort with the state's providers to develop a system that was more useful. A key point is that the usefulness was more a matter of what was useful to the providers than for the state. It was also upgraded in order to consolidate two data collection systems for residential programs and community-based programs. The providers were to submit information regarding valued activities to the Neighborhood Living Project, which in turn was used to generate the comprehensive data for the state. The primary purpose of the process was that it be used to measure overall progress for the administrative purposes of the state and more particular progress measurements for the individual provider teams. The data is not used for either incentives or sanctions as a condition of the program's goals. The Neighborhood Living Project also published a *Semi-Annual Residential Lifestyle Outcomes Evaluation Report*, which tabulates the data and offers some analysis of the data. At the time, they had about a 70% provider participation rate and expected to improve on that as time passed.

Some of the key points made by the Neighborhood Living staff also shed some light on considerations for effective outcome systems. First, they emphasized that any data collection system used by the state should be useful for the providers themselves: Never ask anyone to collect data that they don't personally use. They also strongly encouraged that a high priority be placed on being certain that data related to planning, analysis, and implementation be consistent. This reinforced a position offered by the state agency staff which recommended congruence throughout the system with respect to reporting and core competencies. One of the more profound positions offered by the Neighborhood Living Project is that data cannot be used for any incentive system. They argued that, based on their experience, any time data is tied to incentive or sanctions the numbers become suspect. This was contrary to what the accreditation associations had suggested. However, their arguments seem more valid based on the norms of social science. Earl Babbie in his, *The Practice of Social Research*, emphasizes the point that any data collection must be free from influences that would prefer one result over another [4]

There is certainly good reason to believe that if providers are going to be compensated based on the outcome data, they would tend to present the numbers in such a manner that would best serve their own interests. This is not to say that the providers would be dishonest. Whether or not they are is irrelevant. Rather, this is just recognition of normal human behavior, especially as it relates to business practices. People ordinarily will not go against their own interests.

An example that is particularly revealing was offered by the Neighborhood Living staff. The earliest reports showed that the achievement of outcomes was actually considerably higher than anticipated. In other words, the providers had indicated in the individual plans that they were striving for a much lower level of activity than they ended up achieving. This would suggest that the initial expectations tended to be much lower. The best explanation for this is that the providers probably did not completely believe that the numbers would not be used for sanctions. Consequently, the providers would tend to set out low aspirations to be sure that they did not end up reporting figures which fell short of the mark. The average achievement rate in the first semi-annual reports for activity was over 1,100 percent! This is not an insignificant result. It suggests that the mere perception that the data *could* be used for sanctions was enough to affect the numbers rather dramatically. The most recent reports continued to show a 400 percent achievement level.

The ROS process was designed to be as useful to the local staff as possible. In fact, the team at the Neighborhood Living Project stated rather emphatically that they encouraged all of the providers to use the data at their bi-weekly team meetings. It was clear that the staff of the Project were in the field frequently, which went to demonstrate their commitment to a system more useful to the provider staff. Almost all of them had been providers at some point. They were genuinely committed to helping to improve the system and to a consumer-centered philosophy. They also reiterated the belief that it was ineffective to mandate quality. The emphasis must be on the commitment of local staff and teams to seek quality. The major impediment to such a goal, however, is the constant need for monitoring and enforcement. The conclusion of our discussion was that there is probably no *system* that can in itself bring about quality.

The interview with the California Department of Developmental Services revealed other impediments to designing systems. The major discovery from this discussion stems from the likelihood that sometimes, it was possible to identify probable future developments by observing what was going on in California. It is fairly common knowledge that however California goes, the other western states are likely to follow. This was the case with the fiscal limits movement, beginning in earnest with Proposition 13; the term limits initiatives; and the general condition of state administration. It was in California that the movement to more privatization gathered its momentum. Developments in the field of services to the developmentally disabled were no exception. The priority of deinstitutionalization found its greatest strength in California as did community-based services. Since this is the case, the conversation with the California staff gave rise to some very serious concerns indeed. The most recent trends were actually precursors to re-bureaucratization.

Reform efforts dating back to the 1970s are what one might expect to have occurred. The movement away from institutions began early. The use of private providers also has a long standing in the state. However, recent events had prompted the Legislature and the courts to push in the other direction. The unions for the staff of the residential centers, along with the parents/families of the residents, were promoting their interest to keep the centers open. This alliance had proven quite potent in its ability to push public policy both through the courts and the legislative process. Coupled with this force, the media had pursued the idea that community based systems are more likely to result in abuse than residential programs. This was partially instigated by a report published by Dr. Strauss of the University of California Riverside which alleged that the data revealed that community programs were more dangerous than residential ones. The study was premised on the finding that the mortality rates among community clients were higher than those of residential clients. There had been appropriate responses from the state agencies but they appeared to have fallen on deaf ears. The fact was that no one had ever suggested that community-based programs would extend anyone's life. Quite the contrary, since the consumers were more independent they were also exposed to the same amount of risk as people in the general population. Resident life is much more protected than living in the community. Risk in its various forms is something that all of us consider a part of reality.*

California did have one factor that made it somewhat unique. Services for the disabled are specifically defined as an entitlement under the Lanterman Developmental Disabilities Services Act. Furthermore, current trends suggested that the definition of entitlement was being expanded to mean that such individuals should be protected from harm more than the general population. In addition to these legislative interpretations, the system was being governed by lawsuits. This caused the agency and the providers to spend much of their time on

---

* This was mostly a matter of misuse of the research data by advocates rather than poor research. The research was accurate; the interpretation of the policy ramifications was not.

the defensive. As opposed to the lawsuits that have driven the services to the developmentally disabled to deinstitutionalize, these suits were pushing in the opposite direction by requiring the agency to have greater administrative control and monitoring capability than they did at that time. This could be seen as a direct counterforce to privatization. One result of this dynamic was that Individual Program Plans (IPP) were tied to the entitlements. Consequently, whatever is included in the IPP, the Regional Center must fund. This stimulated greater rule enforcement strategies from the agencies. It seems rather ironic that the same state that gave us privatization was pushing for more administrative management.

The major difference here from other reform pressures was that the push for such administrative control was coming from the legislative branch rather than the executive. This demonstrates how direct pressure from the electorate for protection from risk can be more ominous than bureaucratic strategies. It also signifies where the bureaucratic ethos finds its roots. This will be discussed further in the Chapter 4 on philosophical challenges. At any rate, the resulting administrative strategy was about the same but even more difficult to change than the previous model of the welfare state. Legislative involvement in administrative practices presents serious obstacles to more outcome-based strategies. The more recent budgetary crisis in California and other states is likely to increase the pressure on providers to be more efficient. This will probably further dampen efforts toward outcome-based strategies. I say this because the natural response of agencies to budget crisis is to circle the wagons. This typically means to tighten the reins of control over providers. This is a clear example of the conflict between efficiency and effectiveness.

In summary, the document review and interviews yielded considerable information. The documents revealed that an extensive effort had been put into developing consumer-driven outcome systems. They also presented some of the more important underlying conceptual developments regarding such systems. The interviews were most helpful in filling in the gaps so to speak. They disclosed the genuinely human factors that come into play with any organizational change. Between the two sources of information it was possible to develop a greater understanding of what will be needed for the implementation of an outcome-based system and what is more likely to be effective. The following section is a more in-depth analysis of the findings regarding outcome-based models, setting the stage for a clearer understanding of the larger issues tied to public administration and rationality.

Observations of the Attempts at Reform in Human Service Systems

The DD Service systems exhibited some interesting attributes because they were some of the more mature systems in terms of moving to a contracting out approach. So the movement away from institutions was begun earlier than most of the other human service systems. This would seem to suggest that these state systems have evolved a new relationship between the policy making entities and the providers. However, my observations suggested that this was not entirely the case. Even though the states had been contracting out to private providers for over 20 years, the relationship remained largely bureaucratic. This is due to the fact that considerations of organizational structure were focused more on who was to carry out the various functions and not on how to replace or even the need to replace the bureaucratic ethos. As noted in the previous chapter, like it or not, bureaucracy is a preferred model in many respects and the desire to avoid risk maintains it.

The evidence that the bureaucratic model still dominates was found in: (1) the continued emphasis on rule enforcement, (2) the focus on accountability in the contracts themselves, as well as the related multiple layers of accountability, and (3) on the general philosophy of avoiding risk. Part of the problem relates to the fact that little was known about public entrepreneurship when the state began contracting out. There were many similar instances where services in many previously public programs were contracted out all around the country. However, these were usually those services easily assigned to private sector behaviors. These ranged from road construction to health services to space exploration. The early experiences with contracting out to private entities were generally moderately successful. However, in most cases, what evolved was a cooperative approach in the relationship between the private entity and the public agency. Consequently, the efficiencies or quality improvements being sought were generally not realized. Instead, the longer a private enterprise was responsible for a program the more it began to resemble the public agency that was its predecessor. The National Aeronautics and Space Administration (NASA) is a prime example of this phenomenon. After the Challenger accident, NASA instinctively moved to risk aversion even more than before. There was a similar reaction to the Columbia accident. The irony is that many analysts suggested that the fact that the agency, although mostly private, behaved in bureaucratic ways prior to the accident was, at least in part, responsible for the accidents. The organization was so caught up in overlapping rules that basic elements of safety were actually overlooked. Many analysts identified the essential problem as a need to move from the modified versions of privatization (cooperative or contracted services) to one more substantially different from its public predecessor. This is one area from which the concept of public entrepreneurship was developed. Ironically, even this concept remains mired in the Rational paradigm and will not lead the service providers out of the bureaucratic ethos. Nor will it address the fundamental issues that must be faced if there is to be movement away from Rationalism. This will be discussed further in later chapters.

In other service areas, local governments began to seek methods to deliver services in the community in a way that would satisfy the voters by contracting out as a way of reducing expenditures. The fiscal limits movement of the late 1970s and 1980s initiated some very serious reflection on the very premise of local governments themselves. As these governments faced more and more fiscal limits from the voters as well as from the state governments, they began to explore ways to completely reconstruct the manner in which they delivered services. None of these strategies seemed to work. The voters continued to reduce fiscal resources for their local governments. The citizenry seemed to lack the aptitude to connect the reduction of resources to diminished services. It was through this discovery process that governments began to recognize a need to redefine their role.[5] From this also sprang the idea of the New Public Service. The point of this description of the history of the idea of public service is that states like Montana were contracting out DD services prior to the recognition that a rather ambitious effort was needed to redefine the role of government. Consequently, the system exhibited many of the drawbacks of the earlier efforts to privatize. Basically, it was no one's fault; the knowledge was just not available at the time these reforms took place.

Some examples of how the DD Services systems continue to reflect the bureaucratic ethos will help to clarify the situation. It was particularly noteworthy during the interviews with various parties both in the Department of Public Health and Human Services and in some of the other bodies that the issue of health and safety of the clients arose as a primary value. This is an important observation because it reflects the priority of risk aversion. Of course, no one wants to see any of the clients harmed or neglected in any way. However, if this is the primary value, the programs would be designed to remove as much risk as could be identified. The agency continued to emphasize accountability as the guiding principle in its relationship with the providers. There were a couple of cases where the story of an incident in Deer Lodge County was repeated as an example of what can go wrong. This story was also consistently tied to the threat of liability for such an error. This is risk avoidance in its purest form. Anytime I hear someone in an agency talking about lawsuits and the like, I see a dominant value of avoiding risk or negative effectiveness, i.e., ensuring that certain things do not happen.

This was also clearly demonstrated in a recent evaluation system created by the agency. While a process of involving clients' families and advocacy groups was used to develop the evaluation system, it was clear that the old bureaucratic tendencies won the day. Remember, bureaucracy is something that will result when the constituency wants all risk removed. Consequently, there are numerous documents that include incident reporting and prescribed procedural responses. Even though the process began with a statement that it recognized the responsibility of the provider to determine procedures and that primary interest was in outcomes, the end product is loaded with expectations related to process.[6] What results is essentially an iron fist in a velvet glove. There are repeated statements of the need to acknowledge accomplishments and to respect the independence of the providers but the substantive result is extensive rule enforcement.

This tendency to rule enforcement was also visible in the contracts used by the state with the providers. Some specific examples are the requirements for including reports involving the number of staff available during specific hours and that the availability of certain personnel be assured. There were also provisions for multiple reports on the use of funds. Fiscal accountability is the primary mechanism for maintaining leverage over process. While it may seem harmless enough to require such reports, it was the contents of the reports that alerted me to the fact that the state intended to retain control over all procedures. If one has to track every dollar and be certain that it went to the exact line item that was budgeted in the beginning, it requires a rule enforcement system that is very much like the public agency's. This is a practice that is justified over and over as a way of protecting the taxpayer. Under an outcome-centered system, the taxpayer is protected by agencies focusing on successful endpoints. There is no evidence that strict enforcement of public accounting procedures will improve the quality of service. Yet, that was the area that was given the greatest emphasis in the contracts.

Another piece of evidence that the bureaucratic ethos was still very much in place was the existence of multiple layers of accountability. The providers were subjected to inspections by various regulatory agencies, some of whom were examining the same things. The evaluation handbook even acknowledged that the health department, the fire department, Occupational Safety and Health Administration (OSHA), Sanitarian, and the accrediting body all perform inspections but still requires that the Field Service Specialist (FSS) conduct inspections of those areas. Even though documentation of these inspections was provided to the FSS there was a list of areas to be inspected that were identical to those of the others. This is a rather compelling example of the priority of risk aversion. There was no reason to believe that the FSS was any more qualified to inspect these areas of health and safety but the requirement continued to be imposed.

Finally, the contract monitoring currently being used by the agency emphasized process rather than outcome. While some language in the contract called upon the provider to demonstrate that the clients' quality of life needs had been improved and that accomplishments were relevant, the rather exhaustive description of procedures related to reports and activities suggested that the greater concern was process. This was an important feature of the relationship between the agency and the contractors. One point that should be perfectly clear is that if the primary value selected by the system is the avoidance of any risk and strict accountability, then this relationship and the features that have just been described will serve that purpose quite well. That is why the process of value clarification must be taken first. If this was what the participants had decided was the most important goal of the system then there only needed to be some fine-tuning of the procedures and a clear statement made at the outset to all of the providers that such was the intent. However, the description of the desired values of the system did not clearly state that as the goal. Actually, the goals were stated more in terms of outcome with some qualifying language that emphasized safety and health.

This brings me to the next important point with respect to any human service or other administrative system. All the evidence suggested that values had not been agreed upon in the beginning of the contracting process. The state agency emphasized health and safety as a value. Interestingly enough, this is actually a reverse value in that it focuses on what should not happen. In that sense, it may be viewed as a focus on effectiveness. The larger providers in the state emphasized the need for clients to have a greater freedom of choice of services as well as greater personal opportunity. This is more closely tied to the value of education. The mid-level providers stressed the need for independence of the clients in a different manner. That is, they sought the value of the clients being able to live in their community of choice. This was mostly tied to the value of equality. The small providers appeared to value security for the clients and for themselves. This is most closely tied to the value of efficiency or perhaps, economy. Finally, the clients, their families and advocates, emphasized the value of quality of life and choice. This most closely related to the value of excellence. In any event, this is a serious issue when it comes to designing any system. The lack of agreement on values was probably mostly responsible for the confusion that I discovered at the outset. Each person in the agency that I spoke with was alarmed that any of the providers found it necessary to hire a consultant to analyze administrative strategy. They were under the impression that things were moving in the proper direction and that they were very accommodating for the providers. The fact is they probably were very accommodating and certainly demonstrated the highest levels of professionalism and concern for the system. The difficulty was not in how they carried out their duties; it rested in the incongruence of values. As noted earlier, it is very easy to assume that everyone is operating on the same set of values. The perception was that the set of values chosen by each of the parties was the obvious one, at least to them. Thus, no one was to blame for this incongruence. This is perhaps the most common difficulty being faced by almost every human service system, from health care to welfare.

The evidence also suggests that the policies and procedures in the system had been developed on a rather *incremental* basis. This incrementalism was described as the probable method of decision making in organizations by Charles Lindblom.[7] He attributed this to political considerations and risk avoidance. Generally, as issues were confronted, policies were developed. This is not uncommon at all. Governments are constantly faced with this dilemma. Democracies tend to operate on such a reactive basis. This is demonstrated by the fact that the most significant planning to take place in recent years was as a result of court orders. This can be a common attribute of a democratic system. If some parties are offended by particular practices in the system they may assert their right to bring their case to the legal system. There is also a track record of developing programs or opportunities as a result of a federal grant program. This is a feature of state governments that has been around for a very long time. Again, this is part of being a democratic society. A particular political party or interest group campaigns to take a different approach to policy. That group gains power and implements their policy through a grants-in-aid program. Then another interest group advocates for still another means of addressing a policy area and they gain power and implement a new grant program, and so on. Over time, state and local governments find themselves responding to these initiatives in order to get funding.

The answer is not to get rid of the democratic system, as some may suggest (and believe me, that is partly what has been suggested) but to redefine the role of government. This does not mean simply dropping programs because they cost money. It also does not mean succumbing to the belief that government is the enemy (which is rather ludicrous in a democracy.) Rather, it means to recognize that the role of government rests in the public forum. That public forum should agree on sets of values first and then some mechanism for delivery of services that emanate from those values. The system of services to the developmentally disabled is an excellent case in point. There is a need to move away from such incremental decision-making. However, this does not mean that there should be a movement away from a system tied to the democratic process. As a matter of fact, a managed care option is a strategy that moves away from democratic principles. It places the decisions regarding values into the hands of a private organization. Instead, the system should incorporate means for consensus building to establish values and then call upon the system to achieve the outcomes that extend from those values.

This brings us to a very significant positive attribute to the system. Generally, there was agreement on the basic value. That is, the state generally agreed that it should provide services to the developmentally disabled. There was also general agreement that these services should include opportunities for this special population and not try to isolate them or return to earlier warehousing practices. This was very promising indeed. It gave the system much to build upon. Part of what needed to be done was to define exactly what was meant by opportunities. It was also essential to come to some agreement on the priority of each of the values. The community needed to decide whether it was more concerned with personal growth, personal choice, or safety for this population. That brings us again to the need to develop some consensus on the values to be served by the system. This high degree of agreement is generally not found in public programs or services. Consequently, if the DD Services have such a high level of agreement and yet still face these kinds of challenges, it would suggest that rather substantial reforms are needed in all areas of governance, particularly as it relates to the field of public administration.

Finally, there is one area of concern that could bode ill for the system. While there was a high level of agreement on the need to provide services, there was a growing sense of fear among the general citizenry (at least those who were active in the political process) that they could not expend so much funding on it any longer. The current wave of fiscal limits in the states and national government is more ominous than its predecessor of the 1980s. The movement, essentially defined by Proposition 13 in California, was an attempt to slow the growth of government expenditures as a matter of efficiency. The sentiments of the up and coming groups suggest that government should begin dismantling the social services system altogether. This would present a formidable challenge to all services including those to the developmentally disabled. If we cannot commit to providing basic protection to the poor and disenfranchised then it is not much of a stretch to also eliminate services to the more fragile members of our population. This factor is included here because it challenges the very existence of the system itself. Unless, a high level of agreement can be reached on the values to be served and some consistency in the goals of the participants, the system can easily become a target of those who claim that government cannot do anything but provide for the general defense. Some of those interviewed described the system as virtually sacrosanct. There have been many other programs that made that assumption which are no longer part of the public system.

There is little doubt that we can actually afford to provide these services, there is some doubt as to whether we may assume we can retain the political will.

Moving to the heart of the matter, it became clear that there was an imbalance between the shift in emphasis to outcomes and the administrative structure to carry them out. Bureaucracies are not by their nature outcome-based. In reviewing the documents of the other states in the region, it was apparent that Montana was not unique in this imbalance between stated goals and program design. All of the planning documents stressed procedures as the desired outcomes. These are not outcomes. The value statements provided information closer to outcomes than the goals. Placing value on empowering individuals and their families is a reflection of a desired outcome. Now the only question to be answered is: how do we know when we have increased empowerment? There are a variety of ways that can be observed even if not measured. This can best be set by the providers not by the oversight administration. This is just one example of the imbalance between stated intentions and actual practices. The imbalance is reflected in the fact that the providers were being assigned the responsibility for services but being required to respond to administrative procedures that influence the services. In other words, the bureaucratic ethos dominates even if cloaked in language of empowerment. The emphasis needed to shift and the balance between intent and outcome established.

---

1. Breul, Jonathan, "Three Bush Administration Management Reform Initiatives: The President's Management Agenda, Freedom to Manage Legislative Proposals, and the Program Assessment Rating Tool", *Public Administration Review*, 67, no. 1 (2007): 21-26.
2. Wilson, Woodrow, "The Study of Administration," *Political Science Quarterly*, 56, no. 4, (1887).
3. Henry, Nicholas, *Public Administration and Public Affairs*, 6th ed., (Englewood Cliffs: Prentice Hall, 1995).
4. Babbie, Earl S., *The Practice of Social Research* 5th ed., (Belmont: Wadsworth Publishing Co., 1989), 472 ff.
5. Edgar, Patrick B., *Fiscal Limits in Montana: How Counties Learn to Cope*, (Los Angeles: University of Southern California, 1991).
6. *Draft Comprehensive Evaluation of Services Handbook*, State of Montana, The Developmental Disabilities Program of the Department of Public Health and Human Services, March 1996.
7. Lindblom, Charles E., "The Science of Muddling Through," *Public Administration Review* 19, no. 2, (1959): 79-88.

Chapter 5: Locus of Control, Procedures and Human Service Outcomes

Drawing upon the apparent difficulties associated with moving to outcome based strategies, one may conclude that the solution to the resistance of bureaucracy to such innovation rests exclusively or even primarily in the need to be consistent in values and improve communication within the service area itself. However, solutions rest in much more complex adjustments. One of the principles of moving away from Rationality is to resist the temptation to identify individual factors as causes. Instead, there are multiple interrelated variables that explain how real systems work. Continuing to use the Analysis of Administrative Strategies of the DD Services as a case, along with others, we can extract other issues that elaborate other equally important factors. Among these are locus of control, structural arrangements, and procedural norms.

Locus of Control

This brings me to the consideration of administrative structure related to location of authority. Initially, a key question of the study regarded whether a regional approach was the best way to distribute authority. As noted in Chapter 2, this is closely tied to the structures described as bureaucratic, cooperative, contracted services, or public service. The current system, being mostly bureaucratic with supervision of contracted services, continued to be largely centralized with offices established in five regions. These offices were responsible for the application of the bureaucratic requirements to the contracted services. Thus the question was not whether the regional offices should exist but what was their proper role. In a public service model, the proper role of regional offices is to facilitate rather than control.

This is not just using language to conceal a continuation of the bureaucratic approach. It is a genuine shift in the relationship between the regional office, especially in the person of the Field Services Specialist (FSS) and the providers. Rather than enforcing rules and conducting inspections, the FSS acts as a conduit for the exchange of information relative to the best use of resources. The regional office acts more as a clearinghouse for the network that is developed between providers. If there is a way to share resources or ideas, the FSS will serve as a contact point and actively encourage such sharing. This is a much more rewarding role for all those concerned, including the FSS. The monitoring information should be channeled through the FSS but not as a matter of rule enforcement. This information is drawn upon to enhance the learning of the system and if there are needed corrections, which the providers are perfectly qualified to identify, the regional offices work with the providers to identify strategies for so doing. The way this is done is to review the plan of action devised by the provider as a part of the employees' personal growth plan. This review is to be seen primarily as an opportunity to share ideas and to offer other suggestions. The role is then not hierarchical but supportive. This is much more than a subtle change. In addition to the enhanced role of the providers in terms of advancing knowledge, the administrative design must incorporate the public forum into its activities. This will be discussed further later but suffice it to say that the interaction of citizens with the system is a crucial missing element.

Further insight may be gained by examining the general pattern of locus of control in the several states observed. The observations of the surrounding states involved conversations with providers and agency personnel. Planning documents and literature that was distributed by the providers also proved very useful. The analysis of the systems was necessarily brief but to the point. The limits of resources, especially time, restricted the ability to be particularly comprehensive in this analysis. However, I focused my efforts on areas that I found to be pivotal in the human service systems in general. I was mostly interested in (1) the level of control exerted by the agencies, (2) the emphasis on procedures/process, (3) the apparent values that prevail in the planning documents, and (4) types of arrangements that have developed *vis-à-vis* the agency and providers. Generally speaking, the differences between the systems were rather subtle. All states observed rely on contracting with providers. The stated general philosophies do include community-based approaches to these services. The desire to provide a system that promoted the dignity of the clients and involvement of the families was also universal. In other words, the philosophical preferences identified in the literature were found in the surrounding states. The results of these observations for each of these surrounding states do lend some further insights relative to the administrative strategies that were most applicable. They also clarified some of the issues already presented as matters of concern.

Idaho - The DD system in Idaho had only recently moved to preferring contracting out services to providing them directly through ICF/MRs. They had moved to a regional approach with the regional directors having day-to-day control. These regional offices determined eligibility and resource allocation.

Colorado - The system exhibited some interesting elements of division between the urban and rural providers. This offered an opportunity to contrast what is possible in a rural state as opposed to those with significant urban populations.

North Dakota - While considerable movement had been made to community-based services, there remained extensive emphasis on the ICF/MRs. The planning documents stressed the need to continue to move away from the more institutional approaches.

Utah - The planning documents emphasized the need for advocacy for clients on several levels. This would suggest that the level of support by the general public as found in the legislature was not as high as found generally. This is important in that the administrative agencies exhibited a need to spend considerable effort justifying their existence. This will ordinarily generate a vibrant bureaucracy bent on defending itself.

Wyoming - There was little information available on the Wyoming DD system. This is partly due to the fact that the system found itself in a state of flux. This state was also more or less in the process of developing a more comprehensive community-based system.

Oregon - As noted in the earlier part of the discussion, Oregon had developed some very promising systems of moving responsibility for process to the providers. The interesting twist to this observation was that it had largely taken place within the institutions and was moving to the private providers. There was apparently a willingness to take such risks as allowing front-line personnel to take measurements of success. The difficulty was in moving to a system where the private providers were given the same latitude.

California - While there were several examples of successful outcome based programs, they were overwhelmed by the concerns over risk and the ongoing budget struggles after Proposition 13. As noted already, California provides the best example of the life cycle of programs leading to rebureaucratization.

What is of particular interest here are the strains being experienced by systems attempting to incorporate ideas that are generally foreign to the bureaucratic norms. The state institutions continued to function in a manner of rule enforcement and standard operating procedures. At the same time, the mandates coming from the institutions encouraged strategies that would instigate learning and creativity. This level of incongruence showed itself particularly in terms of the relationship between central authority and individual providers. Clearly, there was broad confusion and even levels of anxiety on the part of both institution and provider. To understand this even further, a closer examination of the specific procedures revealed the tensions that resulted.

Observations/Analysis Related to Outcome-Based Systems

There is surely much that may be said about outcome driven systems. Much of the material that had been gathered through the research on strategies for services to the developmentally disabled described the purposes of such systems, the procedures that should be used, the underlying philosophy, and the experiences of providers and consumers with respect to using outcomes as the primary assessment principle. In another study conducted in 1994, I found hints of similar strains. One of the major initiatives of the Clinton Administration was to reform the welfare system. The primary program for the welfare system at that time was Aid to Families with Dependent Children (AFDC). As part of this reform process, I was hired to analyze the population of AFDC recipients. In this study, I found that the relationship between the central institution and the field personnel, especially eligibility technicians, was similarly strained. One of my recommendations was to move to a case management model that would enable the field personnel to customize benefit packages for clients. This was relevant to this discussion in that this would also involve an outcome-based strategy in terms of moving individuals from dependency to self sufficiency. This turned out to present enough of a challenge to the institutional leadership that my entire report was initially set aside. Viewing these two studies side by side shows how the "devil was in the details." The idea of outcome-based programs makes sense at the outset but the implementation strategies turn out to be the major challenge.

There was no immediately apparent reason that any provider or case manager could not draw on very well developed tools to design an outcome-based model. The elements of these were clearly spelled out by researchers and experts in the respective fields. Yet, the reforms themselves could not seem to take hold. As previously described, the tendency was to resort to the previous bureaucratic models. The task then was to review the materials as a way of examining the strength and weaknesses of each in order to assess whether or not the models themselves contained the elements of their own failure. Generally, the models had been designed to focus on the gathering of preferences by the consumer, observe levels of satisfaction, and measure whether or not the plan was being followed. This is in keeping with the finding in the previous chapter which indicated that quality of programs linked with consumer preference were prevailing values throughout the country. In order to more clearly understand the problems associated with implementing the outcome strategies, I will briefly review the models, indicating anything that is particularly unique. Following this, I will describe the general patterns that had been observed in the implementation of these models. This will lead to the discussion of the relationship between the models and administrative strategy which offers a basis for a return to further consideration of the depth of the need for a paradigmatic shift.

Specific Outcome-Based Models

The most effective way to summarize these models is to describe specific ones that were obtained during the research, indicate the general principles being applied, and identify any unique features of the model. When I speak of models in this context, I mean rather intricately designed plans and procedures intended to guide the provider through the steps needed for an effective outcome-based strategy. Generally, the models had fairly consistent features. The description of each of the major elements of outcome-based models will contain a brief assessment of strengths and weaknesses. Just the same, the point is not to suggest that any of the models themselves are more or less effective than any other. The depth of analysis required to accommodate such needs would take much longer and involve more expertise in the field of specific services being delivered. The primary purpose of this overview is to illustrate the state of outcome-based models and to set a context for later analysis.

In the case of the DD services, the models provided by the accrediting associations were certainly the most detailed. These provide extensive sets of possible measurements for outcomes for the consumers, their families, communities, and employers. They rely heavily on a structured interview process wherein the consumer preferences are identified, a plan is devised, and regular reviews occur. The materials from CARF were the most exhaustive. Therefore, I will use their model to describe a typical outcome-based system. CARF prefaces its model design with a clear statement of the desired result:

> The movement to which CARF has subscribed says that we as service providers should help determine what is important to people, then hold ourselves accountable for it, make our performance visible, and establish efforts to get better. This is a radical departure from definitions of quality and assessment procedures that have subjugated the lives of the individuals served to bureaucratic needs.[1]

The manual quoted above described in some detail a suggested method for developing an outcome management system. The method involved what they called four components and six steps. The four components are actually a set of larger operating principles that guide the system:

Components of Outcome Measurement Management System (CARF)

1. Develop an organizational policy on outcomes.
2. Devise a system to measure or describe:
   a. Effectiveness
   b. Efficiency
   c. Progress
   d. Aggregated individual service satisfaction
   e. Characteristics of persons served.
3. Share the outcomes information in appropriate reports to customers, the public and purchasers of services, as well as the core service's staff and governance authority.
4. Continuously use the results to improve individual services.

Figure 5.1

The steps go into some more detail of the procedures to develop an effective system to satisfy the requirements of the components. These steps were generally found in all of the systems reviewed. Any significant differences in the steps for any of the other models will be noted in the description of the models that follow:

> *Step 1: Conduct a Service Provider SWOT Analysis:* This is a critical first step because it focuses on assessing the assets and liabilities of a provider in light of the needed change. The SWOT stands for Strengths, Weaknesses, Opportunities, and Threats. This analysis will help in the later stages and will assist in any needed efforts to mobilize resources to the outcome emphasis. This is a very popular model in business management systems. The source of this device is unclear but it continues to be very popular in strategic planning circles.[2]

Step 2: Select a Core Service or Service Design, and Identify Its Customers: A core service is the set of services that identify the organization's capability to its customers. This process should involve considerable brainstorming with staff and customers since it is not always clear what comprises the core service(s).

Step 3: Define Quality and Outcomes Expectations for Each Key Customer: Once the core services have been identified, along with its customers, a comprehensive set of statements that indicate what is meant by quality is developed for each area. This should include some process for setting priorities for each customer.

Step 4: Design Outcomes Data System Components: For each core service, at least three measurements (and where practical a fourth progress) for each individual receiving service must be developed. The needed measurements are tied to:

    a. Effectiveness
        i. Results and achievements
    b. Efficiency
        i. Responsiveness
        ii. Costs
        iii. Time
        iv. Ratios of resource use to outcomes
    c. Aggregated Individual Service Satisfaction
        i. Customers' responses regarding how they feel about their individual service plans and outcomes
    d. Progress
        ii. Increase in wages, transition to new tasks (for persons served more than six months.)

Step 5: Design Consumer Satisfaction System Elements: This involves the use of survey methods of the consumer as well as more aggregate results for the purposes of directing organizational resources to areas of need. There are lists of questions that may be asked of the consumers in each of the accreditation association's manuals of standards. This is the most common element of all the models. The questions vary but the general information being sought is clearly tied to outcomes/satisfaction.

Step 6: Use and Share Outcomes Information: This is viewed as a crucial step to continuously improving services. The use of the information is primarily an internal process for the organization. It is important that the information be incorporated into on-going organizational planning. The sharing is not only with governing authorities but with funding sources, and the public. This is a means of facilitating the community integration considered vital to quality of life for the consumers.

This model is rather generic and could easily be used to guide any organization in developing an outcome-based system. However, the details of what must go into each of the steps may be found wanting if the management or staff is unfamiliar with the idea of outcomes as opposed to process. This process is extracted rather directly from Deming's Total Quality Management (TQM) literature. This, in itself, presents some difficulties. The carryover from the TQM model that was designed for production in the private sector is not always clear when moving into human services. As noted by one of the staff at the Neighborhood Living Project: there is a tendency to "widgetize" the services, meaning that the numbers may be taken on face value inappropriately.

The Accreditation Council's model encourages a very similar process for developing a system of outcome management. The documents that I received, however, focused more on the description of the variables that should be included in the measurement. They had developed a rather comprehensive set of questions that should be addressed for each of the consumers, including the individual, the families, the employers, and the community. This can certainly prove useful when designing a system. However, it is important for the individual organization to decide which questions should be included in their strategy. The list of questions provided by CARF, AC, or other source should be viewed as a bank to be drawn from rather than a laundry list of essential questions. Customizing data collection systems is a crucial element in any quality assurance arrangement.

The materials provided by Paradigm Systems have some very attractive features. The most influential of these is a very simplified information gathering device for setting the baseline of quality outcomes. The questionnaire for the initial phase of the process of determining the level of quality has only 29 questions. The questions are a bit lengthy but they provide more extensive explanation than the other survey devices. This actually makes them more efficacious as an instrument for establishing baseline data. The clearer explanation and the use of observable elements make it much more likely that there are consistent definitions of quality. They have also designed interview guides to measure consumer and staff satisfaction that rely on very few questions (13 for consumers and 8 for staff). This makes the process less intimidating for all parties and resists the proclivity to get overly wrapped up in process. Their premise is that much of what needs to be learned about quality and satisfaction is gained by observation that is not particularly systematic. The drawback to these devices is that they cannot be used for program implementation. As noted in the description of CARF's implementation model, a great deal of information must be gathered in order to design a consumer-driven system. These short questionnaires should be used more as interim checks on the progress of the system. The underlying assumption is that if the outcomes are not achieving some level of satisfaction then it is time to reexamine the Individual Plan. This makes sense in that it encourages the use of more intuitive measures as an on-going procedure. This will go far in preventing excessive procedure requirements that interfere with the direct care staff's ability to conduct their work.

Paradigm had also developed some training materials for staff and management that facilitated the implementation of an effective quality assurance system. By their own admission, these materials clearly have evolved from the TQM literature. The weakness of the model is that it emphasizes the feel good nature of quality systems more than it should and it can too easily be viewed by staff as a control device by management. The concepts that are used in this system really do rely heavily on very competent management. This has been one of the primary weaknesses of TQM in general. It is a sad but true condition that managers are usually poorly formed. This is mostly because in our culture we promote people to management because they have seniority not because they have demonstrated the skills that should be associated with effective leadership. Thus, there is a need to develop very aggressive management assessment strategies along with any efforts at quality assurance that would depend on the application of TQM.

As previously described, the DD Service Bureau of the State of Oregon offered some interesting insights into outcome strategies. However, there was no specific outcome-based model that is included in the information they provided. Instead, this encounter was something of a departure from gathering models and more of a critique of the efforts to date. This will be incorporated into the discussion below as it relates to the observations of the success of such models. The agency did provide a rather useful document though. Oregon had recently turned its attention to core competencies as a means of improving quality. A key finding on their part was that they found that the most significant determinant of quality services was the quality of staff and management. In fact, their perspective was that effective management was the single most influential factor. They had developed a rather aggressive program of advancing core competencies. Recently, the DD Services Bureau had published a *Core Competencies Resource Guide* for the purpose of promoting better services. This guide specifically addressed the needed skills of direct care staff. They were working on a similar guide for management. Even though these efforts do not directly guide the implementation of an outcome-based model, their point is well taken. It is extremely important to include professional development that is also outcome-based as a part of any larger strategy to move toward outcome enhancement. The challenge remains regarding the form of professional development that is needed, especially in terms of management.

The outcome measurement system, presented by the Neighborhood Living Project at the University of Oregon, also provided some crucial elements. The Residential Outcomes System (ROS) was their primary measurement tool. Their development of measurement models were genuinely related to *observable* outcomes. It was their experience that this was the only way to develop a meaningful outcome-based system which delivers some way of measurement that is both useful to the provider staff and the program administrators. Thus, they had determined that the focus must be on activities as they relate to the various components of any outcome based model. To quote from the preface to their semi-annual report:

ROS is activity- and outcome-based. ROS makes it possible for residential staff to obtain information concerning the activities and lifestyle outcomes a person experiences. This information is used at weekly staff meetings to ensure that a person's Individual Support Plan (ISP) is being implemented with fidelity, and to ensure that the person's ISP-related activities and other activities help to provide the lifestyle he or she prefers.[3]

The emphasis, therefore, was on activities rather than responses to survey questions by the consumer. Their assertion was that this is a more reasonable measurement. While I cannot argue with this point of view, I must caution that it should not be taken as the only way to measure outcome. However, for purposes of a system that is useful to the provider, the state, and the general public, it certainly has its merits. The premise of the measurement system is presented in the following manner:

VALUED LIFESTYLE OUTCOMES

The purpose of using the information system is to improve the lifestyle of someone with intellectual disabilities who is receiving residential services [this can include community based or supported living services as well]. One way to improve the lifestyle of a person is to ensure that she or he is experiencing valued lifestyle outcomes.

Most people would agree that the following are some of life's valued outcomes:

- Doing activities in the community (sometimes called Aphysical integration.)
- Doing activities with friends and acquaintances (social integration)
- Doing activities more independently and skillfully (independence)
- Doing activities that are preferred (activity preference)
- Doing a variety of activities (activity variety) [4]

The Operations Manual for this system, while a bit complex, guides the providers through the process and is certainly an improvement over other, more convoluted systems. The procedures are easily integrated with daily activities and provide useful tools for observation. There are many external variables that will determine whether or not this system can stand the test of time.

Another consideration which was identified by both the DD Services Bureau and the Neighborhood Living Project was related to the quality of staff. The major difficulties being encountered in Oregon related to the perception of the professional nature of staff. The general impression was that they were not considered professionals at all. Consequently, it had been increasingly difficult to retain staff. This was due to the very vibrant economy of the area and the ability of the state to compensate personnel competitively. The economy was such that many service jobs in the private sector were then paying much higher wages than would be expected, so much, in fact, that the direct care staff were often making less than retail clerks or entry level management trainees. This made it difficult to keep people in what may be described as rather stressful jobs of direct care. Related to this phenomenon, was the result that the staff that were recruited were less qualified than they had been in the past. This challenge was being partially met by implementing the core competencies programs and through what the Bureau Chief described as a very substantial training and technical assistance budget. While not all states encounter this problem of a hot economy, it is important to recognize that the quality of personnel will be a vital feature of any outcome-based program and economic conditions may play a significant role in their success.

Along with somewhat disconcerting observations of evidence of re-bureaucratization, the California Department of Developmental Services contributed some materials on their outcome-based systems. While generally consistent with the steps and measures suggested by the accreditation associations, the materials do provide some useful approaches to implementing such a system. The materials they distributed take on a less formal tone in the consumer preference discovery. The title of the guide for interviewing suggests the nature of the material: *A Conversation with a Friend*. This material was developed by Partners in Consulting, a group of consultants who also use regional service centers, to help friends and family talk with a person about life quality. The strength of this material was in its exhortation of involving friends and family in the process in a more direct fashion. This is accompanied by *Looking at Life Quality: Visitor's Handbook*, which is a guide to the person visiting anyone with developmental disabilities who is charged with evaluating the quality of life experienced by that individual. The appeal of this material is that it was designed to also accommodate the consumers who were recipients of supported living services. Thus, it was not necessary to make modifications to assess the outcomes for those not in residential care. The guides provide clear instructions for conducting the assessments and mostly narrative entries as opposed to forced choice. The measurement indicator is simply whether the variable being assessed is okay at this time or Needs Follow-up. This precluded many of the difficulties associated with weighted scales. Frequently, there are inconsistencies in the applications of evaluative terms such as average, good, fair, etc. What is considered good to one person is not the same to another. This also prevents much of the rating creep associated with evaluation systems, wherein ratings tend to climb whether there is discernable improvement or not. The evaluation findings are explicit in the desired course of action resulting from the assessment.

It is difficult to suggest that the California system was effective however. The dynamics surrounding re-bureaucratization which have resulted from the political environment preclude anyone from suggesting that the programs are a success. These are not unrelated matters though. One has to believe that if the programs were truly successful, the reactionary forces would be less likely to be effective. Suffice it to say that the evidence suggests that some element in the philosophical underpinnings of the outcome-based program prevented the programs from withstanding these enormous challenges.

Patterns Observed in Implementation of Outcome-Based Models

Even though the experiences of all the states had not been observed in this study, it is possible to identify some patterns that follow the implementation of these strategies. This analysis is drawn from personal observation of the states specifically considered, secondary analysis (e.g., Best Practices literature, professional journals, and various studies,) and the broader literature in the field of public administration. Needless to say, not all states or regions experienced every one of the conditions described. However, the process is consistent enough in the experiences of the states to be considered a factor in the success of the strategies. Patterns are most useful as they clarify the factors that contribute to the effectiveness of organizational strategies. They do not suggest that such consequences are unavoidable. It is not a description of fate. Rather, it is useful as a tool to observe the issues and activities that are influenced by social dynamics. In this case, it is particularly useful to describe the pattern because it leads to some rather profound conclusions relative to strategies intended to stress outcomes.

The Analysis of Administrative Strategies of DD Services is but one study I have completed that exhibited these patterns. I use this material so extensively because it provided details necessary to make the point. I found a similar pattern in local governments that had hired me to conduct studies of various kinds. One community has contracted with me on six occasions to provide a survey of citizens' satisfaction with services. In the beginning the leadership enthusiastically used this as a means to develop new programs and engage the citizenry in a manner that incorporated their feedback into the policy making process. However, over time as the surveys continued, the city took on a more conservative approach to the survey, using it instead to justify decisions they had already made.[5] The Study of the AFDC Population revealed a similar behavior in that the state leadership initially stated that they wanted to use the information to design innovative programs that would move the population to self sufficiency. Again, once problems arose related to concerns about risk, they elected to use the information to justify policy decisions already made. These "reforms" involved a clear pattern or re-bureaucratization and aggressive rule enforcement.[6] In almost every consulting experience I have had over the last twenty years, I have found the tendency to revert to the bureaucratic ethos to be very intense. No matter how enthusiastic the clients were in the beginning of the process to use innovations tied to public engagement and outcome-centered models, invariably some element of risk would arise driving them back to the safety of rules and procedures. From these experiences I draw the following general pattern of behavior in program implementation.

Stage 1: Initial Enthusiasm. Whenever organizational or policy reforms are initiated, there is typically an enthusiastic response. The promoters of the change are typically zealots of a particular perspective as described by Anthony Downs in his book, *Inside Bureaucracy*. Zealots are ordinarily drawn from an ideology which is extracted from a larger theory of human behavior. It is not unusual for these advocates of change to come from the academic community in some way or another. Consequently, the changes are sold with considerable vigor to overcome normal institutional resistance.

For example, outcome-based models for services to the developmentally disabled are an off-shoot of Total Quality Management and deinstitutionalization. TQM and deinstitutionalization are strategies that result from an assumption of human behavior that argues people are generally happier when they are more productive. This is more likely to have arisen as a natural conclusion from the social psychologists who hold that personal environment is the primary determinant of personality. At any rate, these kinds of strategies evolve from a larger body of knowledge which makes them more robust. Without belaboring the issue, it is valuable to consider what epistemology is operating when viewing reforms. In this case, the philosophical roots of the application of these concepts of TQM and deinstitutionalization in services to the developmentally disabled can be traced to Bellamy, and O'Brien. [7] The value of community-based services has achieved a position of fairly wide acceptance in the last twenty-five years. The subsequent advocacy of outcome-based systems was a rather natural consequence of this shift. The literature reveals that emphasis on outcomes has gained equally energetic support in the past ten years or so. This was certainly the case in my discoveries through the documents and interviews. This is also a movement in the larger field of public administration. Some of the notable figures responsible for this philosophy are Peter Drucker and Osborne and Gaebler in their *Reinventing Government.*

Once an innovation such as an outcome measurement model is selected as a reform, it is usually the creators of the model who are charged with its further design and implementation. Ordinarily, this is accomplished through a project funded by grants or special set-asides. Those assigned this responsibility, therefore, are typically those who have been successful in drafting a proposal. This means that they are adept at selling their ideas. However, it may not mean that they can also recognize the weaknesses of their strategy or that they can apply the principles in the real world of the practitioners. This is fairly evident in this first stage of program development. The innovations associated with outcomes emphasis were developed and presented by academics or consultants in each of the cases observed. This resulted in an implementation strategy largely driven by the individuals most convinced that the new innovation was the way to go. Naturally, the initial reaction is widespread enthusiasm. The challenge is converting that enthusiasm to genuine commitment on the part of the providers themselves.

Stage 2: Implementation of Pilot Programs. While the enthusiasm of the promoters of innovative strategies may be considerable, it is usually equally true that the decision makers are a bit more cautious. Whether it is a legislature, governor, agency director, or regional manager the willingness to risk all on a new strategy is highly unlikely. Consequently, the implementation begins with pilot programs rather than any comprehensive effort. This is a reasonable approach to new strategies in most cases. However, in many instances, especially those in the human services, there is the very real possibility of the Hawthorne Effect coming into play.* Since the pilot programs are showcase efforts, the staff and management in these programs will tend to be on their best behavior. The pilot programs also tend to obtain more favorable resource allocations. Both of these factors generally improve the programs' probability of initial success. This has been largely the case in outcome-based programs as well. Many of the agency and association people correctly pointed out that the programs which have used this strategy are generally small. The fact is that the organizations that are used as pilot test sites are those which have the greater ability to be innovative. Those that are aware of innovations are the ones who are in touch with the field, usually indicative of an active, competent staff. It is highly unusual for any pilot programs to be attempted with mediocre or marginal organizations. This ultimately plays a role in the strategy's overall success.

Stage 3: General Implementation Yields Mixed Results. After the strategy/model has been pilot tested, its application is broadened. For example, this may be a matter of announcing that funds are available for any provider wanting to develop an outcome-based approach or through a general Request for Proposals (RFP). Sometimes, the implementation is done by region. In any event, the programs incorporating the new strategy move away from those which are ordinarily innovative or having highly qualified staff, to those which are more average. This may or may not mean that they will be effective in incorporating the new program. There are apparent predictors of success, however. The experience of the states observed indicated that the likely outcome is what one might expect. The solid, well-managed programs with generally good track records show improvement and incorporate the outcome measurements as they were designed. The average organizations with generally acceptable performance in the past, absorb the strategy in stride, achieving rather unimpressive results. The marginal to poor performers, remain largely unaffected. So overall, there is some improvement with the ordinarily successful providers and no substantial change otherwise. The measurable impact on the overall services to the consumers is likely to be minimal change. Some might argue that improvements in performance probably would have been essentially the same with or without the addition of the outcomes model. However, that is entirely too hypothetical to be given much credence.

Stage 4: Problems Arise. After the reform is put in place and there is some time for the procedures to become truly operationalized as part of the routine, there are usually some events that suggest that there is a "problem." I have put the term problem in quotes because what are described as problems may or may not be so. This is a matter of how one views the situation. One of the more explicit situations that arise is the difficulty associated with monitoring. Movement

---

* For those who may not be familiar with this phenomenon (or who have forgotten it), the Hawthorne Effect was discovered during a study conducted at the Hawthorne Plant of Western Electric in Cicero, Illinois. The essence of the findings was that no matter what variables were altered in the plant to the positive or negative, the levels of production increased. After some prolonged consideration, the study team concluded that the very fact that the people were being observed altered their behaviors.

to outcome systems necessarily requires that more individualized programs be developed. That is why they all relied on Individual Plans (IP), Individual Program Plans (IPP), Individual Service Plans (ISP) or whatever label was given. This caused considerable difficulty at the aggregate level that the state agency needed to confront. It is very difficult to standardize individualized plans and provide meaningful data to oversight authority. This is no small matter to the agency personnel. Consequently, they will normally continue to apply the pressure for the more standardized reports to be submitted. This will place higher demands on the provider for administrative costs.

The other typical problem to arise is that the reform fails to bring up the floor. This was stated a number of times by state agency staff. Even though the expectation of the outcome system was that everyone should benefit from this innovation, it just did not happen. As noted above, the more marginal providers have problems much greater than any slick innovation will be able to repair. The skill level of these providers was probably not sufficient to incorporate the outcome system in the manner that would bring about the desired change. The fact is that with any innovation that contains a one size fits all quality there will be such difficulties. The other factor that came into play was that there were many such marginal performers that had adopted a dependency approach to services or were minimalist in their expectations. If they assumed dependency, it applied not only to their consumers but to themselves as providers. They were apprehensive about making any changes or undertaking any activities that were not clearly defined either by the agency or past practices. If they were minimalist, they focused on staying out of trouble. This meant that they would typically make decisions based on what was the least they were expected to do to satisfy requirements.

It is just a matter of time before something goes wrong somewhere to the extent that there will be some kind of scandal. Montana had certainly had this experience in the past. The California example is particularly noteworthy for this occurrence. The scandal does not even need to be real. It can be a rather contrived accusation that has very little merit as with the reaction to the study produced by Dr. Strauss. Of course, there can be incidents that are genuinely matters that must be addressed. If one asks whether or not there will be future episodes of neglect or abuse, the answer is most likely, yes. There are no risk-free strategies. Nevertheless, the response to these scandals is almost always forceful and immediate. The Legislature may intervene and demand satisfaction that any such future occurrence will be avoided. The Department Director will need to respond in any event. The one device at the disposal of any agency is the power of rule enforcement which will almost always be used. This was evident in all the cases that were reviewed.

Stage 5: Rebureaucratization. Once these problem areas surface, the likely response is an effort to return to strategies that are more consistent with the bureaucratic ethos. This includes increased monitoring of providers, additional rule enforcement, and standardization. The monitoring of providers had been the one area that had caused more tension between agencies and providers. The agency needed some form of control over the services being provided because they operated on principles of self preservation. Since they were being pressured by either the legislature, governor, agency director, or even the press, they needed to find some way to preserve the institution. The best way to increase control and so demonstrate to the oversight authority that future problems will be prevented is to increase methods of monitoring. It was interesting to observe that the state agencies reviewed were quick to note that they had no resources for facilitating the outcome systems because they were too busy conducting inspections and producing reports. It does not matter whether or not the number of problem providers was a significant percentage of the overall system. The increased efforts at monitoring were a natural response to any deficiencies.

The other mechanism employed as a result of noted problems was increased rule enforcement. The agencies, whether they are regional or statewide, will develop standards manuals and reporting requirements to be satisfied that corrective action is being taken. Specifically, they become interested in the corrective action as they (the agencies) define it. As long as the bureaucracy exists, it will use rule enforcement at the first sign of trouble. So if someone was not properly medicated at a particular time, and the agency is made aware of it, they will institute several rules (not just one) to be sure that this neglect is not repeated. For example, the providers were expected to put all personnel through training on the dispensing of medicines. Perhaps, a specific chart will be required for all direct care staff to sign. A set of policies will be published regarding the dispensing of medicines. All of these are forms of rule enforcement.

Finally, as a result of the responses to problems the sets of standards will be increased. The bureaucracy must return to its comfort zone. That is, it must establish order by ensuring that there are no future problems. The new policies were incorporated into the contracts and enforcement mechanisms were added. As a rule in the end, rather than a single response to each single incident, there are sets of standards that are imposed on all providers. This allows the agency to assure the authority to which they answer that accountability is being fully maintained. I must point out here though, that the process of rebureaucratization is not necessarily the creation of the agency. It may be the result of very specific demands by the courts, the citizens, the legislature, or any number of other non-bureaucratic entities.

---

1. *Managing Outcomes: Customer-Driven Outcomes Measurement & Management Systems, A Guide to Development and Use,* Tucson, AZ, CARF, The Rehabilitation Accreditation Commission, 1997, p. ix.
2. G. Pangiotou, "Bringing SWOT into Focus," *Business Strategy Review* 14, no. 2, (2003): 8-10.
3. *Semi-Annual Residential Lifestyle Outcomes Evaluation Report,* Eugene, Oregon, Oregon Office of Developmental Disability Services, Research and Evaluation Unit, Specialized Training Program, 4, no. 1, (1996-97).
4. Newton, J. S., Anderson, S. A., Ard, W.R., Jr., Horner, R. H., LeBaron, N. M., Sappington, G. & Spoelstra, R. J. *A Residential Outcomes Systems Operations Manual,* Eugene: University of Oregon, Center on Human Development (1994) p. 1-1.
5. Edgar, Patrick B., "Report of Findings: City of Lewiston, Citizens' Satisfaction Survey," (Missoula: PBE Research, 1998, 2000, 2002, 2004).

6. Edgar, Patrick B., "A Study of the AFDC Population of Montana," (Missoula: Northwest Community Consultants, 1994).
7. Bellamy, G. T. *Vocational Habilitation of Severely Retarded Adults,* (Baltimore: University Park Press, 1979); Bellamy, G. T.. Rhodes, L., Wilcox, B., Albin, J., Mank, D., Boles, S., Horner, R., Collins, M., & Turner, J., "Quality and Equality in Employment Services for Adults with Severe Disabilities," *Journal of the Association for Persons with Severe Handicaps* 9 no. 4, (1984): 270-277; O'Brien, et. al., *Accomplishments in Residential Services,* (Olympia: Governors Council on Developmental Disabilities, 1981).

Chapter 6: Outcome-Based Models and Public Administration

Based on the review of the prevailing outcome based models being employed, the experiences of the other states, the basic components, and the general pattern of their implementation, we reach a point at which we must be able to draw some kind of conclusion. To do this, I focus on what was found in this process in a more comprehensive sense to help direct attention to what stands out as important. Then, I will offer an assessment of the state of these models emphasizing overall strengths and weaknesses that have been identified. Finally, I will suggest the implications for outcome-based models in general, which will point out particular strains on the Rational paradigm.

There are several attributes which were consistently found in outcome-based models in both the study of DD Services and other studies that I have conducted, including citizen satisfaction surveys and housing studies. The prevailing principle that guided all the systems was that they should be inexorably tied to consumer preferences. This will turn out to be a vital consideration in the development of any system. The devices used, while differing in specific approaches, contained the essential element of using an individualized or at least localized plan. Each of the systems included some systematic way of gathering information related to consumer preference. This may be in the form of a consumer survey, a team meeting, or an advocate interview. The importance of this step was made clear by all of the models and cannot be neglected. Each of the systems addressed the same general categories of outcomes: social integration, individual choice, independence, and productivity. This has a certain amount of applicability to all human service systems. While the models identified success in these categories somewhat differently, they still considered these the basic values to be served. All of the models required that there be the broadest participation possible on the part of any of the people involved with the individual consumer. The models also encouraged that every means possible be used to identify personal preference so that no assumptions are made regarding an individual's desires.

A very significant aspect of these outcome systems was that they all were tied to the quality assurance programs that have grown in popularity, especially TQM. Quality is the core concept following consumer choice. Systems are being encouraged to focus on improving quality throughout the organization. This requires a commitment on the part of all the staff and an environment that encourages any and all innovations that will contribute to the improvement. Thus, there is almost always a component of staff development included in the models.

To shift one's perspective to focus on quality is not automatic by any means. People need to be taught how to be quality conscious since their experience in organizations has more typically been one of following rules and procedures and not pursuing quality. These are very different kinds of expectations. Along with the need for quality, there is a crucial insertion of self monitoring. This extends the responsibility to every staff member to observe their own performance and, even more importantly, set personal goals to improve. This is generally not something to which people are accustomed.

The outcome based models were largely appropriate in their conceptualization. They were focused on what would seem to be the right set of priorities. It is extremely important to turn the attention of services to the preferences of the consumer as any one of us would want for ourselves. It is essential that an environment which seeks quality and extends personal responsibility be incorporated into these services. These models were designed to take the services to the next level. They called for creativity, choice, and personal commitment. However, (there is always a however) there were some very important considerations that needed to come into play. The models do have some apparent deficiencies that should be addressed as part of any implementation strategy. The one that should be obvious at this point is that they tend not to last. At least, they do not remain in their initial form and fall victim to rebureaucratization. The concerns that bring this about should not go overlooked.

Success is minimal with these models for a variety of reasons. Now, one might argue that minimal success is an expected outcome; that each reform leaves behind some remnant that permanently alters the system and contributes to overall progress. However, the outcome-based models are comprehensive enough in nature that it would be difficult to identify a remnant that would be meaningful. Minimal success is, therefore, a rather significant deficiency. One reason for this minimal success is that they are usually implemented piecemeal. As described in the patterns, they are placed in pilot programs first to work out the bugs. The problem is that the bugs are normally not identified because it is the exemplary organizations that are usually the pilots. Thus, when they are broadly implemented the weaknesses are only then discovered. Furthermore, the nature of these systems is such that they cannot be put in place piecemeal.

Another factor that comes into play leading toward minimal success is that the oversight authority, whether it is the agency, regional centers, or an advocacy group, ties the data from the outcome system to incentives or sanctions. Consequently, the system was driven to become more of a production line than a human service. The suggestion that the outcomes become "widgetized" is all too true. The numbers become issues in and of themselves and the organizations are compelled once again to focus on their own survival rather than the needs of the consumer. It may not seem that these two values would be in conflict but they are because there truly are two competing interests for the providers' efforts. The numbers tend to become tainted and the agency must take some action to improve the ability to report accurately for purposes of accountability. As a corollary to the use of outcomes for sanctions, the fear of risk is generated again because the system is being driven to eliminating error. Thus, the agency, the providers, the advocates, and the general public all get caught up in preventing problems. Rather than emphasizing success, the effort reverts to removing failure. Even though the system may be enjoying a 95% success rate, the attention is given to the remaining 5%. This fear of risk, (rather than a fear of failure because the system is successful by all objective measures) paralyzes the entire system. Very few are willing to take any kind of risk in the interest of improving the quality of life for an individual.

In the end, the outcome-based systems' greatest weakness is that it cannot bring about the perfect result that the Rational Model insists upon. The innovative programs only tend to make the good providers better and do very little to effect the others. There is very little success at bringing up the floor, meaning improving the performance of the worst providers. Consequently, the public is unable to see the successes of the program because it does not hear about them. The marginal service provider continues to operate as a provider rather than a facilitator. This is related to what John O'Brien refers to as operating within the crooked map zone. Basically, he describes the difficulty that we encounter in human service systems whenever we try to improve quality and become more responsive.

Bearing all of the strengths and weaknesses of these models in mind, I continue to recommend that administrators proceed toward outcome-based strategies. There is no need to reinvent the wheel in this case. The existing models are designed very well. In general, then I find these to be suitable strategies. Having said this, I must also admit that I have found that it is not a good idea to implement an outcome-based system. Rather, it is much more appropriate for each service provider to select the model that works best for them. Instead, I suggest a framework for any statewide system. This is different in that it identifies the general values to be pursued but places the responsibility where it should be C with the individual providers in concert with the consumer. Beyond this, I recognize that a fundamental change in philosophy must accompany the implementation. The reason that attempts at outcome based strategies have failed rests in the failure to make such fundamental change. The desire for outcome based strategies in public policy is obstructed by the continued reliance on the Rational model. Invariably, agencies return to an emphasis on deficiencies as opposed to a focus on outcomes. It is nearly impossible to implement a strategy that aims at continued growth within a climate which can only see failures. In the New Testament, we are cautioned that one cannot put new wine into old wineskins (Luke 5:37, 38.) The same metaphor applies to public administration.

Institutionalism vs. Enactment

Conceptually, these behaviors lead us to a consideration of further philosophical insights. The prevailing Rational paradigm also rests on the acceptance of Institutionalism as a matter of fact. There are many who argue that this may be a false premise which leads us to conclusions, or even more significantly, principles of administrative behavior. This is partly a matter of needing to deconstruct one of those hyper-realities that confine us to a set of alternatives that limit our ability to get beyond the bureaucratic ethos.

Institutionalism is the prevailing theory in public administration today. However, there are a variety of forms of institutionalism which may cause some confusion. The three main veins of institutional theory are Rational choice, historical institutionalism, and sociological institutionalism.[1] *Rational choice* refers to theories such as rational choice theory and other forms of analysis based on the assumption that decision-makers are rational, self-interested optimizers, or social choice theories based on rational voters, principal agent theories, focusing on contracts and incentives linking superiors to subordinates or agents, or market theories in general, which also focus on optimization by individuals in markets. That is, in rational choice theories, social phenomena are interpreted in terms of preference-maximizing strategies pursued by individuals. Because of preference-maximization, Hall & Taylor refer to the rational choice tradition as the "calculus approach" to institutionalism. In the public arena, preference-maximizing strategies revolve around exchanging compliance for preferences in a social bargain which, if not kept, may lead to the breakdown of existing institutional patterns of power.[2] While rational choice theories do seek to analyze decisions affecting institutions, this tradition is often seen as a contrast to rather than part of institutional theory for reasons given below.

Historical Institutionalism

Historical institutionalism grows out of group theories of politics and structural functional theories in sociology, both popular in the 1960s and 1970s. Group theory in political science reacted against behavioralism's attempt to generate class-wide generalizations, instead preferring to study each case as a unique constellation of cooperating and competing actors shaped by unique historical backgrounds. Concepts such as incrementalism and "muddling through", rather than rational planning or even rational choice, dominated historical institutionalism. Structural-functional theory in sociology reacted against economic determinism, instead emphasizing the power of culture, values, and norms in institutional change. Pierson's work on *path dependence* fits in this tradition, emphasizing the inertia of institutions as self-reinforcing systems.[3] Historical institutionalism in general emphasizes the constraints institutional factors place on decision-making and individual discretion.

Sociological Institutionalism

Sociological institutionalism is the type most today equate with "institutional theory." The sociological tradition is in explicit contrast to rational choice theory, and has overlap with historical institutionalism insofar as it also emphasizes the socio-political-cultural intractability of institutional decisions. Hall & Taylor thus contrast the "calculus approach" of the rational choice tradition with the "cultureal approach" of the historical and sociological traditions. Sociological institutionalism is differentiated from historical institutionalism by less emphasis on power (as in group theory) or even norms (as in structural-functionalism) and more emphasis on the socio-cultural construction of "realms of meaning" which in turn guide individual behavior within institutions. Sociological institutionalism does not view social patterns as tending toward equilibrium, as do rational choice theories, nor does it view change as being as tightly constrained by norms and traditions as does historical institutionalism. Themes in the sociological tradition include the symbolic functions of institutional forms, which are not necessarily optimized in functional terms; the cultural specificity of different institutional enactments of the same technology; and the quest for organizational legitimacy as the dynamic behind the diffusion of innovation. Change is seen as a necessary institutional process in pursuit of legitimacy.

I am not convinced that there is such a clear demarcation between these theories and prefer to combine them in terms of how they tie into Rationalism. Elements of the rational choice model are used to explain the resulting behaviors attributed to sociological institutionalism. Organizations, it is believed are created as a result of a rational choice to respond to an identified problem. Within the organization, decisions are made through a process inextricably tied to the organizational structure, with those higher in the organization having primary responsibility for major decisions associated with policy. Members of the organization then behave in accordance with the policies and procedures which emanate from the decisions made by the leadership of the organization. This is closely associated with the bureaucratic paradigm described by Barzelay and Armajani:

- Specific delegations of authority define each role in the executive branch. Officials carrying out any given role should act only when expressly permitted to do so either by rule or by instructions given by superior authorities in the chain of command. Employees within the executive branch are responsible to their supervisors.
- In exercising authority, officials should apply rules and procedures in a uniform manner. The failure to obey rules should be met with an appropriate penalty.
- Experts in substantive e matters—such as engineers, law-enforcement personnel, and social service providers—should be assigned to line agencies, while experts in budgeting, accounting, purchasing, personnel, and work methods should be assigned to centralized staff functions.
- The key responsibilities of the financial function are to prepare the executive budget and to prevent actual spending from exceeding appropriations. The key responsibilities of the purchasing function are to minimize the price paid to acquire goods and services from the private sector and to enforce purchasing rules. The key responsibilities of the personnel function in clued classifying jobs, examining applicants, and making appointments to positions.
- The executive branch as a whole will operate honestly and efficiently as long as the centralized staff functions exercise unilateral control over line agencies' administrative actions.[4]

This, I suggest, is closer to the kind of institutionalism that prevails in public administration today. While many academics see a shift to the sociological form, I have not found that to be true in my experiences.

Enactment Theory

Enactment theory stands in contrast to institutionalism in that it does not assume a formal structure as the determinant of behavior. Rather, it relies much more heavily on the process of sense-making on the part of the members of the organization. Weick describes the term enactment as representing the notion that when people act they bring structures and events into existence and set them in action.[5] Weick uses this term in the context of 'sense-making' by managers or employees. He also describes how they can enact 'limitations' upon the system to avoid issues or experiences. It is also seen as a form of social construction. To date enactment is related to organizations and their environment and strategic management.

Enactment theory deals with life in general and organizations. Individuals and organizations are constantly in the process of self-formation.[6] Employees form themselves in organizations. According to Eisenberg this formation occurs in two different ways.[7] Firstly, they achieve stability through enactment of interaction cycles. Secondly through the development of rules for appropriate behavior. Enactment theory can be seen as a process whereby people achieve continuity and coordination. This process requires rules and roles, so that people can coordinate their activities with another. Enactment theory gives a rationale for distinguishing strategic and routine behavior. Much enactment is scripted. People employ routine communication plans when they can; when they cannot, their ability to devise new plans is crucial to their success as organizational members. In practice, a great deal of what occurs on behalf of the organization is routine, scripted, and random rather than strategic.

According to Weick, organizations are in the process of organizing, they undergo constant change. Enactment results because people are conscious of relationships. Enactment theory is related to organizations. Members of an organization cannot separate themselves as an individual or a member of the organization about how they think about the meaning they impose on themselves, other actors, and the environment. Working in an organization reflects a person's products, services and activities. "The external environment literally bends around the enactments of people, and much of the activity of sense-making involves an effort to separate the externality from the action."[8] Weick formulates it in a way that people engage each other, their organizations and their environment.[9]

Qualitative methods, such as dialogue and discourse analysis are used to develop the organization rather than rules and procedures. Dialogue strives for a balance between individual autonomy and organizational constraint through incorporating diverse voices. Discourse refers to language, grammars, and discursive acts that form the foundation of both performance and voice.

Analysis of consultation between management groups is another method that can be used. With storytelling the impact (in focus groups) can be measured. Enactment can help identifying the structure of an organization which goes well beyond an organizational chart. Relationships center on the need for action as a response to the ecological shifts rather than a permanently fixed standard of positions. The communication structures of organizations are the center of study in order to comprehend these relationships not official documents. The communication structure is the most important predictor of informal networks. The predictor can be used in relation to the duration of networks and the strength/weakness they have.

The role played by enactment goes well beyond the relationships, however. In this theory, the organization is depicted in terms of its interaction with the subject ecology. That is, the

Enactment Theory

- Ongoing Updating
- Retrospect exacted cues
- Identity plausibility
- Ecological Change
- Enactment
- Selection
- Retention
- Feedback

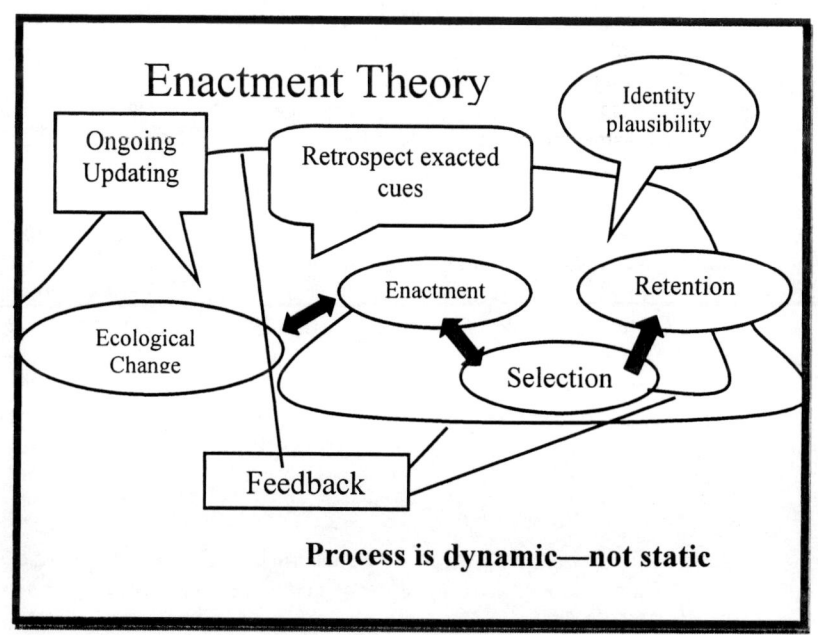

Process is dynamic—not static

Figure 6.1

Organization itself responds to ecological change in a dynamic and on-going process. This is a key difference with the institutional perspective which views the organization more in terms of permanent relationships and a structure which does not change. The figure above depicts the processes associated with enactment. The first thing to note is that there is no beginning per se. Rather, there are multiple stimulus points that include ecological change, retrospect, identify plausibility, and ongoing updating. Strictly for the sake of conceptualization, the process may begin with some form of ecological shift. For example, the public may see value in community center services to the developmentally disabled. The organization responds by beginning an enactment process of deinstitutionalizing, which in turn generates a variety of possible reforms. Through extensive conversation and role negotiations (frequently associated with power, which I will expand upon in the next section) certain strategies are selected. Meanwhile, the ecological change continues which may or may not continue to support the strategy selected and stimulates ongoing updating. The members of the various organizations also interact with these strategy selections through identity plausibility, determining whether that fits with their perception of their role and abilities. Plausibility is a key concept in enactment because it is tied to the subjective belief system of the members of the organization. There must be some kind of belief that the strategy selected is possible. Recall that in the DD Services case, some organizations accepted the outcome-based strategy approach and others did not. This is not so much because the strategy did not or could not work for the organizations that did not accept it. Rather, it was because they did not see it as plausible. Throughout the process of enactment, there are multiple feedback loops which influence the perception of plausibility as well as stimulate ongoing updating within and outside the organization.

The importance of viewing organizations in terms of enactment is that it gives us a vehicle through which we can move outside the Rational paradigm. It removes the essential principle of direct cause-effect relationship. Whereas the institutional perspective depicts the process as more linear with the structure beginning with the problem or cause leading to the creation of the institution, enactment has no single point of entry. Enactment also does not assume that the choice of strategies is tied to a rational decision process. It incorporates the relationships and the less objective process of plausibility identity as part of strategy selection. Enactment does not attempt to remove the organization from its environment in order to observe it. Institutionalism requires that we do just that. Enactment allows the process to take place on many planes and centers on the participants' constant need to answer the question: "What is the story?"[10]

The Role of Power

In all of this, there is a matter that must be discussed further, the role played by power. While we are all intuitively aware of power in organizations, as a rule, we do not like to talk about it. Generally, it is easier to talk about money or sex than it is to talk about power. First, this seems to go against our grain as a democratic society. Second, it causes discomfort to think that some people have power over others. Power theory is a recent development in organizational theory. It differs from the institutional and systems perspectives in various ways:

- In the other theories, the assumption is that organizations are about accomplishing goals of some kind.
- The other theories assume that personal preferences of individuals are restrained by rules, authority, and norms of rational behavior.
- The power theorists find these perspectives as being naïve and of minimal practical value

- Organizations are complex systems of individuals and coalitions, each having its own interests, beliefs, values, preferences, perspectives, and perceptions.
- Coalitions continuously compete for scarce organizational resources.
- Conflict is inevitable.
- Influence—and the power and political activities through which influence is acquired and maintained—is the primary "weapon" for use in competition and conflicts.
- Power politics and influence are critically important and permanent facts of organizational life.

Rarely are organizational goals accomplished by those with formal power. Goals result from ongoing maneuvering and bargaining among individuals and coalitions. Coalitions tend to be transitory. Organizational goals shift with the balance of power among coalitions. Goals provide the legitimacy for resource allocation decisions. Power relations are permanent features primarily because specialization and the division of labor result in the creation of many small interdependent units. According to James D. Thompson, "a lack of balance in the interdependence among units sets the stage for the use of power relations."[11] Jeffery Pfeffer expands on this concept, "[t]hose persons and those units that have the responsibility for performing the more critical tasks in the organization have a natural advantage in developing and exercising power in the organization."[12] There are many forms of power that exceed the legitimate power, i.e., power that is based on some form of legal authority or the office. This flies in the face of much of the institutionalist theories that abound and is certainly contrary to the bureaucratic ethos. These other forms of power include:

- Control over scarce resources – in organizations some resources are naturally scarce. These may include items (e.g., paper, tools, etc.), skills (e.g., computer technology), or funds. The need for particular resources may shift over time and thus, the person who acquires the power based on scarcity.
- Easy access to others who have power – this may simply include the person responsible for setting a key person's calendar, such as an administrative assistant. It could also include those who have access to others outside the organization that will have power (e.g., a legislator).
- A central place in the potent coalitions – some individuals are placed in an organization where they provide the information conduit for key coalition members.
- Ability to work the informal rules – frequently, it is the person who understands the informal rules and networks who wields much more influence than those

with formal authority. Simply knowing how a key figure should be approached will have more influence than going through the formal process.
- Credibility – this is ordinarily built up over time. The person who has demonstrated that they are reliable and able to overcome obstacles will be given more sway than those who either have no track record or have failed to demonstrate such skills.

Power is the ability to get things done the way one wants them done; it is the latent ability to influence people. It is not vested in a position held within the organization or even necessarily the force of personality. The important feature of power is the end point, i.e., accomplishing something that is seen to have value by members of the organization. Power is typically tied to dependence or, probably more accurately, interdependence. If one is going to accomplish much they must be able to see that they require the cooperation of others. The autocrat typically has less power than the one who delegates because the actual knowledge, skills, and abilities being applied to problems is broadened and the members recognize how important it is to work together.

Power can emanate from expertise that is valued by the members of the organization or those influenced by it. This expertise may not be specifically associated with what the organization does but is valued nonetheless. Effort and interest are key elements in the development of power. This means that power does not come on its own but requires some effort on a person's part. Just because the son of a company's owner is placed in a position of authority/responsibility does not mean they will automatically have the associated power. They will have to earn it. I have personally observed this on a number of occasions where the new supervisor assumes that he/she has power because they are placed in the position. Only later do they discover that they still have to earn that role in the relationship with the other employees. Failure to work at this will invariably result in a person with low power based on the definition of the ability to get things done. The subordinates retain power in such a case and undermine the power of the supervisor. Interest in what is being done and where coalitions exist is also critical in the development of power. The person place in a presumably more powerful position will soon discover that they must develop relationships and show interest in the culture of the organization or they will be highly ineffective.

Attractiveness (charisma) does play a role in power. Although, I would argue this role is not as great as many think. Other members of the organization will soon come to recognize incompetence even in the most attractive or charismatic leader. Location/position also plays a part in the development of power. Here we have a crucial point in terms of our understanding of organizations. The bureaucratic ethos assumes that the power is found in the position. In fact, that is the essence of the bureaucratic model. However, this has not been shown to be true. In almost all of my consulting projects I found that I needed to spend some time discovering where the actual power laid because it did not exist as the organizational chart indicated.

Coalitions are a key factor in the development of power. An organization is a collection of coalitions held together for a common purpose. The power and influence of any given coalition will vary over time.[13] At any given moment there will tend to be a dominant coalition, although, it is not unusual for there to be more than one dominant coalition. I found in many organizations there were easily two or three loci of power found through coalitions. It would largely depend on the issue upon which was being enacted. A coalition is a collection of entities that share resources and information to achieve a set of common goals in a controlled way, with plenty of prejudice.[14] The participants have varying amounts of trust amongst each other and such partnerships and trusts change dynamically. Participants will tend to move in and out of coalitions, sometimes willingly. The composition of the coalition will change depending on the issues or stakes. There are a number of factors that contribute to the degree of any coalition's power: formal authority, control over resources, information and access to it, and the reduction of uncertainty – that is the ability to increase predictability and thus, control.[15] Rules may be another contributor to power. However, my experiences have shown that it is much more a matter of using the rules to one's advantage than a close adherence to them. Sometimes, it is actually being able to work around the rules, which enhances power.

The important point to remember is that power does not always reside where the institution intends. This runs contrary to the bureaucratic ethos and is frequently the explanation behind unintended consequences. Rosabeth Moss Kanter in "Power failure in management circuits" states that there are three groups particularly susceptible to powerlessness: first-line supervisors, staff professionals, and top executives.[16] She goes further to point out that: higher organizational levels have the power to punish, prevent, sell off, reduce fire, without proper concern for consequences but this does not give them the power to accomplish. Managers who perceive of themselves as powerless tend to use more dominating or punishing forms of influence. This can be a problem of considerable dimension since it can be destructive. Kanter's descriptions arise from her experiences in organizations. I have to say that my observations have yielded similar insights. When I began working with a client and observed that a person in position of authority was autocratic and controlling, I noticed that they had very little effectiveness. Ironically, so many of these individuals sought to increase their use of aggressive devices not realizing that the more they took such actions the less they were likely to gain any power. I liken this circumstance to one of Aesop's fables in which the sun and the wind were debating which of the two of them was more powerful. To test their power they spotted a traveler on the road wearing a cloak. The proposition was that the one who could get the cloak off the traveler was more powerful. The wind began blowing harder on the traveler below. As the wind blew harder and harder, the traveler clutched the cloak more and more firmly. After this futile effort, the sun took its turn and simply raised the heat a bit. Naturally, the traveler feeling the heat, removed the cloak himself. The point is that when members of the organization sense that they are more in control of their contribution, they are more likely to contribute in a constructive manner. They must want to put forth the needed effort. Motivation comes from within the individual not from anything that a manager may or may not do. Thus, power is more properly understood in terms of each individual and is something that is given never taken.

Our understanding of power will go far to increasing our effectiveness in organization. It will also show that the rational model of power is false and may be counterproductive. There are basically three forms of power—power over, power within, and power with.[17]

- a. Power over – sees the world as an object, made up of many separate, isolated parts that have no intrinsic life, awareness, or value... Human beings have no inherent worth; value must be earned or granted... Power over motivates through fear.
- b. Power from within – sees the world itself as a living being, made up of dynamic aspects where there are no solid separations and no simple cause and effects. In such a world, all things have inherent value... Its motivations are erotic in the broadest sense of the deep drives in us to experience and share pleasure, to connect to create, to see our impact on others and on the world.
- c. Power with – bridges the value systems of power-from-within and power-over. Power-with sees the world as a pattern of relationships, but its interest is in how that pattern can be shaped, molded, shifted. It values beings, forces, and people according to how they affect others and according to a history based on experience.

Understanding power in these broader terms leads us to conceive of organizations differently as well. Under the Rational paradigm, the primary form of power is power over. It uses rule enforcement which is attached to fear. If one violates the rules they expect some form of punishment. Punishment is only effective if one is afraid of it. In the case of the DD Service providers, their fear was that they would be subjected to sanctions, including a cancellation of their contract. The agency leadership was more than willing to use this fear as a vehicle for leverage, or power. Power within plays a role in individual development and can be useful in terms of administrative strategy. However, there is still a need to coordinate all individuals in terms of being either organization or coalitions. Suffice it to say that movement away from the Rational paradigm involves greater use of power with, as it centers on the empowerment of all participants. This will also reach beyond the organizations and to the community. It is the decay of community that is a major contributor to disconnectedness. What is needed is an administrative strategy that will bridge the gaps inside the administrative agencies and between citizens and the agencies.

---

1. Hall, Peter A. and Rosemary Taylor, *Political Science and the Three Institutionalisms*, (Chichester: Blackwell Publishing, 1996).
2. Cook, K. S. and M. Levi, eds., *The Limits of Rationality*, (Chicago: University of Chicago Press, 1990).
3. P. Pierson, "Increasing Returns, Path Dependence, and the Study of Politics, *The*

American Political Science Review, 92 no. 2, (2000): 251-267.
4. M. Barzelay with B. J. Armajani, *Breaking Through Bureaucracy,* (Berkeley: University of California Press, 1992): 116.
5. Weick, K.E. "Cognitive Processes in Organization" *Research in organizational behavior,* ed. B.M. Staw, 1 (1979): 41-74.
6. Eisenberg, E.M. "Dialogue as democratic discourse: Affirming Harrison," *Communication yearbook 17,* ed. S.A. Deetz (Thousand Oaks: Sage, 1994), 275-284.
7. Eisenberg, E.M. & Goodall, H.L. *Organizational Communication: Balancing Creativity and Constraint* 2nd ed. (New York: St. Martin's Press 1997).
8. Weick, "Cognitive Processes in Organization," 130.
9. Weick, K. E. *Sensemaking in Organizations,* (Thousand Oaks: Sage 1995).
10. Weick, Suttcliffe, and Obstfeld, "Organizing and the Process of Sensemaking," *Organization Science,* 16, no. 4, (2005): 409-421.
11. Thompson, James D., *Organizations in Action: Social Science Bases of Administrative Theory,* (Columbus: McGraw-Hill 1967).
12. Pfeffer, Jeffry, *Managing with Power,* (Harvard: Harvard Business School Press 1992).
13. Banner, David K., *Designing Effective Organizations: Traditional and Transformative Views,* (Thousand Oaks: Sage 1994).
14. Dasgupta, Partha, Vinjay Karamchet, and Zvi M. Kadem, "Efficient and Secure Information Sharing in Distributed, Collaborative Environments" http://cactus.eas.asu.edu/Partha/Publications.htm
15. Banner, *Designing Effective Organizations: Traditional and Transformative Views,* 8
16. Kanter, Rosabeth Moss, "Power Failure in Management Circuits," in L. Maniero and C. Trombley, *Developing Managerial Skills in Organizational Behavior: Exercises, Cases, and Readings* 2nd ed., (Englewood Cliffs: Prentice Hall, 1994), 322-329.
17. Wink, Walter, *Engaging the Powers: Discernment and Resistance in a World of Domination,* (Minneapolis: Fortress Press 1992).

Chapter 7: The Human Sacrifices to Rationalism: The Decay of Community, Responsibility, and Reason

Before we get carried away and put the entire onus for disconnectedness on bureaucracies, we need to turn our attention to the role played by members of the community, be it local, state, or national. I cannot stress enough that the rational organizational forms were not created in a vacuum. Bureaucracy is a fairly natural consequence of choices made by members of society, that is, all of us. This was not a usurpation of power by the bureaucrats. It is a result of an exchange. Decisions have been made over the years that have resulted in this exchange. In exchange for the bureaucracies assuming responsibility to solve social/community problems, the populace avoided having to make difficult decisions. This was partly a matter of deciding that the use of rational agencies was the best way to solve our most elusive problems. This is also a result of being averse to risk-taking on the part of the general public. It is not something that began with the New Deal either. It began much earlier than that. So many people assume that this reliance on government agencies is the result of the creation of the welfare state. I would argue that this is very far from the truth. Americans started expecting the government to take care of their problems almost from the beginning. While they did create a democratic republic, the early Americans were still in the frame of mind that government had a paternalistic relationship with the people. Those who are called our founding fathers, the framers of the constitution, took full advantage of this tendency. It is true that in the first century or so of this constitutional state, little movement to the purely rational state occurred. Once the westward expansion began to slow, the growth of the bureaucratic state took off.

In addition to a dynamic of the relegation of responsibility by citizens, the process of regulation and resistance has stimulated the growth of the bureaucratic state. As laws were passed to regulate undesirable behaviors, to a greater extent on the part of organizations rather than individuals, strategies were developed by those being regulated to avoid the consequences of the law. This resulted in the development of laws to counter the avoidance behaviors. The cycle repeated itself until regulations became so complex that innumerable unintended consequences resulted. Today, citizens and organizations find themselves caught in an insurmountable tangle of laws and regulations. The bureaucrats are also hamstrung by these convoluted rules. In short, we have managed to victimize ourselves with a complex web of limitations.

A Very Brief History

After the idealism of the American Revolution had waned and the more practical matters of economy came to bear, the leaders of the nation (mostly rich landowners) framed a system of government that preserved the stability of government, primarily through the form of the U. S. Constitution. This also preserved the status quo for these same framers. Thus, from the start, the institutions of governance were framed in a rational manner. However, full-blown Rationalism had yet to develop. Nevertheless, this government exhibited very paternalistic tendencies in the beginning. The fact that only male landowners had the right to vote contributed to this predisposition. Women and those without land were viewed as needing to be controlled and/or protected. The initial system of electing representatives and senators ensured that the rabble were not able to send uneducated delegates. The rule of law was given absolute primacy, laying the groundwork for a rule-driven government. This particular constitutional system of government was quite appropriate at the time and has served us well since. The truth is that most people did have little education and could be easily duped by those who were educated. The size of government in the beginning was quite small, both as a matter of available resources and a more *laissez faire* approach to public policy. Most of the governance that was relevant to the general public was conducted at the local level. These localities were mostly small communities. This allowed some level of ownership of problems by the citizens. Equally significant, in the first century of the existence of the U. S., most social problems were ameliorated through migrations west, especially facilitated through homestead acts. So social problems were readily moved to a new location and change was able to evolve within these new communities without undue pressure on the older metropolitan areas.

This style of governing and social relationships was quite effective overall. That is, until the Industrial Revolution came along. This challenged the workings of society in extremely profound ways. The Civil War was as much a result of these principles as it was a result of confronting a moral question, if not more. Urbanization began to concentrate human interaction in a way that had not existed before. The new factories required these concentrations of labor so it was no longer desirable to move people to new lands. Consequently, the local governments needed to deal with issues of crime, sanitation, and transportation much more aggressively. It did not take long before local governments were unable to manage the stresses of industrialism. Thus, quite early on demands were being shifted to the states and national government to address these needs. At the same time, the need for more universal education became prominent. Workers needed to be able to understand instruction, which was frequently written, while at the same time, a new management class was being created. Local governments were the primary providers of this education. Nevertheless, national standards were being created because of the nature of the industrial state. Books were mass produced and the information being passed on was increasingly rational. The Industrial Revolution also brought with it larger and larger corporations. In a relatively short time it became logical that only a larger government could control the excesses of these corporations.

The social challenges that sprang from the Industrial Revolution were enormous. Sudden concentrations of working class people, including immigrants, created demands on government for which it was poorly equipped. The capitalists needed a workforce that was under control and some means for protecting its property. The workers needed an aggressive government for regulating the excesses of the industrialists. This included the need for labor protections, safety, education, and public works. Since government had already been framed in a rational manner and since this was the method of choice in the private sector, it was an obvious choice to use Rational methods to conduct this type of regulation. As the needs of the middle class increased, the demands on government increased further. For each new set of challenges, new sets of rules and their responsible bureaus were created. All the levels of government in the U. S. took on bureaucratic solutions to the demands of the public. This suggests that the development of the bureaucratic ethos began with the people, not with the government. In the beginning, this demonstrated that it remained the government of the people.

Once this process began, it became more and more self replicating. From the perspective of the Founding Fathers as described in the *Federalist Papers*, the purpose of government was that it was to prevent tyranny of any one group over another or that it was to provide for the common defense.[1] This began to change with the Industrial Revolution. Over time, the common perception became that government's primary role was to provide services. The initial priorities were providing public safety and education. With the growth of Industrialism, the services grew to include other areas of people's lives. Programs were developed to protect workers. These included child labor laws, safety laws, labor laws, benefit laws, wage laws, and so forth. Another rather ironic aspect of this is that the bureaucracies grew because they needed to respond to industry's attempts to circumvent the laws that were implemented in earlier periods. The more capitalists misbehaved; the more necessary it was to create bureaus to regulate them. Programs were also developed to care for the vulnerable. These included those for handicapped, developmentally disabled, elderly, and eventually the poor. Such programs were largely created at the convenience of industry. It was much more efficient to care for these populations through industrialized methods. Thus, institutions created for care and other benefit programs were developed so that these populations could be controlled. This also freed the working class to be more mobile and not be distracted by having to care for those in their families who were so vulnerable. Eventually, we began developing programs that actually protected lifestyles. These included park systems, highways, subsidizing of other transportation, and some housing programs. *

---

* This is one explanation for many people to believe the American Dream is owning their home. [Actually the American dream, if there is one, is found in the Declaration of Independence and it is social justice.]

As these programs multiplied, the perception grew that government's role was to assume problem-solving responsibility. Whenever an issue arose that may have been viewed as something that undermined the quality of life, the general pattern of turning it over to government resolution persisted. The key point here is that it actually involved a process of turning power over. This is tied to my contention that power is always something that is given and never taken. As problems increased in complexity, the agencies increased in expertise in the various fields. The agencies became more complex and the number of technocrats increased as well. These were highly skilled professionals who confronted the problems of society. Through their own use of complex language and principles they became more elusive to general comprehension. Thus, rather complementary forces were at work. The public was turning complex issues over to the bureaucrats. The bureaucrats were assuming these responsibilities and distancing themselves from the general public. The separation grew to a point that the bureaucrats had developed their own procedures, rules, language, and power and the general public was largely oblivious to how problems were being addressed and felt little responsibility for what was being done in their name.

The Emergence of the Disconnected

By the time we reached the middle 20th Century, it was clear that the expectation was that government was the vehicle to solve almost every kind of problem in society. This is a result of an increasingly assertive middle class and the incredible increase of wealth in the nation and the enormous consequences of a massive economic system, i.e., the Great Depression. This was also related to the emergence of the U. S. as the world superpower. At the onset of the post-World War II period, the U. S. stood as a military and economic colossus. Such a status brought with it immense responsibility. Americans were forced to be aware of the enormous problems of the world. Not only were we facing the rise of Communism but we were also being made aware of vast poverty, human exploitation, and environmental catastrophe. This was more than most citizens could bear. Consequently, the responsibility for facing such challenges was further relinquished to government. A former colleague of mine, Donald Spencer, described it in terms of needing to face the challenge of global distribution of wealth and power. He suggested that the choice came to either applying a triage strategy to the community of nations or a new international economic order. Neither of these approaches was viewed as particularly attractive. The triage approach would force us to identify nations that should be helped and those that should not. There really is no reasonable way to make such a choice. The new international economic order would have required us to make very significant changes in our own society because it calls for us to allow for the leveling of the economic playing field. I suggest that neither choice has been made and the general public has largely vacated the decision, leaving it to its government. This is where the disconnected population appears relative to the international sphere.

The international arena is but one place that finds people disconnected. At the national level, there is plenty of evidence that citizens do not relate to their government. While some may go so far as being openly hostile to it, most are just distant. The difference rests in the continued reliance on the state and national governments to solve problems. It is not so much a matter of people trying to resist government as it is one of preferring not to want it until they need something. This has been identified as a form of anomie. Anomie refers to a breakdown of social norms and is a condition where norms no longer control the activities of members in society. Individuals cannot find their place in society without clear rules to help guide them. Changing conditions as well as adjustments of life, lead to dissatisfaction, conflict, and deviance. Durkheim observed that social periods of disruption (e.g., economic depression) brought about greater anomie and higher rates of crime, suicide, and deviance.[2] The fascinating thing about what is happening in the U. S. is that the sense of not finding a place exists to a high degree. However, there are few indicators that this will result in any kind of revolt. Nevertheless, the rates of crime are rather high for a wealthy nation. When compared with other developed nations, the U. S. has the highest incarceration rates. The occurrence of suicide, particularly among young people is also quite high.

McKnight and Kretzmann point out that this is a rather widespread phenomenon:

> No one can doubt that most American cities these days are deeply troubled places. At the root of the problems are the massive economic shifts that have marked the last two decades. Hundreds of thousands of industrial jobs have either disappeared or moved away from the central city and its neighborhoods. And while many downtown areas have experienced a renaissance, the jobs created there are different from those that once sustained neighborhoods. Either these new jobs are highly professionalized, and require elaborate education and credentials for entry, or they are routine, low-paying service jobs without much of a future. In effect, these shifts in the economy, and particularly the disappearance of decent employment possibilities from low-income neighborhoods, have removed the bottom rung from the fabled American ladder of opportunity. For many people in older city neighborhoods, new approaches to rebuilding their lives and communities, new openings toward opportunity, are a vital necessity.[3]

I suggest that this is not just a problem of inner cities, as many might contend. Rather, the tendency is for communities of all sizes to be facing the same phenomenon. In many cases, the communities have so separated themselves through gated communities and suburbanization that they fail to see the extent of the challenge.

Kretzmann and McKnight go further to suggest that vast segments of society have been labeled and label themselves as victims or clients of one sort or another. They refer to the common practice of needs maps in communities. This has come about as a result of years of service providers -- government, non-profit, and others requiring clients. By using the perceived deficiencies of the community, the providers' justify their existence and sustain themselves. This is closely related to the process I described earlier as cooperatives and contracted services. Nearly every community has these needs maps. It is not an issue confined to urban areas. Kretzmann and McKnight describe the consequences of these needs maps quite well:

- Viewing a community as a nearly endless list of problems and needs leads directly to the much lamented fragmentation of efforts to provide solutions. It also denies the basic community wisdom which regards problems as tightly intertwined, as symptoms in fact, of the breakdown of a community's own problem-solving capacities.
- Targeting resources based on the needs map directs funding not to residents but to service providers, a consequence not always either planned for or effective.
- Making resources available on the basis of the needs map can have negative effects on the nature of local community leadership. If for example, one measure of effective leadership is the ability to attract resources, then local leaders are, in effect being forced to denigrate their neighbors and their community by highlighting their problems and deficiencies, and by ignoring their capacities and strengths.
- Providing resources on the basis of the needs map underlines the perception that only outside experts can provide real help. Therefore, the relationships that count most for the local residents are no longer those inside the community, those neighbor-to-neighbor links of mutual support and problem solving. Rather the most important relationships are those that involve the expert, the social worker, the health provider, the funder. Once again, the glue that binds communities together is weakened.
- Reliance on the needs map as the exclusive guide to resource gathering virtually ensures the inevitable deepening of the cycle of dependence: problems must always be worse than last year, or more intractable than other communities, if funding is to be renewed.
- At best, reliance on the needs maps as the sole policy guide will ensure a maintenance and survival strategy targeted at isolated individual clients, not a development plan that can involve the energies of an entire community.
- Because the needs-based strategy can guarantee only survival, and can never lead to serious change or community development, this orientation must be regarded as one of the major causes of the sense of hopelessness that pervades discussions about the future of low income neighborhoods. From the street corner to the White House, if maintenance and survival are the best we can provide, what sense can it make to invest in the future? [4]

I argue that this condition reaches much farther than inner cities or low income neighborhoods. This is a widespread situation in large and small communities alike. It is also a significant part of the process used by rational bureaucracies to exert the level of control that is a part of Industrialized society.

Anomie in the Local Community the Anomia Scale

In an effort to take this concept of anomie to a practical level, I find it useful to examine some specific cases. To do this, I will draw upon studies that I conducted for communities in Montana and Idaho. As part of their process of developing needs assessments for the local government, I recommended that we include a measurement of anomie. This would provide some insight into how likely certain strategies might work. Thus, I included a set of questions in these surveys as part of a Likert scale that addressed the feelings of respondents toward their neighbors, the public sector, and expectations for the future. This scale is commonly referred to as an anomia scale. A set of statements was presented that called for the respondents to agree or disagree, or strongly disagree or agree. The statements were sentiments drawn from Srole's Anomia scale, a device which has been highly tested in rural areas for the measurement of anomie.[5] I modified the scale to accommodate changes in the last 40 years and adjusted the calculations to demonstrate positive and negative outcomes. Anomie is viewed as a somewhat negative term in this context, in that it means a level of separateness or distance from the community. The scale is designed to measure the sense of belonging from two dimensions, the feeling that the respondent feels a part of the community and the sense that they feel that they are accepted as members of the community. This acceptance is measured in terms of the formal and informal community, that is, the official representatives of the community (i.e., government officials) and the unofficial leaders (i.e., prominent citizens). The ideal situation would be found by two distinct outcomes. The first desirable outcome is that there is a definite balance between these two perceptions; that one affirms the other. The second ideal result is that the measured outcomes are positive.† The scale used in this case measures the outcome as falling between 1 and -1 with 0 being a neutral outcome. As reported in the table above, then, the scale has been adjusted to show a positive number as being low anomie and a negative number being high. The reason for using a range equally distributed between positive and negative is to emphasize how far away from neutral the result falls. Other analysts have reported this number as a range between 1 and 5. However, I found it to be a more accurate assessment if the result was seen as falling onto a standard curve. Table 7.1 presents the findings from all three communities.

For our purposes, it is important to observe whether citizens have a sense of anomie within either dimension. The results of the scale present several possibilities when it comes to the social environment. If the citizens feel that they belong to the community and it accepts them as belonging, then there is every reason to believe that they (the citizens) will contribute to planning processes and gain some satisfaction from participating in the process. This is a community that will likely retain ownership of their own problem solving. If, however, they do not feel that they are a part of the community, whether or not they are accepted, then they will either prefer to stand on the outside and criticize or they

---

† In this case, the calculation is essentially a double negative. A positive outcome is one that shows that there is little sense of anomie.

will seek to gain entry through whatever means they find available. If they feel that they are a part of the community but are not accepted by the community then they may experience high levels of frustration and work for more acceptance by lashing out at those who they believe have rejected them or they may elect to satisfy this need through participation in special interest groups. If the perception is that they are not a part of the community but have been accepted as such by others, then they may experience a sense of guilt and either work harder at being a part of the community or engage in activities that will convince others that they should not be accepted. Finally, if the perception is that they are neither a part of the community nor are they accepted as part of the community, they will tend to isolate themselves in whatever way is available to them. In rural areas, the means most available to citizens to be separate is physical isolation. In urban areas, however, physical isolation is not available and anti-social behaviors are more likely, as noted above. Finally, if the feelings are not strong in either direction, the citizens are largely ambivalent in their attachment to community. Such ambivalence creates the most difficult setting for community action. The sense of strong feeling is what prompts people to action.

The results shown in Table 7.1 provide evidence of a state of disconnectedness. I must point out that these are small communities, located in predominantly rural areas. It would seem that if the residents of anyplace were going to experience a sense of belonging, it would be in such communities. However, these results do not suggest such a condition. Granted, the respondents indicate a very strong sense that they do belong. In fact, this is what one should expect from a small community. The sense of feeling accepted as belonging is in the negative, on the other hand. This brings us to a couple of significant conclusions. First, there is a high level of imbalance in the two dimensions. Ordinarily, one should expect them to be within two or three points of one another (e.g., .6 to .3). This is because the sense of belonging would tend to result in a sense of being accepted. The leaders of such local governments would be known by the citizens and probably would have had personal contact. These results show a seven point separation. This is rather striking. Second, the fact that the two dimensions fall into different quadrants (one positive and one negative), reveals that the respondents are concerned about their community but feel powerless. If one thinks about this for a while, they should be able to see how this can have an impact on local policy. There is little that can be done by local government that will convince the people that they are being heard. The perception predisposes the citizens to feeling left out.

Disconnectedness As a Result of Advocacy

In the same areas where the surveys were conducted, there were other intriguing results. One that stands out is that the majority of citizens were in favor of ensuring that their neighborhoods were consistent in their appearance (no businesses or multi-family structures) with 74.3 percent supporting this point of view.

The Human Sacrifices to Rationalism: The Decay of Community, Responsibility, and Reason 107

Table 7.1

Anomia Scale					
Self to Community					
Strongly Agree (+1)	Agree (+.5)	Disagree (-.5)	Strongly Disagree (-1)	Rating‡	
290	504	313	75	.26269	
200	564	340	95	.18098	
60	345	608	185	(.21411)	
(47)	(148)	(618)	(395)	.48262	
(234)	(432)	(436)	(103)	(.10705)	
				.60513	
Community to Self					
(273)	(429)	(441)	(55)	(.17696)	
(165)	(434)	(460)	(134)	(.01509)	
152	342	533	163	.08950	
(153)	(370)	(458)	(227)	(.09768)	
(172)	(433)	(896)	(200)	.15256	
				(.10705)	

‡The rating is calculated using the following formula:
$$\sum_{n=10}^{3} \frac{(SA_n * 1)+(A_n*.5)+(D_n*-.5)+(SD_n*-1)}{N(W_n)}$$
Where, SA_n = no. responding strongly agree to question n
A_n = no. responding agree to question n
D_n = no. responding disagree to question n
SD_n = no. responding strongly disagree to question n
W_n = Weighting (+ or -) for question being phrased as a positive or negative.

At the same time, a nearly equal number opposed any zoning regulations imposed on them or their neighbors (72.6 percent.) This means, at the very least, there were around 25 percent who both supported consistency and opposed zoning! Testing for correlation resulted in a finding that there were 53.8 percent of the respondents who actually responded this way (% = .056). This, I suggest, is further evidence of disconnectedness. One would expect that people would be aware that the only way to regulate consistency is through zoning. However, when people are interviewed in these communities, their explanations revealed something quite intriguing. Of course, they could understand that the two were related (after I explained it to them) but they just were not comfortable with government doing it.

In two recent studies I conducted for different cities on fair housing, I found further evidence of disconnectedness. The first thing that stood out was the differing goals between service providers and clients. I found extensive evidence of service providers using the needs map approach described by McKnight in the communities. Added to the dilemma of the needs maps themselves, I found that turf protection and competing services were rather excessive. The programs themselves were designed well and the competence of the providers was quite impressive. There was ample information available through the many groups and advocates in the housing policy area. Those involved in fair housing advocacy were highly knowledgeable and motivated. Therefore, the potential effectiveness was quite high in the jurisdictions. However, there were three factors which impaired the success of the programs. The number of providers presented something of a challenge in itself. It was difficult to determine who did what in fair housing. Some of the advocates were highly specialized. Consequently, it was not uncommon to hear of individuals seeking answers only to be shuffled through several organizations. The number of organizations alone was not the entire extent of the difficulty. The relationship between the organizations also acted as an obstacle. Finally, the bureaucratic ethos, which these organizations clung to, was an impediment because it restricted the possible strategies for reaching an outcome of fair housing.

A significant barrier to success of the programs regarded the number of housing providers and consumers who actually took advantage of the programs. All of those who presented fair housing workshops complained that there were a significant number of landlords, property managers, and owners who did not attend the workshops. Estimates by the respondents consistently suggested that around 50 percent of providers did not attend. The explanation for such poor attendance was that there was no leverage to encourage more. If landlords were not members of the Landlord Association there was no practical way to reach them in order to solicit their attendance. If property owners were not real estate licensees or members of property management associations they were not easily made aware of the program. In addition to it being extremely difficult to reach the people most in need of the programs, there was the matter of the fee charged for attendance. Since many landlords/property managers already viewed regulations as a nuisance, it was highly unlikely they would pay to hear about more of them. This is an interesting twist in the regulatory environment. The regulators came to believe that their regulation was so vital to the quality of life that those being regulated would be willing to pay for it. However, those being regulated felt quite the opposite.

The organizational relationships in one community were particularly worthy of note because they had such a direct impact on outcomes and social climate. While there were many constructive efforts being made toward more collaborative approaches to problem-solving, conflict over philosophical approach and allocation of funding continued to be a significant force. I have already described some of the structural difficulties, such as the multitude of advocates and an emphasis on self interest. Suffice it to say, the energy devoted to conflict was still a barrier to effective solutions. During a time that resources were being stretched, it was more reasonable to arrive at some arrangement that emphasized cooperation over conflict. During the interviews, and within the documents gathered throughout the process of research, it became clear that there were strong differences of opinion relative to how housing should be regulated, provided, and promoted. However, when the representatives of these groups got together these differences were minimized. Consequently, when the individuals I interviewed felt free to express themselves openly, the criticisms of other agencies were very strong but when asked about these conflicts in a more mixed forum, the various parties agreed that they got along well. It was evident that the residuals of prior conflicts carried over without all the parties necessarily being aware of it. Part of the problem related to the clinging to a bureaucratic mentality.[6]

This example of housing policy in a local community demonstrates the bureaucratic ethos and its roots rather well. The key here is that these conditions are a result of communities misplacing the responsibility for problem solving completely into the hands of organizations. It goes beyond the question of government involvement or not. The development of all of these programs came about because we opted for the Rational approach to solving our problems. Once that happened, the only strategy that made sense was to create expert organizations to address the deficiencies. The citizens, especially the clients in need of the programs, are generally out of the loop. The agencies are more concerned with preserving their territory than actually solving the problem. Remember, these are local agencies in a fairly small community (about 75,000 residents each). One might expect that there would be little difficulty overcoming such stresses and connecting with the citizens. However, the dynamics of the bureaucratic ethos, especially as it relates to preservation of the organization, overcome what could be considered as reasonable. We cannot, however, attribute all of this disconnectedness to bureaucratic ethos. There is also a very significant political and social reality that drives these trends.

Communitarians, especially Amitai Etzioni, in his *Spirit of Community* bemoan that American citizens have diminished their sense of responsibility.[7] This has occurred alongside an expansion of the sense of civil rights. So, for example, at the same time most are acutely aware of their right to a jury trial they are unwilling to serve on juries. While we are all certainly aware of our right to free speech, all too many fail to acknowledge their responsibility to avoid speech that will cause harm. I suggest that it has gone further than that. There is also a preponderance of separation from a sense of responsibility for public policy. This takes different forms. One form occurs when people may openly advocate for a particular idea but after it has been enacted and goes awry will blame those in public office. An example of this phenomenon is found in many of the fiscal limits initiatives, such as Proposition 13 in California and I-105 in Montana. In 1986, the voters agreed to freeze property taxes in Montana. When it came out that this would result in the elimination of programs, the citizens objected vigorously. This is extremely common in tax reduction schemes. The voters are quick to opt for such limits but not to make the sacrifices that will result. Of course, one might argue that the politicians are quick to sell the voters on the idea that tax reductions can be made without consequences. That just serves to make my point. If voters honored their responsibility for policy outcomes they would probably not be so quick to accept such arguments.

From the Reagan administration on, voters have been willing to accept an argument that taxes may be reduced, certain services increased (Defense) and there would be no consequences. Since the September 11, 2001 terrorist attacks, there have been plenty of demands for improved homeland security and support for military action. At the same time, there is no apparent willingness to increase revenues. The result was the return of an enormous deficit in the federal budget approaching $500 billion. More recently, this carried over to the demand that the government protect citizens from the excesses of the finance sector. It is clear that the only reason that the Bush administration, followed by the Obama administration elected to bail out big financial and industrial entities is because the public insisted that they be protected from the potential of economic calamity. However, the overall economic picture was likely just as much a result of individual malfeasance as corporate. It is rare to find a person who accepts that there should be personal consequences. Even in the face of enormous deficits, the voters remain in denial. This continues to happen in states across the nation. In 2009, there were 42 state governments facing deficits as a result of the loss of revenue during a recession and the decline of federal grants. The responses to these fiscal crises remain fairly universal—reduce budgets without eliminating programs and increasing taxes only as a last resort. This trend has been around for some time now. I examined the larger issue of fiscal limits and the responses of local governments back in 1991. The approach to fiscal limit has changed little since then.

Fiscal Limits and Local Government Responses

Local governments in Montana, as in California, Massachusetts and several other states, suffered fiscal crises which seriously impaired their ability to provide services to their communities. Although voter-mandated limits on property taxes had been important causes of these crises, constraints had also been imposed by the termination of federal revenue-sharing and reduced revenues from resource-based taxes such as those on oil and coal. For some jurisdictions in Montana the cumulative effects of these revenue losses had been crippling.

In the fall of 1986, Montana voters approved Initiative 105 (I-105), which required that the state legislature enact comprehensive reforms of property and other state taxes. I-105 also mandated, however, that if the legislature failed to enact tax reforms, a comprehensive property tax freeze was to be implemented instead. The Montana Legislature, which meets only biennially for 90 days a session, proved unable to formulate any reasonable comprehensive reforms within such a short period of time. In fact, they have been unable to develop such a reform to date, nearly twenty years later! The legislature has only been able to rehash program cuts and continue to provide an equally wide spectrum of programs on budgets that are increasingly restrained.

As a result of I-105, the 1987 Legislature passed legislation implementing a property tax freeze as stipulated by the initiative. This freeze remains in place as of 2009. While supporters of I-105 justified the measure by asserting that state lawmakers had failed to provide local governments with the flexibility to develop alternative sources of revenue (voters' guide, 1986), the enabling legislation worsened the revenue situation for local governments. Montana Senate Bill 71 froze the state's property taxes at 1986 levels by capping the chargeable millage. In many communities the overall taxable value of property actually dropped in subsequent years, resulting in a net loss in the revenue base for those local governments. The full impact of the freeze was felt as a result of the 1989 reassessments with the budgets in 1990. The reassessments caused losses in counties that generated much of their property tax revenues from resource based properties (i.e., oil and coal fields.) This has continued to date. Many counties have been forced to combat this by adding separate mills or imposing fees for services. The delays in reassessments has played a major role in the strategies of these counties, giving more affective power to property assessors and distancing the people from the control of their own local budgets.

These events in Montana are not dissimilar to fiscal limits experienced in California and Massachusetts in the 1980s, and many other states more recently. The extent of the depth of fiscal crises in 2009 in most of the states has yet to be determined. California faces extreme challenges that place it on the verge of bankruptcy again. Even so, voters turned down revenue enhancement propositions offered by the Legislature, continuing the perception that it is just a matter of the state government finding all the waste and corruption. This level of denial is clear evidence of citizens being disconnected from their own government. This has a fairly long history and is not likely to go away anytime soon. Proposition 13 in California approved in 1978, placed legal restrictions on the ability of jurisdictions to increase property taxes. In Massachusetts, Proposition 22, approved in 1979, placed restrictions on the ability of governments to increase property taxes by limiting the growth of property taxes to 22 percent per year. These along with I-105, provide interesting case studies of how disconnectedness may become self perpetuating. The voters limit property taxes in order to control local governments, the state government enacts legislation to that effect, and local governments are forced to rely on fees for services or other alternative forms of revenue. Even more significantly, local governments are brought to court for failure to provide mandated services, especially education, and are forced to raise revenues. Thus, in an effort to increase control over local government, the voters actually compel the courts, which are generally not elected bodies and are certainly not elected to make policy, to mandate taxes. These responses to fiscal limits are a key in furthering our understanding of disconnectedness. A deeper analysis of the responses themselves clarifies the dynamics.

While much has been written concerning the impacts of fiscal limits, of equal importance are the specific responses that have been undertaken by local governments. The impact of the limitations is illustrated by such responses. The act of limiting revenues is of little importance until such restraints are reflected in some alteration of government behavior. A sizable amount of literature is devoted to discussing such response strategies. One area of particular concern in the field is cutback management. Studies in this area are generally concerned with understanding how cutback management should be done or assessments of the results of cutback management. One of the more prominent authors in the area of cutback management is Charles Levine. The central focus of his work is analyzing and describing management techniques that may be employed by public sector agencies undergoing the process of retrenchment.[8] Other authors offer similar advice on how reductions should be carried out.[9] Such studies offer useful insights into means available for dealing with a difficult set of circumstances for public managers. Unfortunately, advice offered in these studies tends to involve stopgap measures for holding the public organizations together until better days arrive. This has led other researchers to ask: What if retrenchment never goes away? I would suggest that this particular question is of greater relevance today because retrenchment has not gone away.

Many theorists and practitioners in public administration began to realize that the fiscal limits movement was only one source of the ongoing fiscal difficulties confronting public organizations. They began to explore more creative ways to increase revenues so that services could continue to be provided at stable levels. Notice that the public administrators are now attempting to deal with financing programs separate from the citizenry. An idea popular in the mid-1980s was to increase available funds through the employment of creative financing techniques. For example, Maynard and Wheatley suggested the use of private sector methods of investing public funds.[10] Still others suggested that a variety of financial methods, such as variations on the methods of taxing property, would help local governments increase their available resources. Both Hamilton and Martlew, for example, described financing techniques used by local governments that were changing the face of traditional revenue devices, including tax-exempt and non-tax-exempt bonding approaches.[11] While these techniques were not purported to be a panacea, they were widely accepted as an important new direction in financing government. Again, it is significant how much these responses involve a process that is highly technocratic, and separates local governments from the citizens.

Others, searching for innovative responses to fiscal limits, turned their attention to revenue enhancement strategies. Woolsey, for example, offered suggestions for improving the collection of property taxes themselves.[12] The thrust of his suggestions was the need to establish methods through which some equalization of property taxes could be facilitated. Thus, Woolsey presents the importance of taking some action that will be perceived as reform by the general public even though he admits that property taxes are inherently unequal. Angell and Shorter suggest a scheme for revenue enhancement that has become more widely accepted.[13] While their focus is on the more specific practice of charging certain private industries' fees for the construction of infrastructure needed by that industry, the concept has been expanded to include fees for a wide variety of services. During the period following the fiscal limits movement, the assessing of fees for public services in specific instances has become a widespread phenomenon. Finally, Fisher suggests that governments increase their revenues through the sharing of broader tax bases.[14] For example, it would be beneficial to both parties if a municipality and county drew from the same larger tax base and divided the resources after collection. This practice encourages the two governments to coordinate their service provision. Fisher does caution public sector managers that this should not be equated with consolidation of governments but a mere sharing of tax bases so that leveling can take place between jurisdictions. This avoids the problem of some individuals paying much lower taxes simply because they live within a different jurisdiction.

Another group of authors argued that what was truly needed to improve government efficiency is a better understanding and application of budgeting theory and practices. They believed that more effective budgetary systems would be the best means for dealing with the fiscal limits movement. If governments can control performance measures, and therefore the effectiveness of their expenditures, they can prove to the public at large that they are worthy of continued support. Among these are Billingsly and Moore, and Hill and Plumlee.[15] Billingsly and Moore suggest that states have responsibility for ensuring that local governments operate in an efficient and effective manner since states are the architect[s] of the financial framework within which local governments function. Bozeman and Strausman extend this analysis by suggesting that a revision of budgetary theory is necessary in order to deal with the fiscal limits crisis.[16] Their contention is that traditional budgetary theories are ineffective in an environment of fiscal limits. This is especially the case in local governments that have been able to set budgets and then been able to set the mill levy to cover that budget. Thus, rather than preparing a budget based on anticipated revenues, the decision makers are able to set a budget based on their assessment of needed services and to set the revenues accordingly.

These suggested responses tell us a great deal about not only the relationship between government and the governed but the separation between intent and outcome. As already noted, the government experts seem to consistently base their suggested responses on some sort of belief that the citizens need only be assuaged regarding the very specific fiscal device that has been limited. They attempt responses that appear to be rather separate from the citizenry. These are very rational responses to particular challenges. This is at least partly a result of the practice of citizens turning governments loose to solve problems. It is also a result of a common citizen request for governments to behave more like businesses. It apparently escapes their understanding that government is not a business and cannot behave like one and, if it did, most of the decision-making would be removed from public discourse. This brings us to the point of the separation between intent and outcome. Ironically, the act of trying to exert citizen control over government results in more behaviors that remove or distance citizen control. The solution of the public administrators therefore being, if citizens are going to make the job difficult, they need to be kept away from deciding any of the specifics of governance.

Most of the studies reviewed above define approaches for responding to fiscal limits that are based on traditional models of service delivery and revenue generation. However, there is a growing body of literature that suggests that alternative models should be sought. The bulk of this literature is dedicated to describing specific methods used in some jurisdictions that may be described as innovative. The most well-known of these methods involve some form of privatization. Since the Reagan administration offered privatization as a means for achieving greater efficiencies in providing government services, many state and local governments have sought out areas to apply the concept. E. S. Savas is perhaps the most widely recognized proponent of this approach. In *Privatizing the Public Sector*, Savas describes various services that may be privatized.[17] He also provides some words of caution to jurisdictions that will opt for such approaches to providing services. His greatest concern is the tendency for governments to contract out in a manner that will diminish the jurisdiction's accountability. Rehfuss reinforces Savas' concerns by describing difficulties experienced in state and local governments regarding the monitoring of contractors.[18] This, he points out, is the weakest aspect of privatization since it is extremely difficult to construct a method of monitoring that will ensure that the public will is being carried out. I have already described some of examples of this in Chapter 3. While government-provided services have explicit authority lines, the relationship between authorizing body and service provider in a privatized situation has only the limited strength of contract arrangements. Governments must be particularly careful which services they contract out since some services are more politically sensitive than others and involve the vulnerable of society. For example, privatized social services may fail to serve those most in need since they are the most costly cases to handle.

Roehm, Castellano, and Karns provide a detailed analysis of privatization schemes used by local governments around the country.[19] Their study seeks to provide a greater understanding of which privatization practices are actually being employed by local governments. Their survey questions address the means through which contractors were selected and the specific services that were contracted out. Their findings indicate that contract award practices vary from management areas to service areas, but there appears to be for each area of interest a predominate approach. Generally, the lowest bid among qualified companies was the most popular method for selecting a contractor. However, many localities had placed limitations on this practice to be certain that local contractors were favored. They found that local governments mostly privatize readily distinctive services such as vehicle towing and refuse collection. Very few localities privatized vital services such as fire protection and police protection.

Kolderie offers an assessment of privatization efforts by identifying two different goals or concepts that are generally involved in their employment.[20] He suggests that one must distinguish between the primary policy decision of government to provide a service and the secondary decision to produce the service decided upon. He further notes that either function or both may be turned over to private organizations. The importance of these aspects of privatization is that a transformation of the role of government (at least at the local level) is observed. No longer is local government, represented by city managers, commissioners, or mayors viewed as the exclusive source of deciding the levels and means of services that will be provided. Government may be more accurately understood as a broker that facilitates a process through which the citizenry determines what services will be available and then seeks means for providing those services without necessarily providing them itself. At least, that would be the ideal outcome. However, it would seem that more of what has occurred is that public administrators tend to seek strategies that separate them more from the public. Ironically, the most popular responses are those associated with the "reinventing" movement, which moves the decision-making further away from the public by translating the idea of citizen into customer.

This discussion of responses by governments to fiscal limits movements provides some hints at how the process of disconnectedness has been accelerated. While the movement toward Rational responses, at the request of the public, began the phenomenon of disconnectedness, the fiscal limits efforts have pushed them along even further. Remember, these are mostly *voter initiated fiscal limits*. This means that the desires of the general public have pushed disconnectedness even further along. The government organizations, being rational in nature, need to have some sense of control over processes. If the citizens begin to challenge that by limiting money available for the process, the organizations tend to protect themselves. As we saw in the first set of responses, the strategies employed, even at the local government level, amounted to steps to outmaneuver the public. These responses took on characteristics which separated the citizens from the decision-making process. They were frequently highly complex, which only exacerbated the citizens' sense of being disconnected. So the voters pushed on government and the reaction of government went further in the direction of being separate.

Summary and Conclusion

The existence of disconnectedness is not only attributable to the bureaucratic organizations. These organizations were not only a result of an increasing reliance on the Rational paradigm but were equally initiated by expectations of the public at large. From the beginning, the United States was instituted to be a rational and paternalistic system. The Rational Model emerged as the primary means for satisfying the public good as the Industrial Revolution took root. The needs of the industrialists and the needs of the laborers both contributed to the ever growing bureaucracies. The industrialists demanded protection of their interests in an educated, stable work force along with facilitation of their infrastructure needs. The laborers needed protection from the excesses of Industrialism including wage and working conditions. This shifting between the two forces is shown in the dialectic process that is found in the two-party system. The administrative state that resulted from this dialectic became more and more entrenched.

As the United States developed into a major world power, international expectations not only added to the growth of the bureaucracy but also demonstrated the need for the citizens to be risk averse. The complex challenges of being the major international player distanced the people from their own government. In domestic politics, it has become increasingly clear that the citizens have become disconnected from their government and their communities. As more and more programs and bureaus appeared on the scene, there has been a discernable increase in anomie. This is a state of being isolated resulting in a breakdown of social norms. The response to this phenomenon has been the development of more programs, which, in turn, only leads to more separation from government and community. As providers of services base their purpose on needs maps the people become less attached to the need to own the problems. Rights become separated from responsibility.

An assessment of some local communities demonstrated the presence of this anomie. The three communities studied showed that the people had some sense of belonging but that they were not accepted as belonging. This resulted in being disconnected from solutions to problems. For example, people both wanted consistent neighborhoods but no zoning. The complementary event to this is that organizations, especially those with the mission of advocacy, develop more and more for their own sake. This resulted in multiple organizations with the same or similar purposes. These groups enter into competition for resources and self perpetuation and the clients for whom they advocate get left behind. Over time, this has contributed further to the preponderance of irresponsible behavior. People literally become incapable of connecting the programs to the problems that brought them about.

A significant outcome of these patterns is the rise of the fiscal limits movements. The citizens themselves choose to limit the revenue raising ability of their government. Initiatives such as Proposition 13 in California and Initiative 105 in Montana are examples of the more direct effort to limit revenues. These are not the only kinds of fiscal limits, however. There are also ongoing grass roots efforts that find their way into the Legislatures which also try to limit resources without ending programs. The irony of these efforts is that the reaction on the part of the public administrators further separates the electorate from the policy process. Leaders in the field have advocated for a variety of strategies that allow the agencies to enhance their revenues outside of the political arena. These run the gamut from cutback management to budgetary practices. A particular strategy that has gained considerable appeal is the increase in privatization of public services. This further separates the public from influencing the programs and their policies. At the same time, some responses to the fiscal limits movement suggest an emerging paradigm that replaces the Rational Model. These responses are discussed further in the next chapter.

1. "1787-1788: Federalist Papers: No. 10 and 51" http://www.allamericanpatriots.com/american_historical_documents_1787_1788_federalist_papers_no_10_and_51
2. Durkheim, Emile, *The Division of Labor in Society*, cited in Durkheim's Anomie (*hewett.norfolk.sch.uk*, 2002).
3. Kretzmann, John P. and John L. McKnight, *Building Communities from the Inside Out: A Path Toward Finding and Mobilizing a Community's Assets* (Evanston: Institute for Policy Research, 1993), 1.
4. Kretzmann and McKnight, *Building Communities from the Inside Out: A Path Toward Finding and Mobilizing a Community's Assets*, 3.
5. Srole, Leo, "Social Integration and Certain Corollaries: An Exploratory Study," *American Sociological Review*, 21, no. 6, (1956): 709-16.
6. PBE Research & Consulting, *Analysis of Impediments to Fair Housing, Missoula* (Missoula 2001), PBE Research & Consulting, *Analysis of Impediments to Fair Housing, Great Falls* (Missoula 1997).
7. Etzioni, Amitai, *The Spirit of Community: Rights, Responsibilities and the Communitarian Agenda*, (New York: Crown Publishers, Inc., 1993).
8. Levine, Charles, *Managing Fiscal Stress*, (Chatham: Chatham House, 1980); Charles Levine, Irene S. Rubin, and George G. Wolohojian, *The Politics of Retrenchment: How Local Governments Manage Fiscal Stress*, (Beverly Hills: Sage Publications, 1981).
9. Ingraham, Patricia and A Barrileaux, "Motivating Government Managers for Retrenchment: Some Possible Lessons fro the Senior Executive Service," *Public Administration Review*, 43, no. 5 (1983): 393-402; Roger Kemp, "Cutback Management: Coping with Revenue Reducing Mandates," *Management Information Service Report*, 12 (1980): 1-7.
10. Maynard, David and Priscilla Wheatley, "At the Crossroads: Private Sector Perspectives on Public Sector Financing," *Government Finance Review*, 2 (1986): 15-21.
11. Hamilton, R., "World turned upside Down: The Contemporary Revolution in State and Local Government Capital Financing," *Public Administration Review*, 43, no. 1, (1983): 22-31; C. Martlew, "State and Local Government Finance," *Public Administration Review*, 61, (1983): 127-47.
12. Woolsey, D., "Alternative Methods of Taxing Property," *Academy of Political Science Proceedings*, 35, (1983): 180-88.
13. Angell, Cynthia and Charles A. Shorter, "Impact Fees: Private Sector Participation in Infrastructure," *Government Finance Review* 4 (1988): 19-21.
14. Fisher, P. S., "Regional Tax-Base Sharing: An Analysis and Simulation of Alternative Approaches," *Land Economist* 58 (1982): 497-515.
15. Billingsly, Allen G. and Paul D. Moore, "Financial Monitoring of Local Governments," *State Government* 52 (1979): 155-60; K. Q. Hill and J. P. Plumlee, "Policy Arenas and Budgeting Politics" *Western Political Quarterly* 37 (1984): 84-89.
16. Bozeman, B. and J. D. Straussman, "Shrinking Budgets and the Shrinking of Budget Theory," *Public Administration Review* 42, no. 6, (1982): 509-15.
17. Savas, E. S., *Privatizing the Public Sector: How to Shrink Government*, (Chatham: Chatham House, 1982).
18. Rehfuss, John, "Contracting Out and Accountability in State and Local Governments: The Importance of Contract Monitoring," *State and Local Government Review* 22, (1990): 44-48.
19. Roehm, Harper A., Joseph F. Castellano, and David A. Karns, "Contracting Service

to the Private Sector: A Survey of Management Practices," *Government Finance Review* 5, (1989): 21 ff.
20. Kolderie, Ted, "The Two Different Concepts of Privatization," *Public Administration Review* 46, no. 4, (1986): 285-91.

Chapter 8: Various Attempts at Reform within Rationalism

Efforts have been made to address the challenge of disconnectedness and the bureaucratic ethos within the Rational model. These have either focused on outcome-based models or more entrepreneurial principles. They have met with limited success, unfortunately. As previously described, the tendency is to re-bureaucratize after setbacks. Nevertheless, these innovations are worth reviewing. They teach us about some elements of successful strategies, or at least those that offer some promise. They also demonstrate the underlying dynamics of the straining paradigm of Rationalism.

A particularly notable strategy has been to borrow from the private sector with privatization. As I noted before, these fall short of the mark because of the diseconomies related to public goods. More significant efforts to correct such shortfalls are found under the broader concept of public entrepreneurship. Public entrepreneurship draws upon principles much more appropriate for the public sector. A version of this which gained some popularity is reinventing government promoted by Gaebler and Osborne.[1] The concept is much larger than discovering efficiencies by challenging the members of a bureaucracy, however. These only serve to increase the separation between citizen and public administration, as clearly described by the Denhardts.

There are a variety of advances that have been taken by governments in response to revenue restraints, inefficiencies, and disconnectedness. Much of the literature is devoted to descriptions of such responses. While these analyses are useful in a discussion of specific strategies, the first task must be to describe the types of responses that may be selected by governments. Two particularly useful discussions are those of public entrepreneurship along with those associated with sustainable planning or sustainability indexes.

Public Entrepreneurship

Two authors who have contributed to the development of the concept of public entrepreneurship that I relied upon are John Kirlin and Anne Cowden. Kirlin's discussion of alternatives presented in his book, *The Political Economy of Fiscal Limits,* emphasizes the broader response strategies that governments may investigate.[2] His typology is premised upon the assessment of causality of the fiscal restraints by decision makers, be they voters or legislators. The understanding of what brought about the fiscal limits movement will have a great deal to do with how officials chose to respond. These frameworks are briefly described below, indicating the explanation selected, the general strategy for responding to restraints, and the intended outcomes or preferred political system. This is clearly an example of how a system, facing the stress of a major shift in political environment or other challenges, attempts to change within the paradigm. The process begins with an analysis of the cause-effect relationship in order to construct a response.

Grudging Accommodation

According to this view, voters are uninformed and responses, therefore, are mostly a matter of improving the performance of the public sector. The strategy is to outlast the present political climate and minimize the impact of the limits. Thus, the desired political system is one very similar to the existing system with some fine tuning rather than any significant changes.

Centralization of Political Power

The primary stimulus to fiscal limits is derived from a government which is ineffective, inefficient, or, in some way, unjust. The need for some greater power of government to curb arbitrariness is an essential element of the preferred system. Thus, the appropriate strategy is to move services to a larger, bureaucratic government in order to prevent abuses. For example, the movement of welfare services, previously provided by local government, to state government, will enable government to ensure that there is a higher standard of equity throughout the system. Another example is the creation of a Department of Homeland Security which will pull together all the information gathering functions and coordinate them with response strategies to terrorism.

Reallocation of Functions

The root cause of fiscal limits results from the inappropriate assignment of responsibilities to governments. Certain levels of government are better equipped to provide specific types of services than other levels. Thus, there should be some rational method of reassigning these duties so that the most efficient and equitable provision of services will occur. In the end, the desired system should have in place a more rational distribution of responsibilities brought about by careful study of what services belong at which levels. Responses should also include the implementation of some device for ensuring a continued allocation of programs to the proper locus. An example of this is the shifting of responsibilities of the Immigration and Naturalization Service to more appropriate departments in which the same people facilitating the immigration of foreign nationals are not also responsible for policing illegal entries. Another example includes the creation of the Department of Homeland Security.

Tilt Toward the Private Sector

Fiscal limits came about because government has simply become too large and intrusive in people's lives. It is necessary to limit government revenues so that it will be forced to examine its practices and eliminate those that are inefficient or ineffective. This process will reduce the burden on the private sector and individuals' abilities to improve their economic well being. The desired outcome is a vibrant private sector with elimination of inappropriate government involvement. Examples of this are the streamlining of U. S. Forest Service sales of forest resources or the use of incentives for environmental improvements rather than the enforcement mechanism of the Environmental Protection Agency.

Tilt Toward the Public Sector

The fiscal limits movement is explained as a symptom of the conservative movement in the late 1990s and early 2000s. Thus, the responses are an aggressive challenging of these ideological setbacks for those who believe government is largely responsible for social equity. The desired system is a continued growth in government so that the poor and disadvantaged are protected from the wealthy. Standing by these convictions in the face of conservative interests is the aim of government. There are few recent examples of this strategy, since the conservative movement has taken such firm hold. However, the growth of state governments, especially in areas of consumer rights regulation can be viewed as examples.

Re-reform Political Institutions

The fiscal limits are brought about by a crisis of confidence in government. The electorate is expressing its frustration with a process that puts people in office who are not committed to policy changes. The political system has become so ineffective that the will of the people is not carried out because the system lacks devices through which any form of leadership has an impact on policies. The desired political system would be one where the electoral system brings about changes desired by the people. This would be accomplished by strengthening political parties or removing barriers to change such as the seniority system. This framework appears to have taken on a new vitality illustrated by the current mood to limit terms of office. This is also the intent of campaign finance reform efforts like the McCain-Feingold bill.

Reconceptualization of the Political System

The explanation for the fiscal limits movement is rooted much more deeply in the broader theoretical understanding of government and its purpose. The currently accepted theory has failed to provide a set of responses that deal with the fiscal limits efforts in a meaningful manner. Poor theory has led to poor government and weak structures. Thus, the strategies selected should involve a more sophisticated reassessment of theories regarding the proper role of government. These theories should reflect the general understanding of the electorate regarding government. The approaches need to be flexible and sensitive to the changing demands on government. The emerging political system should be one that respects its obligation to provide a public forum through which policy choices are made. The primary purpose of the political process should be to convert public sentiment to a larger theoretical understanding of policy and enable change. Governments must be able to learn in order to be effective. Examples of this can be found in some public choice models in local governments. One example is the tendency of local governments to use survey data to gauge the sentiments of the public. Another is the use of focus groups to design development policies found in many state and local governments.

These alternative models are the basis for response strategies to fiscal limits, which, I suggest are an offshoot of disconnectedness. The order of description is important because it moves from a more institutional approach to one that is based on theoretical roots. These approaches are particularly useful to an understanding of what is occurring in the larger scheme of political/historical forces. The discussion of such issues also leads to a greater appreciation of the profundity of the challenges being faced by governments in general and society at large.

To appreciate what is occurring in the state and local governments' responses to fiscal limits, and by extension to disconnectedness, it is necessary to view these strategies in some context that will facilitate the grouping of the responses into larger categories. Anne Cowden provided a most useful device for accomplishing such a task in her lexicon of terms and concepts which surround the changing fiscal realities.[3] Since this lexicon is used to explore the responses found in California after Proposition 13, it is particularly useful in examining possible responses to the broader disconnectedness. Cowden's typology focuses on identifiable behaviors in local governments. While these behaviors result from the explanations offered by Kirlin, they avoid the normative or assumptive language found in his alternatives and concentrate on procedural outcomes rather than theoretical foundations. These can also be expanded beyond local government to state and federal government efforts, with little imagination. The important point is they describe behaviors indicative of attempts to reconcile the strains on the Rational paradigm.

Transitional concepts

Cowden describes the following four concepts based on transitional values normally encountered during the initial response period. These responses represent the first stage of fiscal stress and involve various strategies.

Load shedding. This includes turning over some public services to the private sector or volunteer efforts.

Cutback management. These are efforts directed at maintaining services while reducing budgets through hiring freezes, across-the-board cuts, eliminating some services, and other similar approaches.

Retrenchment. This is similar to cutback management, doing more with less, learning to live with less, and limiting public sector service involvement.

Public Entrepreneurship. Public entrepreneurship is not a singular form at all but a combination of forms. The essence of this strategy is that it seeks to draw on the strengths of all the other forms for the particular function or service. The first three may be described as initial coping strategies which place heavy strains on governments and often bring about intense self doubt in the public sector about government's ability to provide what they believe are traditional services. They also tend to place governments in an adversarial position relative to the electorate which may lead to further limitation movements by the voters, as demonstrated by Proposition 4 in California in 1980 and many other fiscal limits initiatives and legislation which followed in states around the country. These particular strategies have pretty much played themselves out in most states, which have been battling budget shortfalls for decades now.

Some jurisdictions turned to more creative responses as the pressure increased. These innovations have been grouped under a heading of *public entrepreneurship*. These strategies include a variety of innovative devices such as coproduction, co-provision, organizational mechanisms, investment, and community-based mechanisms. These are similar in many ways to the strategies described by Gaebler and Osborne in *Reinventing Government* and those developed at the national level by the National Performance Review of the Clinton Administration.

Some clarification here is needed since various authors have employed the term entrepreneurship in different ways. The larger meaning of entrepreneurship is derived from an understanding that innovative responses to public challenges must be found through a creative or entrepreneurial process. Creativity must be stimulated, both individually and organizationally, in order for the innovation to occur. The term entrepreneurship may also refer, more specifically, to activities that intend to stimulate economic development. For our purposes the former sense of the term is preferred. Continuing with Cowden's typology then, the innovative strategies are:

Entrepreneurship. These include active efforts to enhance the private sector climate and thus improve revenue bases. This includes such things as the creation of enterprise zones and marketing the state or community.

Public/Private partnership. Public/Private partnership captures part of the profits that accrue from a joint venture between public and private sectors, e. g., sharing of rent payments in a shopping mall.

Coproduction. Coproduction is the voluntary production of goods and/or services by local residents, usually in conjunction with public agencies, e. g., repair of streets by neighborhood residents with city assistance.

Co-provision. Co-provision is similar to coproduction but involving more the contribution of money or time by citizens for the provision of publicly provided goods or service, e. g., neighborhood watch programs that are administered by law enforcement or in some cases, Special Improvement Districts (SIDs).

There are also various mechanisms which may then be subdivided into two broader categories, internal and external mechanisms:

Internal mechanisms. These approaches deviate from standard public sector practices that are used to stimulate creative behaviors within government:

Pay-for-Performance systems. This strategy seeks to redesign incentive systems within organizations. The traditional civil service reward system is viewed as a barrier to innovative behaviors on the part of employees. So a system is designed to incorporate some performance measure with compensation. An example is the use of a salary matrix.

Innovative budgeting. The responsibility for budgeting is either altered or reallocated. This may include multi-year budgeting or decentralized profit centers.

Flexible human resources. The relationship between the contracting parties may be altered so that the time commitment of employees is tied more to the goals of the organization. This may involve the use of part-time or seasonal employees or consultants. To this may be added the use of flex time or innovative job designs.

Intrapreneuring. Such innovations attempt to create a new sense of ownership among managers in the public sector. The goal is to encourage entrepreneurial activities by these managers that will improve efficiency or seek non-tax revenues.

Volunteers/Fundraisers/Citizen Bureaucrats. These efforts involve the active recruitment of volunteers to provide some service. One of the most common of these is the development of neighborhood watch groups which are then coordinated with local law enforcement. These could also include mentor programs or highway litter patrols. Attempts to raise funds for services previously provided by the public sector through grants or fund drives may also be included in this category.

External mechanisms. These pertain to efforts to involve the private sector in the provision of service delivery or the use of private sector techniques by the public sector.

Public/Private sector competition. This incorporates contracting with pubic sector departments while also contracting with private sector organizations in an attempt to identify optimal service systems. The use of competitive bidding by the public agencies compels them to operate in a more efficient manner if they wish to retain their function.

Benefit-assessment. Included in this strategy is arranging to fund various local improvements, distinguished from property taxes or other general revenues on the basis of the levy, with the amount of the assessment based on the benefit to the electorate (SIDs).

User charges or fees. This includes charging those who directly benefit from public sector services. This may be for utilities, where a user fee is charged to everyone, or a more specific service, such as property assessments or inspections. It is also being more commonly used for state and national parks.

Contracting out. The production of services is conducted through a contract with a private sector organization or another government jurisdiction. This may include shared services by local jurisdictions or the transfer of responsibility to a higher level of government. It may also include specific services such as research by an agency of a university.

Enterprise zones. Areas of the jurisdiction are designated for economic growth stimulation. Frequently, this involves the use of industrial parks with reduced taxes or other benefits provided by the government.

Small business incubators. An arrangement established through the cooperation of government and other interests, such as economic development corporations, that assist in the early development of enterprises by providing space, shared business equipment, or consulting services.

Franchise arrangement. Local government awards private organizations the authority to provide public services within a geographical boundary. This may include airport authorities, vehicle towing, or transportation systems.

Subsidy arrangement. A financial or in-kind contribution to a private organization is made by the government in order to increase the level or quality of service. For example, a local government may choose to contribute to a YMCA to provide recreation services.

Vouchers. The government provides citizens with a coupon to be used toward the purchase of a specific local service, for example, discount coupons for public transportation or vouchers for schools.

Regulatory and tax incentives. These techniques allow the local government to use its regulatory and taxation powers to encourage the private sector to provide services or to reduce the demand for public services. For example, regulatory powers can be used to encourage a local transit company to offer handicapped access or tax incentives can be used to encourage citizens to provide their own street maintenance.

Marketing of public services. The local government actively assesses the needs of clients or citizens and then designs services to fit those customer needs. It may also include the promotion of existing services to increase usage. This is an alternative to producing services which may be without consumer utility. The outcome is reducing public services which have little demand by either increasing the demand or eliminating the service.

Investment approaches. Governments attempt to improve their income through the investment of public funds, repurchase agreements, and/or state/local government investment pools.

Bargaining/negotiation/mutual cooptation. Direct interactions between a developer and a jurisdiction are conducted to determine how the capital infrastructure necessary to accommodate growth will be provided. Such arrangements may include the construction of roads or utility lines

Community Facilities Districts. The establishment of a district service by a proposed facility or service is offered by government so that the funding of the facility or service is more directly provided by those citizens that utilize them.
Through this lexicon, Cowden provides the context for studying some recent approaches to government activities. Her typology facilitates the measurement, to some extent, of innovative behaviors in governments. This lexicon also enables the placement of emerging values regarding the proper role of government into a more observable form by linking specific behaviors to these values.

A theme which emerges from the work of Cowden and Kirlin, as well as others, is that politicians are most likely to pursue such alternative or innovative responses where they have been willing to reconceptualize the role of government. The cornerstone of such a reconceptualization is the recognition that government does not exist to provide services across a wide spectrum. Rather, government's proper role is to provide a public forum through which needed services may be agreed upon and a variety of devices employed to provide the services in the most effective or efficient manner. What is important to consider here is the limitation imposed upon this phenomenon by the Rational model itself, since effectiveness and efficiency are the preeminent values. Cowden provides an excellent description of how these emerging values are revealed. The reconceptualization of government is further described by Kirlin in his discussion of the fiscal limits movement itself. While Cowden briefly lays out the elements of the emerging values in California specifically, Kirlin takes a broader perspective to the changing face of governments in general.

Drawing from the works written prior to the fiscal limits movement of the late 1970s and 1980s, and reflecting on the movement itself, Kirlin suggests that governments' roles have come into question. For example, Bish and Ostrum had already described in 1973 a shift in expectations for metropolitan governments based in part on New York's fiscal crisis.[4] Kirlin draws from their reassessment to suggest that the primary importance of the fiscal limits movement is its reflection of the need to develop a different understanding of government and its place in society. No longer should government's effectiveness be measured by its ability to provide services but by its ability to facilitate the public choice process through which the types and levels of services desired by the constituency is determined. Thus, the development of new service provision devices is enabled by a new understanding of government. This theme is supported by a number of analysts and would seem to set the tone for reforming local governments nationwide. This, at first glance appears to be the premise for the public entrepreneurship model itself. However, on further examination it becomes clear that public entrepreneurship continues to begin the process by assuming that government should provide the service. Even more to the point, public entrepreneurship removes the citizen from the decision-making process even further by replacing public service with more of a business-style assumption of ownership by the public administrators.

Public entrepreneurship is purported to center on drawing upon the talents and creativity of all the members of the system. It seeks the organizational form that is best suited to the task being undertaken. In the case of human services for example, it is preferable to grant as much latitude to the local providers and the individual case manager as possible while holding them to specific expectations regarding outcome. The entrepreneurial organization can reach a goal that is outcome based with discretion placed in the hands of a provider or case manager, a bureaucracy cannot. This option also allows for combinations of organizational forms that present structures do not allow. For example, the provider may have direct contact with a private employer to be certain that the clients' needs are being met or the preferences of the client and/or the clients' family may be incorporated into the structure of the program. In a bureaucratic form such lateral contact is actively discouraged. In a strictly private enterprise form the interests of the client are far too easily subordinated to profit. In a cooperative format the survival of the organization may too easily supersede the outcomes desired. In a contracted services model, the adversarial role of the contractor to the agency may expend far too much energy and the proper values overlooked in trying to accommodate such a relationship. In any event, even though public entrepreneurial strategies are advanced as non-bureaucratic, they continue to rely upon Rational assumptions. Worse, they allow the agency to take on a level of independence that diminishes its sensitivity to the preferences of the general public. While they may incorporate client preferences, they do not incorporate citizen desires into their planning and operations.

The public entrepreneurship model moves away from structural solutions to value-centered outcomes. It returns the emphasis to what is the most desired outcome and then moves to designing systems toward that end, retaining a flexibility where needed but adding accountability where it is in the client's best interest. The ability to engage in such flexible behaviors allows the organization to design systems that are individualized where appropriate or standardized in other cases. The main dynamic is not the organization structure but rather the task to be accomplished. When conflict arises between structure and outcomes, it is the structure that is sacrificed. However, this is not a trivial matter. The entrepreneurial process involves careful assessment of what interferes with success. It is not an anarchy so while the organization is granted considerable freedom it is also not inviolable. However, since it typically by-passes the public forum as the crucial element in its conduct, it will tend to either gravitate back to a bureaucratic model when it comes under attack or resort to aggressive marketing strategies intended to ensure its continued success.

It is imperative to recognize that movement away from bureaucracy is not easy. The attempts to do so to this point in many cases have clearly demonstrated this to be true. Remember, the current structure has built-in protection for itself. Its enormity and principles that promote formal structure are extremely difficult to break through. Those in the upper and middle layers of the structure may feel particularly threatened by such strategies. When threatened, they are able to pull out many different devices at their disposal to stop reforms that they perceive as a direct attack on the organization. These may be as simple as selective implementation or as aggressive as controlling information. For example, the agency may opt to implement community based services except that they will not release control on safety inspections. The agency may use information by releasing reports unfavorable to a given provider but not those which are favorable. In any event, while conversion to this strategy of public entrepreneurship may be carried out carefully and a sound support base formed prior to implementing any changes, the essential dynamics of Rationality remain ingrained. My argument here is that Rationality itself acts as a barrier between the public programs and the citizenry. In order to develop reforms that are truly going to be transformative, a new paradigm must be embraced. This is best accomplished by involving those being affected in the design of the reforms, especially the "front line" people, which includes clients and other stakeholders. It also requires a widely expanded understanding of who the stakeholders are and how they should be involved.

An important point made here is that in spite of all these challenges associated with fiscal limits, the members of government agencies, especially human service organizations have performed admirably. They have borne up well under challenges of increasing case loads and procedural requirements. Their responsiveness to clients has been impressive under these conditions. However, the movement to public service models requires a profound philosophical change. The best way to accommodate this change is by drawing upon the creative abilities of those working in the public service occupations specifically. This cannot take place within the bureaucratic environment. This in no way suggests that public organizations cannot be successful. Rather, it suggests that in order to be successful the public organizations need the dramatic shift associated with public service as a foundational principle.

A very profound yet critical underpinning of public service is that it literally redefines the role of government. The other modelsSthe bureaucratic, the cooperative, contracted services, and public entrepreneurshipSare premised on the belief that the role of government is to provide services. Thus, from the bureaucracy to the contracted service all of the emphasis has been on the direct determination of the procedures of that service; literally it has evolved into a victory of process over outcome. Many of the advocates for these various structures have incorporated outcome-based language into their promotional efforts. However, as long as the belief continues that it is government's role to provide services, the need to *control* remains. Instead, the role of government needs to be defined as *to provide for the public forum through which the extent of services will be determined and to distribute resources to those values that are identified through this public dialogue.* There is a profound difference between this and the language used in public planning to this point. No matter how it is phrased, reform language continues to retain government's control over the services themselves. This explains the difficulty that continues to plague all of the efforts to move from the bureaucratic model to more ones associated with public service.

This concept of public service also provides critical insight regarding organizational structure. Frequently, development of the models associated with public administration includes discussion of structure with respect to the location of authority. Specifically, there is mention of the use of regional offices or similar decentralized structures. The issue really is not about the location of offices but is about what kind of relationship should exist. In order to move to a public service approach to providing services, every effort is made to improve the capacity of the system by removing obstacles and encouraging creativity. Thus, a decentralized approach can be effective as long as the role of the satellite providers is properly constructed. The public servant in a regional office should act as a facilitator rather than as an authority. Generally speaking, more decentralized approaches to administration are more conducive to this model. The more latitude granted to the regional offices, the more effective they are at facilitating. The absence of a high level of discretion at all levels dampens the creative abilities both of the region and the providers. The climate of encouraging innovation toward more successful outcomes must be complete. Thus the existence of an effective network of providers facilitated by the regional administrator is more consistent with the overall philosophy related to public service. Since the public service model requires much more energetic involvement of the public at large, it is much more practical to distribute as much of the decision-making to local offices, allowing for more direct interaction with citizens.

Community/Social Indicators

Public entrepreneurship has been limited in its successes. Culminating in the National Performance Review under the Clinton administration, the process of seeking entrepreneurial solutions has lost favor. This is the result of many factors. Perhaps, the most significant reasons have to do with the perceived lack of success as states and local governments continue to struggle with substantial budget shortfalls. In large part, this may be explained by the fact that the root assumption that government's primary role to provide services has persisted. The strategies that are apparently replacing public entrepreneurship are based on the concept of sustainable communities. The central theme is that the use of extensive data, identified as indicators, will direct the actions of government in a way that focuses on the accomplishment of desirable ends. These indicators emphasize the idea of sustainability. One of the earlier sources of this value was Daly and Cobb's Index of Sustainable Economic Welfare.[5] Their focus was on the need to replace tracking of economies by using Gross Domestic Product with an index that included the limits of resources as well as the effect of environmental/social degradation on the overall well-being of the community. Their core thesis throughout their work concerns the need to realign government and social structures toward smaller social and economic units. Consequently, economic and political power must be in balance at any given system level for the system to function in the interests of community. While this appears to leave only two choices either to centralize power in a global government or to decentralize the economy and make economic actors more accountable at the national and sub-national levels Daly and Cobb claim that it is not an either/or choice but a both/and. The emerging global society must develop democratically controlled institutions at all levels: international, national, and local. It also needs to create a decentralizing context for economic activities that returns institutional control to people, roots economic interests in local soil, and reestablishes some sense of human community. They suggest five activities which could be undertaken, leading to an overall shift in practices:

- *Significant university reforms;*
- *Local community-building;*
- *Steps toward a relatively self-sufficient national economy;*
- *Bringing the question of scale into public consciousness; and*
- *Changing the way we measure economic success.*

The influence of this seminal work can be seen in various efforts. There has been more attention directed toward community-building and changing the way we measure economic success. The activities of university reform, a self-sufficient national economy, and bringing the question of scale into public consciousness have not received much attention. I would suggest that this is due to the deep roots of each of these in the Rational model. Notable efforts are occurring in community building and the measurement of success in various areas. These include:

- sustainable growth indexes (an unfortunate term since Daly and Cobb argue that *growth* is not sustainable), also referred to as performance measurement,
- community indexes or outcome measurements in the non-profit sector, and
- community-building through social indicators and focus groups.

It is a bit early to determine any level of success in these areas but they are worthy of attention since they point to the future and suggest the form of post-Rational models.

Performance measurement has become an accepted management practice for state and local governments across the country, no longer limited to a handful of large jurisdictions. Over 120 cities and counties have cooperated with the Center for Performance Measurement of the International City/County Management Association (ICMA). [6] This is, to some degree a continuation of long term efforts to move governments to performance budgeting. The goal of this perspective is to tighten the ties between expenditures and actual performance in the community. From the earliest works on public budgeting this has been a system that has been highly valued. Unfortunately, no system to date has managed to remove the more typical budgetary strategy tied to incrementalism* and line items. Epstein, Solomon and Grifel describe the essence of the practice:

> [M]anaging for results, based strictly on internal development and use of performance measures by government officials, is not by itself, the highest value use of performance measurement.
> It is possible to go beyond internal uses of performance information, to higher value uses that focus on measuring and achieving results that matter to the citizens of a community, region, or state. Performance measures that focus on issues or conditions in the community of greatest concern to citizens will be of greatest interest to citizens and elected officials. Some form of citizen engagement is needed to identify community conditions that concern citizens the most. A government can thus achieve the greatest value from its measurement and improvement efforts when it aligns citizen engagement with its efforts to manage for results, or more generally, when it aligns citizen engagement, performance measurement, and policy and implementation. [7]

Performance measurement applies to measure of both community conditions or broadly defined measurements of outcomes desired by the community, e.g., em-

---

*This is a term coined by Charles Lindblom in 1959 which describes the decision-making process in governmental agencies, especially budgeting. Essentially, it means that changes are only made very gradually and are premised on the previous year's practice/budget. Charles E. Lindblom, The Science of Muddling Through *Public Administration Review 19* (Spring 1959), 79-88

ployment, crime rates, or air quality, and measures of government service outcomes. Government service indicators are rather well established by government accounting standards. Some governments add to these with survey data of citizen satisfaction. I have personally conducted some of these surveys and used the data to guide government decision-making processes.

The more elusive element of the use of community indicators is the measurement of community outcomes. There has been immense discussion of what variables should be included, how the data is to be collected, and to what it should be applied. The general sense of the field is that the number of indicators should be as broad as possible. The more data that is made available the better it is for advancing public service. This becomes problematic when discussions proceed. In almost every case that data sets are selected, some segment of the community will come forth complaining that there are variables that have been neglected. Consequently, the process of selecting indicators themselves is one that must be very carefully and consciously carried out, in order to arrive at a point of agreement. Such procedures must, of necessity, be based on a consensus model.

Summary and Conclusion

The strains on the Rational model of governance have been revealed, at least in part, through the various fiscal limits movements. There have been a number of responses offered by governments throughout the nation, mainly in local governments. These responses may be understood by laying them out in typologies based on either categories of causal assumptions and resulting strategies as done by John Kirlin or through a lexicon using identified behaviors on the part of the government entity as demonstrated by Ann Cowden.

In the causal model, the type of response is derived from an assumption as to what brought about the fiscal limits. They range from an assumption that the public is poorly informed and the agencies need only ride out the temporary condition that has been created by the limits to recognition of a basic weakness in the theory of government. It is not difficult to imagine that governments and their agencies have gone through all of these phases (with the possible exception of the last), but these responses are not necessarily serially related. It is equally possible that a local government may move immediately to the last set of assumptions. It is also possible that a jurisdiction may move in a direction to more restrictive or jump around from one to another with no particular pattern.

The behavioral lexicon helps to sort out how more entrepreneurial responses may be identified. While it is very easy to see that governments have gone through at least some part of the transitional strategies of load shedding, cutback management, and retrenchment, it may be somewhat more difficult to find instances of innovative strategies. One may even argue that the initial or transitional strategies are necessary in order for agencies of governments to be brought to the point of trying any of the more creative schemes. I find that a bit unlikely but it may help in conceptualizing how the underlying theoretical assumptions must change in order for non-bureaucratic strategies to be discovered.

Be that as it may, I have found that state and local governments have tried many of the entrepreneurial strategies with varying degrees of success.

A promising trend is found in the rise of interest in community/social indicators as a public model. There is at least an attempt to redefine what it is that government is to accomplish and what the fundamental issues are based on measurements of existing conditions. At first glance these appear to be overly complex undertakings. However, the reality is that social interaction is very complex. Whenever I hear of someone advocating policies premised on the belief in simple answers, I cringe. Such simple answers invariably lead us into trouble because they fail to consider the nearly innumerable dimensions that are affected by any change in one. This bring us to the point of considering an alternative to the Rational model itself. I contend that we are drawn to simple answers because that satisfies our perception of the world in Rational terms. It is time to consider replacing this manner of thinking with something much more realistic.

The attempts at reforms within the Rational paradigm have shown that change is possible, at least in terms of the ability of leaders to try something different. The barrier to success is not the unwillingness to change but the persistence of the bureaucratic ethos. We must remember that this ethos is not just a matter of government employees' attachment to an organization form. Rather, it is the result of an entire cultural system which has sought out some form of safety. It is not particularly sensible to believe that a select group of people are responsible for the rigidity of government. It is equally the result of a belief system that seeks a reduction in uncertainty. The bureaucratic ethos comes as much from the demands of the general public as it does from government leaders. This suggests right up front that any consideration of reconceptualizing the role of government will rely on educating the general public as much as it is the leadership.

---

1. Osborne, David and Ted Gaebler, *Reinventing Government: The Five Strategies for Reinventing Government*, (New York: Penguin Group 1993).
2. Kirlin, John, *The Political Economy of Fiscal Limits*, (Lexington: D. C. Heath, 1982).
3. Cowden, Anne C., "A Public Sector Lexicon: California Style," *State and Local Government Review* 21, (1989): 116-122.
4. Bish, Robert L., and Vincent Ostrum, *Understanding Urban Government: Metropolitan Reform Considered*, (Washington, D. C.: American Enterprise for Public Policy Research, 1973).
5. Daly, Herman and John Cobb, Jr., *Redirecting the Economy Toward Community, the Environment, and a Sustainable Future* (Boston: Beacon Press, 1989).
6. Epstein, Paul, Randall Solomon, and Stuart Grifel, "High Value Performance Measurement: For Sustainable Results that Matter to Citizens," *The Bottom Line,* (Washington, D. C.: ICMA, 2000).
7. Epstein, Solomon, and Grifel, "High Value Performance Measurement: For Sustainable Results that Matter to Citizens," 5.

Chapter 9: An Emerging Paradigm: Chaos Theory

There have been several modifications to the Rational paradigm. These have met with varying degrees of success. One cannot argue that they have not contributed to the strategies available in organizing and problem solving. However, we may well have to admit that we seem to be falling further away from stability and solving major problems rather than closer. In recent decades, however, there have been some more aggressive attempts to replace this paradigm. Some of these include the holistic models, noetic sciences, and Chaos Theory. Of these the one which holds the most promise is Chaos Theory. In spite of the unfortunate name, this theory presents great opportunity in the social sciences. Interestingly enough, just as did the Rational Model, it has emerged in the field of physics. So even though so many social scientists continue to cling to the Rational Model because it is so scientific and it has served physicists so well, many physicists themselves are now challenging Rationalism. As with any emerging paradigm, it has its fair share of detractors. However, more and more of the world's scientists are turning to this model for more sound explanations of phenomena. The underlying theme in the theory is that our previous notion of order is inaccurate. It also suggests that our goal of averting chaos is not only extremely unlikely but ill-advised.

In the 1970s, some physicists began using computer technology to extrapolate some rather basic laws of physics. At first, using a hand-held calculator and repeating an equation hundreds and even thousands of time (thus replicating the passage of time), they began to notice that there were aberrations in the results. This prompted them to take measurements of some simple physical systems and to enter them into a computer system, apply the formulae for those systems and instruct the computer to repeat the calculations millions of times. The results were quite contrary to what would have been expected. The results began to disperse and significant relationships were eliminated. The linear models normally associated with the laws of physics literally disintegrated. A classic example involves the behavior of water passing over a water wheel. [This is rather ironic since the water wheel was so important in the early development of Industrialism.] The results suggested that the wheel would stop after a while and actually revolve backwards. Then it seemed that the forces would propel the wheel in two different directions. After careful analysis, the research team identified seventeen different dimensions that affected the water wheel system (e.g., time, heat, wind, pollution, biological systems, evaporation, etc.) Not only were there so many dimensions unaccounted for, but the relative importance of each of these dimensions shifted throughout the extended period of observation. Bluntly put then, this study refuted the singular cause-effect relationship altogether. Even an apparently mechanistic system was not at all so predictable!

Other studies focused on the concept of turbulence. This phenomenon, found in natural systems of all kinds, was ordinarily written off as an anomaly. However, some researchers found that turbulence was rather constantly present. This discovery occurred mostly because the sensitivity of measurement instruments had increased so much that previously unobservable levels of turbulence could be detected. One basic system demonstrates this idea fairly clearly. Physicists observed that in smooth conduits for water, periodically eddies would develop. This occurred even if the speed of the water did not increase. The researchers designed incredibly smooth channels to observe the behavior of the water. So as the water flowed, there should have been no shift in its smooth course. However, eddies developed anyway. There were several other experiments conducted on similar systems and in other disciplines (such as demographics) and similar results were found. The conclusion, after many attempts to correct any errors in methodology and measurement, was that turbulence is constantly present in systems.

The finding that turbulence is constantly present is indeed significant. This takes away the notion of stable, predictable systems. It also provides additional understanding of the problem of the water wheel. After considerable effort, the observations of turbulence lead to an even more significant discovery. Not only is turbulence constantly present but its apparent chaotic nature exhibited some fairly consistent behavior. First, the turbulence would be rather minuscule and remain within the bounds of the expected linear behavior. After a time, the turbulence would increase in intensity until observable shifts began to occur in the system. This build-up would eventually lead to bifurcations in the system itself (splitting of the results into two or more distinct directions.) These bifurcations were indications that a different dimension was influencing the system. Unless the level of energy was redirected from the turbulent bifurcations, a chaotic episode would ensue. This chaotic episode is a period of time where the relationship between variables becomes so erratic that the line that once demonstrated the relationship becomes non-existent. In other words, all predictability disappears. After a time, however, a new line indicating the nature of the relationship emerges. The system is completely altered (like the water wheel) and will begin to start this process over. Figure 7 below depicts this process. This graph should be viewed as a three-dimensional chart even though it is on a two-dimensional surface. The points on the graph are those at which the resulting lines intersect a perpendicular plane. In other words, imagine lines shooting through the paper and the resulting holes making up the line. This is the only practical way to add the fourth dimension of time and millions of repetitions of the measurements and calculations in graphic form.

Figure 9.1 shows that initially the system appears stable. The curve demonstrates a relationship that falls within expectation (including, of course, the use of standard deviation to form the line.) After a while, as the frequency of events increase (e.g., if this was a demographics chart the increase would be in the arrival/fertility rate [%],) the line becomes unstable and splits (bifurcations.) The subsequent lines also begin to bifurcate in increasing frequency until the lines disintegrate altogether. After a time a new line emerges which indicates that a different relationship has formed. This line also goes into bifurcations and chaos after a period of time, eventually resulting in another new line. The significance of this illustration is that it shows that systems have a built-in level of instability or turbulence. The result of the chaos is not total disintegration of the system at all but the development of a new system. The concept of chaos has been mostly misunderstood for some time in Western culture. That is why the term itself has such a negative connotation. However, the truth is that chaos is where the creative forces are found. Whenever we try to hold off chaos or contain it through the imposition of some form of artificial order, we are literally interfering with the natural process. This understanding of chaos also alters the belief that we are somehow in opposition to Nature.

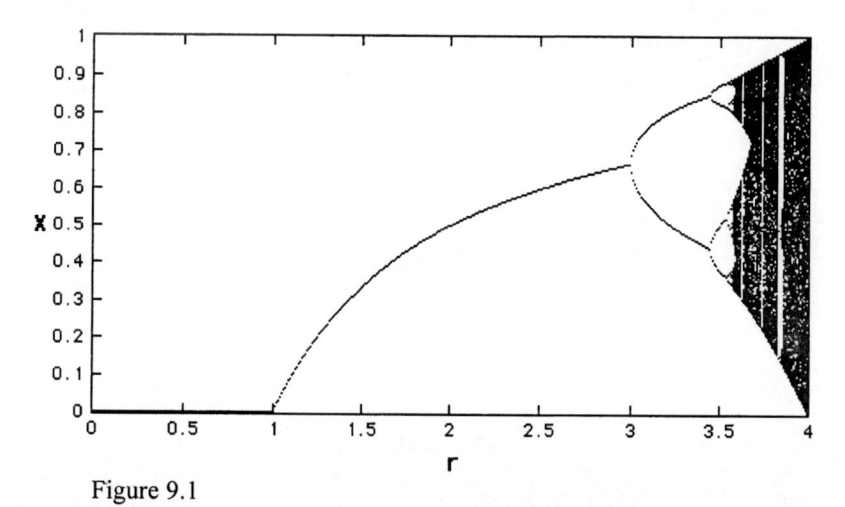

Figure 9.1

Rather, we are a part of nature and contribute to the creative process if we but allow ourselves the opportunity. Further, these dynamics indicate that the systems do not seek equilibrium at all. Rather, they actually move toward disequilibrium as a means of transformation. The suggestion here is that systems in general, whether they are in physics, biology, or sociology, actually are geared to transform themselves. Their interaction with other systems combines with other energy as a means through which this occurs. The energy for this transformation actually comes from within the system. This will have a profound impact on how social systems are viewed and, more specifically, how human organizations should be conducted.

Another important discovery in the chaos literature is that systems are composed of fractals. These fractals are smaller systems within the system that possess the same or very similar features to the larger system. Much as the geneticists have demonstrated that genes are the building blocks of biological systems and contain the messages which determine the composition of the organism, fractals are the messengers within the system which indicate how the system will look and function. This may seem inconsequential but it is very significant. It suggests that geophysics, populations, and social systems rely on the smallest units to determine their properties. In the social sciences, it implies that the larger system (the organization, community, or nation) is the result of the behaviors of all of the individuals and that its transformation comes from them. This is contrary to the Rational beliefs that held that the individuals were influenced and their personalities determined by the social system.

An elaborate but common demonstration of fractals and their interaction is the Mandelbrot design. These rather fascinating images are the result of constructing an image or shape from a mathematical formula and then replicating the formula millions of times. The resulting image is an extraordinary design. Close examination reveals very tiny sub-units that appear remarkably similar to the larger units. The larger image is not simply a larger version of the small sections but an expansion of it which also takes on relational features that demonstrate the change. In other words, these images are the very essence of Chaos. Even though the results begin to appear random, the extrapolation reveals that the chaotic systems present their own form of order. This continues to occur as the process proceeds and accelerates. The point is that the system, when allowed to undergo such expression of its properties, unfolds as something remarkable, orderly, and actually quite beautiful. This metaphor can certainly be carried over to human systems. Figure 9.2 presents an example of fractal.

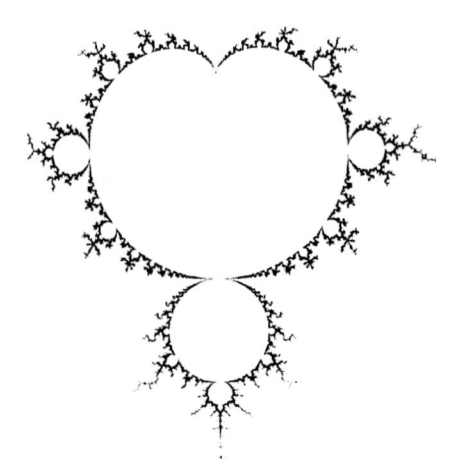

Figure 9.2

The presence of fractals, along with the inherent turbulence explains what is referred to as the butterfly effect. The butterfly effect is drawn from an old Chinese proverb which states that the breeze produced by the wings of one butterfly may result in a typhoon on the other side of the world. Chaos theorists argue that this is more than just poetic but an accurate description of the interaction of systems. The true energy in systems is found in the smallest units. These small units combine to form complete systems and, more importantly, lead to its transformation. This will play a very significant role in the understanding of social systems. This has a direct bearing on implementation strategies in human service systems which are most concerned about outcomes. The following table provides a summary of Chaos Theory in comparison with Rationality.

Table 9.1

Comparison of Rational and Chaos Theory	
Rational Model	Chaos Theory
Strong cause-effect relationships	Weak cause-effect multi-dimensional
Systems seek equilibrium	Systems seek disequilibrium
Systems remain stable	Systems transform through chaos
Hierarchical order	Fractal order
Turbulence destructive to system	Turbulence provides creative force

Applying Chaos Theory to Human Organizations

I can well imagine that many readers are already asking what all this has to do with implementing an outcome-based model in human organizations or communities. Actually, it has everything to do with it. The major argument is that the movement to outcome-based systems is antithetical to the Rational paradigm. Consequently, another paradigm must be sought that is more appropriate. A major development in the natural sciences has been the emergence of Chaos Theory. Several individuals have suggested that this model should be carried over to the social sciences. I submit that not only is the model applicable to the social sciences but it is even more useful than it is to the natural sciences. To be frank, the Rational Model has not been particularly successful in the social sciences. The expectation that a mechanistic, linear model is sound when studying human beings defies common sense. Nonetheless, it is what has been tried for over two centuries. Any reasonable person would admit that it is time to try something else. Taking the basic premises of the Chaos Model and applying them to human organizations, as shown in Table 2 above, provides some rather convincing evidence that this is a promising approach.

There Are No Cause-Effect Relationships But Multidimensional Ones

This should require no stretch of the imagination at all. The strategies employed in the human organizations to this point have largely ignored this. Procedures are standardized because it is assumed that the deficiencies may be dealt with one at a time and that if a response works in one case it will work in all (or at least nearly all.) This is clearly singular cause-effect thinking. If, on the other hand, the multi-dimensional influences are recognized and that these are different in composition and proportion for each individual, no administrator in her/his right mind would promulgate standard operating procedures in the human organizations. Instead, the capacities of each individual in and out of the organization would be emphasized.

There are many examples where this would seem to be a much more sensible approach in human organizations. A case management approach in welfare programs for example, would not require standard processing of claims or one-size-fits-all programs. Instead, each individual would begin by identifying what it is they want and what is interfering with their progress. Then a plan of action that stresses this capacity is prepared with clear understanding of the consequences of any failures within the individual's control. The only sensible way to carry this out is to honor individual responsibility for success. The differences in each case would be too great to have standard sanctions (such as community work after a set period of time.) Employment programs are then tied to the desired outcome as well. Rather than imposing a standard process on every person and hoping they find a job in the end, specific job tracks could be identified during the planning process. The case manager is expected to facilitate this and remove any unnecessary impediments. *

In the services within organizations and communities this understanding will also have very profound impact. First of all, programs must be designed for the individual since the influences are so complex. The idea that every person should be channeled through the same process would make no sense since the interest is in developing the individual capacity instead of treating standard deficiencies. Furthermore, the idea of protecting each individual from risk would be seen for what it is, ludicrous. There is no way to avoid risk since the existences of dimensions that come into play are virtually innumerable. Instead, the focus would be on growth and learning, not only for the citizen-client but for the manager as well. This is very different from the present established procedures.

Systems Seek Disequilibrium in Order to Transform Themselves

This makes more sense than one may first assume, especially in human organizations. Those who work in human organizations know, at least intuitively, that equilibrium is virtually impossible. Whenever the situation with clients appears

---

* I suggested just this kind of strategy in my report to the Montana Department of Social and Rehabilitation Services, *AFDC Population Study* Northwest Community Consultants, Inc. Missoula, MT (1994)

to reach some form of stability is exactly when something goes wrong. Even in institutions where everything is ordered by the book, stability is rarely seen. If the system was, in fact, seeking equilibrium, one would think that it would have at least come close to finding it at some point. In fact, examples abound which demonstrate that the most innovative and successful experiences in human organizations come about through chaotic episodes. For example, in mental health services, the greatest progress came about when court cases caused considerable disruption and forced deinstitutionalization. If Rationality were accurate this would run counter to logic. However, it makes perfect sense within the Chaos paradigm.

Taking this a bit further, the concept of attempting to impose stability or equilibrium brings about its opposite. In viewing the chaotic model, it should be easily seen that the intensity of the chaos is increased with each successive episode. This is because the suppression of turbulence (or chaos) only contributes energy to it. When the Army Corps of Engineers used the best of Rational technology to control the turbulence of the Mississippi River, the result was a much more intense event of floods in 1993 than would have otherwise occurred. When the National Park Service used all of its rational expertise to control fires in Yellowstone Park, the result was an extreme conflagration in 1988. There is no reason to believe that this does not apply to human systems. Each time a set of controls is designed to reduce instability, the result is typically a rather dramatic event. One could argue that the two World Wars are classic examples of this dynamic. Each was the result of a strong belief in the rational paradigm and the imposition of controls on economics, ethnicity, and nature itself.

In human organizations, the relationship is very similar. The more effort that is put into maintaining stability, the more energy there is in a period of turmoil that results. Most of the ways that attempts are made at retaining stability focus on deficiencies. For example, the emphasis in welfare programs over the years for seeking stability was the elimination of fraud. Other attempts included the addition of work programs and various other methods of meeting immediate needs like teen pregnancy prevention programs. However, all of these efforts stressed keeping the system intact by removing one more deficiency, each seen as being a cause of current problems. The result was a very turbulent period of welfare reform that has been largely a matter of intense turbulence. People are being thrown off the programs in large numbers. The programs are being dismantled in many ways. This, however, is probably only the early experiences of bifurcation with various strategies being tried which are on very different tracks. The true chaos occurred when the first economic downturn arrived and the system has been completely incapable of handling the pressure. Recently, the rash of states having to undergo drastic measures to bring their budgets into balance is one outcome of the reform efforts. This, of course, was not the only cause of the deficits, which is exactly the contention of Chaos theorists. It is the multidimensional nature of systems that prevent policy makers from anticipating the consequences of their decisions.

A brief review of other human services reveals some of the same kinds of experiences. After the shifts away from institutions, there were some differing strategies developed. These included community residential centers, group homes, sheltered workshops, and supported living. These may also be viewed as bifurcations. These attempts continued to be constrained by rational responses which attempted to limit and control the deficiencies. The pressures have only increased to move toward change. I believe one can fully expect the next ten years to undergo very profound shifts. This will either happen through well developed plans for change and responding to the paradigmatic pressure or it will occur through a very chaotic episode. If the events in California are any indication, the chaotic episode is the more likely event. The process of rebureaucratization is specifically a result of trying to isolate deficiencies and apply standard procedures. While the specific nature of chaotic episodes are virtually impossible to anticipate (otherwise they would not be chaotic) one may envision that there could be massive exodus of providers from the system or series of countersuits as consumers are restricted from pursuing the quality of life they had been promised. By allowing some smaller deficiencies, as the providers continue to learn, the smaller turbulence will be allowed to run its course and help to transform the system with less disruption. Speaking of California, the fiasco of the recall of the governor and the turmoil of the budget can be attributed to the events described earlier, from Proposition 13 to human service reforms.

Systems Transform Themselves Through Chaos

This aspect of chaos is particularly intriguing. The researchers have found that there is considerable evidence that systems, including species, do not evolve strictly through natural selection or *survival of the fittest*. Rather, systems are actually driven toward transformation through the internal turbulence. In other words, evolutionary forces may be more *by design* than *by accident*. This also may be easily observed in human systems, intrapersonal, interpersonal, and social. Individuals tend to intentionally place themselves in situations within which they learn to adapt. This is not always easily explained. Ordinarily, these callings to growth are viewed as intuitive or spiritual. In any case, the evolution of the individual is not through accident but by intent. The same is true in personal relationships. Social systems undergo change through their experiences with turmoil. Most historians recognize that the most profound changes in the macro-societal sense occur following wars, economic collapse, pandemics, or the like. However, what drives us toward these events is very unclear. Logically, it is easy to see that human beings would rather not experience these things but drive themselves toward them nonetheless.

In the human organization, the value of this concept is rather significant. Since the conditions of culture are constantly changing, it is important for the human organization to respond. The Rational systems do not allow for this. Instead, they are reactive in nature, trying to resist the changes. This results in the systems being behind the times frequently. By contrast, if the people in organizations are allowed to enter into the turbulence of cultural shift, they stand a greater chance at learning and adapting. If it is true that through these chaotic episodes, systems transform themselves, then it would indeed be quite valuable for human systems to benefit from this dynamic. Systems perform much better if they become the learning system which seems to be more natural for humans. By this, I am suggesting that the organization must be geared toward learning from error rather than being so averse to it that it tends to be concealed. Things go wrong, but rather than react in a manner that is fear-driven, leadership actually challenges itself and the organizational participants (which includes staff, clients and the public) learn from the mistakes. Rather than treating deficiencies through Standard Operating Procedures, the human service providers should be encouraged to learn from the smaller chaotic events. To impose standardized responses, cuts off this learning opportunity. For example, if a case worker in a welfare department finds that some of the consumers are taking advantage of a fuel assistance program, she should be able to apply a learning model. The bureaucratic, rational response would be to notify the fraud division or to invoke a policy for sanctions. However, if the case worker is given the discretion, she may find that the contributing factors to the abuse were not fraudulent at all but that either the consumers were unaware of the expectations or that some undisclosed need entered into the case. In the future, this would be incorporated into that case worker's intake interview process. Thus, the event is used to learn rather than assume. The routine was altered to reflect that learning and the agency, the consumer, and the community could all benefit from this learning.

In many human services, there are numerous instances where this understanding could change how activities are conducted. For example, as part of an individual plan process, it is more than appropriate.† As the plan unfolds, the consumer, the case worker, and the other participating individuals share in the responsibility for its success. When events seem to be interfering with success, even though the specific procedures or activities are taking place, rather than being fixated on the plan as a mandate from on high, the team seeks to discover what is impeding progress. Through each of these experiences, learning picks up momentum. The consumer, the case worker, and the other participants (such as the family) all begin to learn more about the underlying nature of the consumer preference and actually to overcome fears. The experience of risk or failure is not seen as a deficiency but as an opportunity for growth. Consequently, a greater level of personal responsibility and intrinsic rewards for those involved also unfolds. Rather than taking on the plan as something restrictive or as a source of potential sanction from the hierarchy, they actually use it in the manner it was intended, as a means to growth.

To the Rationalist this may seem a bit pie-in-the-sky but there is ample evidence that this is not only realistic but closer to human nature than what is assumed most of the time. The rational assessment of human nature is in itself

---

† The individual plan process is taken specifically from a case management approach to human services. The concept has been particularly useful in mental health and services to the developmentally disabled. It is based on the idea that each individual has different needs and consequently, needs a specific plan to address those needs. This plan is then used as a guide for the provision of services. As noted earlier, this strategy has met with limited success because it runs counter to the Rational/bureaucratic culture within which it exists.

restrictive and artificially constructed. It is based on a manner of observing reality that is largely negative and intentionally narrow. In cases where this view of people has not been accepted, there are repeated stories of incredible success. Unfortunately, the perspective of most of us is so clouded by the Rational Model that we cannot even see these successes. When we observe any occurrence of considerable accomplishment by individuals or groups, it is likely that the deficiencies were ignored and failures were not barriers but steps toward success. That is the very nature of true entrepreneurial accomplishment. The success stories are invariably those which overcame adversity and would not allow stumbles and obstacles to deter them. In human organizations, we continue to be constrained by the Rational Model because it is official. Allowing the normal turbulence in trial-and-error to run its course, is the more effective way to create a learning organization and one that accomplishes *outcomes rather than procedures.*

Systems Made Up of Fractals

This feature has more relevance than it may at first appear. The importance of fractals is that they explain part of the complexity of managing any kind of system. The suggestion is that the manipulation of the tiniest parts of a system can potentially alter the whole thing. Either the fractal will conform to the characteristics of the larger system or vice versa. Upon further examination, it becomes easily recognized that the former is probably more likely than the latter. If the larger system is altered in some way, it is very likely that the fact that the smaller fractals have not changed will force it back to its original form. The power of the system is found in the fractals not in the whole. However, if the smallest units of the system are altered, the change draws upon the internal chaos of each of the surrounding fractals to begin making systemic transformation. Consequently, not only is adaptation brought about with the least disruption but the expectation that the system will return to its original

> **Transformation begins at the top, energizing individual staff and consumers**

> **Knowledge is made available through the coordinating role of hierarchy and transformation is facilitated**

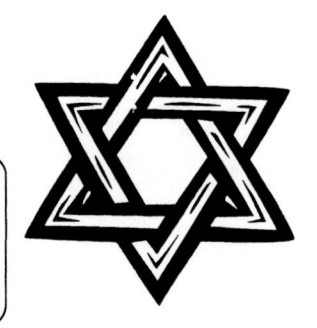

form is quite remote. Transformation through the chaotic process actually brings about relative order. This may run counter to our current logic but once the rational belief system is set aside, this presents itself as very reasonable. It fits much better into past experience than the hard and fast rules of rationality and empiricism.

In much the same manner, this has very profound meaning in the human organization. For the most part, efforts in human organizations have relied on attempts to alter the larger system in hopes that the smallest units (individuals) will conform to the change. This has met with very little relative success. Naturally, changes occurred in the society but not to the extent that had been intended nor necessarily in the manner that was desired. Human organizations tend to be forced to be reactive which has results in enormous amounts of energy being dispensed with very little result. If, however, the recognition of the fractal relationship is employed in human organizations, we have a very different set of norms. Changes are sought at the most basic level using the internal chaos as a vehicle for transformation. This is accomplished by stimulating the learning process gained through overcoming obstacles and mistakes. The transformation of the individuals stimulates the same energies in the surrounding individuals and the system changes. The basic fractal units are the individual staff members as well as the clients/consumers.

The human services sector provides an example of how this might work. I emphasize human services because they have been notorious for trying to alter human behavior patterns using Rational methods with rather poor results. The failure in human organizations rests in the unwillingness to turn the clients toward their capacities through chaotic episodes. The focus on process is a result of trying to stem these chaotic episodes and get all of the individuals to conform to some larger set of norms. Clearly, this has not brought about the desired ends. This approach to human organizations essentially inverts the bureaucratic model. However, since it no longer relies on two dimensions, it does not eliminate the hierarchical structure. Instead, it energizes the structure to function in a manner that facilitates rather than controls. The role of the hierarchy is no longer to dictate procedures and rules. The role becomes to encourage and to connect the resources to the need. This is not only a different role but a more significant one, if one assumes significance is related to success. Instead of spending endless hours invoking rules, which is an attempt to curb the transformational energies found in the internal chaos of the fractals, the agency professionals spend their time working with providers and individuals to help them discover solutions to challenges. The learning through the transformation process must take place at the lowest level though. The agency acts as the resource through which this can take place.

Outcome-based strategies become a reality because they are being carried out at the appropriate level with genuine leadership demonstrated through encouragement. The type of organization that results from this system is multidimensional, empowering, and evolving. The image that is more realistic is not a hierarchical pyramid but a three-dimensional Star of David. Figure 6 above illustrates this point. [Since I am confined to a two-dimensional presentation device, I ask the reader to envision these as three-dimensional.] This approach to organization is actually much more natural than the pyramid. Anyone who has worked in an organization any length of time is aware that the most powerful influence is found somewhere in the middle. The true movers and shakers are those with experience and skill, not necessarily the top management. In the Star of David the energies double up in the middle. These people are both transformers as staff and facilitators as leaders. This also recognizes the truth found in the principle that those who head an organization are both responsible to the staff and to the task. A skilled manager recognizes that she/he serves the staff through support and encouragement as well as managing the staff by coordinating knowledge. The less effective managers are those who fail to recognize one of those roles. The creative energy made available to the organization increases geometrically as the capacity of each individual is increased.

Releasing the creative energies of each staff member also increases the opportunity for community integration. Rather than relying strictly on specific individuals for community/public relations, each staff member has an interest in improving the involvement of others in the community. The concern for the staff members is no longer survival in the organization, avoiding risk, or following rules. Rather, their interest is in accomplishing the outcome. Under the Rational Model, the hierarchy constantly reminds the staff that they are not to take risks and to remain within the boundaries. In an organization governed by the Chaos Model, the opposite is true. They are reminded to be creative and learn through risk taking and to explore beyond the boundaries. The more successful they are at discovering effective means of improving the quality of life for the consumer, the more the entire organization benefits. The transformational organization is also more beneficial to the citizens. Once the resistance to change is ameliorated, the belief that the citizen is a threat is minimized. The public service model encourages everyone to increase the amount of citizen input not reduce it. The main reason administrative staff in public organizations develop a form of antipathy to citizens is that it threatens consistency. The citizens are the enemy of stability and undermine predictability. Adopting a model that encourages creativity through risk taking also opens the team up to more input. This shift in philosophy may seem all too simple but it only becomes simple once the paradigm shift takes place.

Conscious Shift in Paradigms

A basic practical and theoretical question is whether or not it is possible to consciously shift a paradigm. This is particularly problematic within organizations as it would also require a change in culture. Many social scientists and leaders of organizations argue that paradigm shifts must be evolutionary, i.e., the shift in paradigm must take place on its own when the conditions are right. This idea has been largely supported by those who have written the history books. The shifting of ideas at such a basic level has appeared to require very subtle changes until the pressure is so great on the existing paradigm that there is an urgent need to accept a new way of thinking. In other words, the paradigm follows the changed beliefs but cannot change them. Major developments have occurred through what appear to be largely accidental discovery or through subtle influences. Thomas Kuhn, in his *Structure of Scientific Revolution* describes the process through which paradigmatic shifts occur.[1] He argues that the buildup of pressure on the existing paradigm must become very intense before the shift can take place. The exact point at which this occurs is unclear. Some may argue that Kuhn's description of paradigms is limited to science and cannot be applied to social science much less public administration. While such a claim is partly true, I would argue that public administration occupies a unique place in this discussion and that the shift I describe here relates more to paradigms. Kuhn compares the development of paradigm shifts with revolutions in the political sphere.[2] He further argues that the scientific shifts in paradigm come about as a result of a buildup of anomalies within the sciences to the point that it is not longer possible to sustain the *status quo* and preserve its integrity. It would be appropriate to use the term "revolution" to describe the needed shift in public administration if all we were concerned about was the political dimensions of the field. However, what I argue goes further than that. It is necessary to shift in all the underlying disciplines of the field in order to bring about the needed change.

Since I am using the Chaos theories as a possible alternative in terms of shifting ideas in public administration, I would also assert that using the idea of paradigms is appropriate. A brief overview of the movement of the scientific metaphor demonstrates how this works. There were numerous discoveries related to the physical universe and methods of inquiry, prior to Isaac Newton. There were also many changes in the social fabric that made the change possible. People were able to pursue individual exploration more and the flow of information was increasing such that changing the paradigm was facilitated. The church was being forced to cede authority over scientific matters to the states which allowed for the construction of ideas that were less metaphysical. Printing presses and improved transportation made the exchange of ideas more widespread. Reintroduction of Aristotelian logic allowed for the examination of knowledge through a process that attempted to establish a beginning point instead of accepting what was proclaimed from a higher source. All of these things had to be in place prior to the rise of the Rational paradigm. The basic idea, then, is that it takes considerable pressure to experience disequilibrium sufficient to drive an entire culture toward such profound change. In the view of Kuhn this relies mostly on accidental discovery or an evolutionary force like natural selection. New paradigms only come to replace the old because they are strong enough. Survival of the fittest is applied to paradigms. This is the case because the system of ideas, like all systems, seeks equilibrium which would make them resistant to change.

The primary problem with this widely held belief is that it is also a product of the Rational Model. Interestingly enough, the eyes through which the evolution of ideas is being viewed are those of rationality. However, employing the Chaotic Model to the very same historical events produces a rather different interpretation. Major changes have come about because the existing one contains the turbulence that drives it toward a transformation. The compulsion for discovery is a very large part of that turbulence. The human system continuously drives for its own evolution. Thus, it projects itself toward chaotic episodes that move the paradigm along. The events leading up to Newton are only examples of that. The string of discoveries prior to Newton was not accidental. Gaps in understanding became more and more unacceptable because each person was driving for some form of improvement in their condition. Jacob Bronowski stated that the purpose of knowledge is to reduce uncertainty.[3] The elements of uncertainty were built into medieval society. The opening up of independent thought was brought about by the very self destructive nature of the church and empire. The more each exerted its authority unfairly, the more it stimulated the need for change. All of the other factors can easily be interpreted in the same way.

Paradigmatic shift happens not because pressure builds from outside the paradigm but inside. The seeds of change are built into the belief system itself. Turbulence or restlessness is distributed throughout the system. Paradigms must be pushed toward change as a function of utility and growth. In other words, the change is not the exception but the rule. Furthermore, since systems do not seek equilibrium but disequilibrium, the assertion that societies are resistant to change is largely contrived. The apparent resistance to major change is merely an additional means of contributing the energy needed for the change. In fact, if one examines the history more closely, it becomes apparent that the resistors to change are ordinarily a minority. Their impeding change contributes to the desire by the rest of the population to move toward it. So ironically, the attempts to hang on to a paradigm, to claim stability, only increase the intensity of the chaotic forces that bring the change about.

Therefore, the intentional, active movement toward a paradigm shift is not only possible but desirable. This argues for revisiting underlying beliefs on a regular basis rather than as a last resort. Beliefs and principles should be examined regularly and compared with our experiences and our sense of success or failure. This should be encouraged at all levels, especially at the individual level, not constrained by higher authority. This allows human systems to move forward by stimulating change. Another way to understand Future Shock is to recognize that it is mostly brought about by the resistance to change that is part of the Rational paradigm.[4] The longer a paradigm is preserved, especially if it is done to preserve stability, the more disruptive the process of ultimate change will become. The act of preservation finds itself in increased control over natural forces. Thus, individuals are compelled to honor the paradigm and not wander outside its boundaries. This causes added discomfort at all levels because the chaos found within all people is not allowed to follow its course of transformation. This is also a dynamic of fractals wherein the frustration within these individuals soon becomes a major feature of the larger system. It is not difficult to make the case for rampant levels of frustration throughout human systems.

Implications

Considering the dynamic for change within the conceptualization of the Chaos Model then brings us to the point of defining the implementation of substantive change in organizational/community behavior. All systems must change, both because of the internal turbulence and since all surrounding systems are also transforming. This certainly applies to most organizations and communities. The recent drive toward outcome-based strategies is a clear symptom of transformation. The diversity of ideas and procedures for these systems as methods of providing services are also extensions of these transformational forces. The experiences of the states in recent years have shown that there are increasingly significant forms of turbulence at work. That is part of the challenge in systems described through the Chaos Model. The transformation is nearly impossible to predict. This much is known: the longer the transformation is deterred, the more intense and disruptive the ultimate chaotic episode becomes. The other known factor that comes into play is the longer a centralized, rational approach to administering the system is continued, the more disruptive the episode will be. This is being evidenced by the very disturbing trends of cynicism toward government in general. Thus, the sooner substantial change can be implemented, the better. The more the transformational process can take place at the lowest fractal level, the more likely it is that successful strategies will result.

---

1. Kuhn, Thomas S., *The Structure of Scientific Revolutions, 93ff.*
2. Ibid., 92.
3. Bronowski, Jacob, *The Common Sense of Science*, (Cambridge: Harvard University Press, 1953).
4. Toffler, Alvin, *Future Shock* (New York: Bantam, 1984).

Chapter 10: Applying the New Paradigm

Using any new knowledge is as complex as the knowledge itself. The one factor that stands out is that if one accepts the premises of the Transformational Model, they must also accept that it is not possible to craft generalized principles that will apply in all situations. Thus, it is highly problematic to serve up either an organizational design or any strategies that will apply in all cases. In fact, to lay out sets of principles of operation will revert back to the Rational Model's use of laws and rules. Having said this, it is reasonable to offer some general guidelines regarding how one can initiate the process of change. Since the results of these initial changes are bound to take a nearly infinite number of subsequent directions, the critical point is that managers/leaders must be prepared to facilitate the learning process, stimulating change wherever it asserts itself.

The following suggestions are offered which describe the needed steps for transformation of organizations, which include agencies and communities, at three points of entry: organizational, (including, individual staff and management) community, and public policy. However, this does not suggest that these three points are in isolation from one another or that they are the only possible points. In fact, quite the contrary is true. Public administration requires that more holistic strategies be adopted in order to avoid the typical regression back to the bureaucratic ethos. Implementation of the changes for any of the levels without one or both of the others will make it highly unlikely that the strategy will succeed. Then again, we must accept that some form of change is the one thing that is inevitable. The question is whether or not the change that eventually materializes is one that is desirable. While the Transformational model describes a dynamic that is elusive to control, it does not preclude the possibility of some steerage.

The primary thesis here is for public administrators to stimulate search procedures that are more likely to alleviate some of the tyranny of the Rational models. These have been defined for us in advance and frequently preclude a broader exploration for solutions from perspectives that may not be in what is called the main stream. Thus, through these recommendations I intend to encourage non-traditional sources of learning. I resist the idea that solutions can only come from the "leadership" or the dominant culture, whether it be organizational or communal. Furthermore, these recommendations are not to be viewed as comprehensive. They offer suggested formats for change that will be conducive to implementing outcome-based programs at large. The participants who include citizens, clients, and staff should all take as their personal responsibility the discovery of other steps that will contribute to success. The dynamics of the Chaos Model stipulate that the most important necessary energy for creative transformation comes from within the system. However, the system must be as broadly defined as possible. It also infers that the best strategies are those which are allowed to evolve out of the turbulence. That means that energized discourse and the infusion of risk must be highly valued. This precludes the utility of incorporating the ideas of someone from outside the system *in toto*. Systems are to change from those guided by self preservation and administrative rules to those which learn and re-emphasize the values being sought. These recommendations should be taken as they are intended C guidelines for discussion and the release of creative forces.

The Organizational Level

The important consideration for embarking on a significant change of direction for any organization is that it demands a serious reflection on what is about to happen. The very premises of the organization are going to be challenged. At first, this may be rather frightening to many of those involved. There will be a real fear that the very survival of the organization is at stake. Leadership must be prepared to respond that if the process of moving to more outcome-based, as well as value-based, operations threatens the organization then the need to do so is even more urgent. The only way to overcome the counterproductive energies of the bureaucratic ethos is to discard its primary purpose of self preservation. Moving from that point, the organization will suddenly give itself permission to really learn. Almost all of the strategic planning episodes I have experienced both as a member of the organization and as a consultant, get trapped in the assumption that survival of the organization is the highest priority. This acts as such an impediment to genuine learning adjustments that it fails to focus attention on the mission or *raisson d'etre* of the organization itself. In the absence of such a self examination, there is little hope that moving to outcome/value based methods will succeed. Thus, we begin with an examination of the needed adjustments from the individuals moving up to management. This reasserts the importance of a very different kind of thinking.

Staff

The primary objective for the staff is to unleash their creative abilities as well as tie them to the concept of outcome emphasis. In order to do this, they must be able to adjust their thinking from one of fear of failure and sanction to constantly looking for opportunities for growth. The following steps should contribute to this change:

Development in outcome-based thinking. All development efforts should be turned toward functioning within an outcome-based system. This necessarily includes learning critical thinking skills. No longer should the development of critical thinking be confined to the academy, especially at the graduate level. The difference here is that the staff themselves should be visualizing where the consumers/clients/citizens want to go and how to get there. This means that concerns for following mandated procedure should operate as a supporting element to the outcomes rather than the dominant concern. This also means that whenever problems arise, they are not viewed as setbacks but as opportunities to learn. This will require some effort since the current system has so conditioned people to fear problems. A second aspect of outcome-based thinking is the ability to genuinely set personal goals. It is extremely difficult to concentrate on the consumer's goals and the ultimate outcomes if one does not use goal-setting personally. The concepts of goals and objectives are so frequently misunderstood in many ways. Frequently, the staff see goal-setting as a busy activity with little relevance to them personally. It is not unusual for such planning efforts to be misused by management as another control mechanism. This usually results in a rather cynical response on the part of staff so that the process is not viewed seriously. Finally, this thinking includes the need to learn about risk management. Rather than viewing risk as a pariah, everyone needs to view it as a part of the growth process. This may seem rather obvious but the truth is most people who work in human organizations believe that risk-taking is wrong. This is especially the case in human services. There is even a sense that risk-taking of any kind with public resources is unethical. However, not taking risk is a greater problem since it denies the citizenry the chance to grow through trying. The following is a more specific description of one method which will enhance success:

Incorporating Job Expectation Agreements. In order to build an administrative system that promotes this model there is a vital need for the development of Job Expectation Agreements. These are statements that are drafted in addition to the position description for each member of the organization. Essentially, they identify explicitly the desired skills, the goals for professional growth, and indications of areas of strengths and needs. There are two primary points at which these are developed: (1) when an employee is initially hired, and (2) as a part of the annual performance review.

Initial Hire. After an individual has been selected for a position, an entry interview should be scheduled. This is a transition point between the hiring selection process and the beginning of employment. The fact that this is a point of transition is very significant. Transitions of any kind are difficult. The literature abounds with descriptions of the process of transition and how difficult it can be.[1] The fact that the new employee is going through a transition means that they have some important work to do in terms of their own emotional well-being. They must be able to undertake proper endings. This means that they have to be willing to acknowledge that they are experiencing an ending. They must then be able to go through a luminal period in which they are likely to feel lost and uncertain. Finally, they must be able to accept the changes and embrace the new environment in which they are now immersed. This all must be taken into consideration in the process of developing the new relationship of the employee with the organization. If either employee or employer fail to incorporate the process of transition, this will likely result in a rough period of adjustment. The transition time is typically not immediate and may require a certain amount of patience. I have found that this critical step accounts for the highest amount of turnover. Recognizing that the employee and the organization both experience transition will be helpful in smoothing the process.

To begin the process, the supervisor and the employee schedule an hour or two during which the detailed expectations of the position are discussed. This must include any skills that must be learned, working conditions, scheduling, and team-building. It goes beyond the basic position description because it must clarify the specific needs of the position for which the individual is being hired. This should then be integrated into the probation requirements. It is crucial that this be clear, approved by management, and reinforced. This way, the employer and employee have a firm footing from which to begin. A key difference between this process and those more traditionally employed is that the expectations are mutually negotiated. There must be an element of the expectations on the part of the employee included in the process. The employee is encouraged to develop both expectations for themselves and for the employer. Another key difference is that these expectations can change. The principles associated with turbulence in any system suggest that change is both constant and desirable. Rather than lay out rigid requirements this process facilitates a certain amount of fluidity. It is not that some predictability is not appropriate. Rather, it is that the more important dynamic is transformation.

Annual Performance Review. This should be used as a means to clarify issues and improve performance. It is not to be employed as a punitive measure but as a constructive way to enhance the work environment for all concerned. The process must begin with the supervisor and employee sitting down for one-on-one discussion regarding the work environment and performance. Every effort must be made to ensure that this is a positive experience. Thus, the employee must be given every opportunity to provide input and to be encouraged to set goals. As a result of this discussion, the supervisor can then draft a Job Expectation Agreement containing the expectations for both the organization and the individual. Note that the actual expectation agreement is not formulated until after the employee has been in the organization for a significant amount of time. This removes some of the considerable disadvantage that is experienced by new employees who are typically in no position to develop expectations since they are not sufficiently familiar with the task environment. It also takes into consideration the need for the process of transition to be nearly complete. Things that may be included are professional growth needs such as formation or skill practice, goals for personal enhancement (e.g., learning about other parts of the organization, improvements in performance [e.g., punctuality], or even personal health goals), and any statements of areas of challenge (e.g., scheduling difficulties, improvement in peer relations, or consumer needs). Finally, the document must conclude with an overall statement of expectations for the upcoming year. I must emphasize that this should be as positive as possible as well as specific. Supervisors should use it as a guide for performance rating throughout the year, not just for the annual review. Thus, they should refer to it whenever they want to acknowledge positive performance and/or negative performance. The supervisor may also want to use a Critical Incident approach wherein a journal is kept for each employee which is shared with them on a regular basis.[2] In fact, nothing should go in the journal without being shown to the employee; the employee should have free access to the journal; and effort must be made to keep it balanced (i.e., accomplishments should be noted as well as other less constructive incidents.) If this is used properly, the employees will all know where they stand.

I also stress the need for an underlying principle in supervision of *NO SURPRISES!* This means that every employee should be aware of how they stand at all times. It may seem a bit of a nuisance, but this will do so much to alleviate any unnecessary conflict and increase comfort levels for everyone. Thus, if there are performance issues, they should be brought up immediately (one-on-one), the desired corrections clearly stated, and reinforcement for either correction or continued deficiency clearly delivered. So, for example, if an employee is having difficulty being on time, the supervisor needs to relate to him/her immediately that it is a problem, provide clear standards of expected punctuality (e.g., no more than 3 late arrivals per month) and seek feedback from the employee regarding any reasons for their difficulties. Sometimes, it is possible to make simple adjustments to help the employee meet the standards, even something as simple as shifting the schedule by fifteen minutes. If the standard is not met during the prescribed period, explicitly stated (e.g., the first month after discussion), then a verbal warning is issued that this cannot be accepted and that the employee has a particular period to correct it. Again, using the example of a month, if the employee is late more than three times in the following thirty days, he or she will receive a written warning which will be placed in his or her file. The warning is issued not at the end of the month if he or she is late three days in the first week. If the behavior persists then they may be suspended or released depending on the gravity of the issue (e.g., if their tardiness is placing a consumer at risk, they may be terminated at that point.) Obviously, if they persist after suspension, they must be terminated. One aside here that should be considered is whether or not punctuality is a genuine need of the organization or if it is merely a method of control with no purpose beyond the existence of a rule.

Most of the time when this approach is used, combined with the Job Expectation Agreement, it is extremely uncommon for employees to be terminated. They will either recognize that they are in the wrong job and leave or they will work with the supervisor to correct the deficiency.

Incorporating Learning Strategies in the Job Evaluation Process. Evaluation programs are all too often geared to instilling fear and imposing discipline. This is not the appropriate use of an evaluation system. The correct use of evaluation is for professional growth and development. As staff learn how to use critical thinking, evaluations should be used as one mechanism for encouraging them to take personal responsibility. The idea is to avoid punishing as much as possible.* During the evaluation process, staff should be asked to identify any skills they feel they need in order to accomplish the desired outcomes. It is so

---

* Personally, I believe that punishment should *never* be used. However, that may be too much for organizations to accept immediately. I certainly encourage organizations to aspire to such a standard, though.

important for this to be a non-threatening encounter so that they will not hesitate to acknowledge such needs. The process should also call upon the staff to identify areas of risk and how they plan to deal with them. This includes describing how any of the potential problems will be addressed. This specifically employs sound critical thinking skills and contributes to the personal growth of the staff member.

Increasing Levels of Individual Discretion. This is a logical outcome of developing critical thinking in staff. In fact, if the skills are taught and encouraged and then staff are not given the increased discretion, the result could be regression. What I chose to refer to as the law of rising expectations could stimulate considerable resentment on the part of these employees. The more the organization makes changes that improve the sovereignty of the individual will tend to stimulate increased expectations of such changes. Thus, the likely response of employees to the expansion of their discretion is to want more. The increase in discretion can be developed by using the Job Expectations Agreement as a guide for employees to construct a work plan. This gives them the real opportunity to take initiative and be creative. Another element in this change is to use local teams to discuss plans and exchange ideas. It is not particularly desirable to leave employees in a position where they feel left alone in planning, especially since risk-taking is being encouraged. There must be a balance between personal responsibility and team-building. This is another way to improve the risk management aspects of the outcome-based program.

Emphasizing Self Monitoring. Filling out an environment of creativity, risk-taking and personal growth, management must be willing to incorporate self monitoring as the primary accountability mechanism. This means that the supervisor(s) should only enter the process as facilitators of evaluating progress. The staff member should be regularly monitoring progress of their own areas of responsibility. This is especially important to any self-monitoring system. So many attempts at integrating self monitoring in organizations meets with less than satisfactory results because they are not made a regular feature of daily activities. Consequently, when employees are asked to respond to questions regarding their performance, they typically feel somewhat overwhelmed. The typical result is the responses are less than accurate since the respondent feels a need to give complete answers even though they do not have all the information. Thus, each staff member must be encouraged to use fairly simple monitoring devices on a daily basis. In addition, the monitoring should include honest assessments of resource deficiencies that may impede the accomplishment of desired outcomes. This is not a matter of providing excuses for the staff but one of a more collegial approach to identifying needs. The regularly scheduled reviews should focus on examining areas of capacity for staff and end users. This should be a very positive process so that staff will be less likely to approach the process with anything less than sincerity. One approach to this process would be to rely more on peers than on any authority figure. It is crucial that the peer review process not be used as any part of a system of sanctions or rewards. This may seem a bit odd but the reality is that if the reviews are used in this manner there are other interpersonal issues that interfere with their effectiveness. Since peers are aware that their colleagues will be evaluating them, it can have a deleterious effect. Typically, they may offer only positive, overly glowing evaluations of their peers, hoping for the same in kind. On the other hand, there may be some interpersonal conflict involved in which the evaluation is used as an opportunity to get back at their colleague. In any event, the fact that human beings are involved precludes anything like objectivity in this process. Consequently, the evaluation is to be used as a learning opportunity not as a condition of continued employment or any other motivational tool.

Management

At the heart of the system from the perspective of the Star of David organization, management at the lowest level must be given all of the tools needed to create the outcome-based environment. This means that they must be treated in a manner that assumes that they have the best interests of the citizen/consumer/client at heart. Some ways that this will be accomplished are to minimize the number of rules requiring compliance, increased training in outcome philosophies, and more discretion in organizational structure (scheduling, compensation, and relationships.) As noted earlier, one example of this is to allow inspections by local authorities (e.g., public health, fire) to suffice and only request copies of their reports. The other essential element of creating this environment is to employ collaboration as a matter of routine. *This means that collaboration with all levels of management cannot be viewed as an inconvenience or an after thought.*

Contracts Must be Tied to Outcomes. When speaking of contracts, this is not confined to privatization relationships. Rather, this is more a matter of understanding the relationship within organizations relevant to management as on a contractual basis. Similar to the Job Expectation Agreements, expectations for outcomes and values served should be spelled out in agreements with management personnel. This is far too complicated to describe in any kind of detail here. Nevertheless, a collaborative process should be initiated at the earliest possible opportunity involving providers, consumers, and agency to design a contract that emphasizes the achievement of outcomes. Process should be eliminated from the contract unless required by law. The contract must incorporate the satisfactory accomplishment of specific outcomes as opposed to treating these as a collateral aspect. This stresses the outcomes that really matter in services and avoids the tendency to return to satisfying bureaucratic needs. The measurement of success should also include some device which seeks the balance between planned outcomes and those achieved. The idea here is to avoid the over-achievement experienced in Oregon because providers feared sanctions. All language which implies sanctions should be eliminated from the outcome achievement process, since this will only serve to encourage timidity.

Develop Data Reporting Which Emphasizes Needs of Staff. All data requirements must focus attention on how energies are being applied to accomplishing the desired outcomes. For example, using a collaborative process, which includes providers, consumers/families, and agency personnel, design a data reporting system which serves the needs of the providers. This should be similar to what the Neighborhood Living Project at the University of Oregon used to develop the ROS. The staff from Eugene spent time in the field with the providers to construct the data needs. They then spent time working with the DD Services Bureau to design a process that would incorporate those needs into the Bureau's data requirements. The reporting system is relatively undaunting so that providers are more willing to consistently submit the data. It is crucial that the data be something that providers will use in their regular operations. This should not prove to be all that difficult since the system should be geared to outcomes anyway. If providers emphasize outcomes and the data requirements emphasize outcomes systemic congruence is more likely.

Establish Peer Review Teams. This is another device that should prove useful in encouraging personal responsibility and creativity. The idea of peer review teams is more to share ideas and mutual encouragement. The goal, after all, is the enhancement of the quality of life for the community, citizenry, and consumers. By broadening the field of information and ideas, this can only be improved. Whenever performance is observed as being marginal, rather than bringing down the full weight of the bureaucracy and therefore discouraging creativity, this team will work with staff to identify ways to address the problems. The teams should be organized by Local Planning Districts, which keeps the task manageable. The team members should include: a management representative, a consumer, an advocate, and a staff member. The role of the manager must be as facilitator and not as the bureaucratic muscle. This team is critical to the successful implementation of an outcome-based program since it will be a means of heading off any problems before they are allowed to undermine the transformation.

Allow the use of Funds for Investment. This may seem to fall outside the construct of an outcome-based program but it is a natural complement to it. The idea here is to also allow the staff to be creative on the financial end. Naturally, this does not allow for misuse of funds or any unnecessary risk-taking. There are ways to invest in funds that are safe but will give the providers a way to increase their available resources. This is one more way to reduce the provider dependency on the state for day-to-day decisions and encourage greater discretion. The investments should probably include some requirement for the use of endowments. This means that the principle will remain safe and the interest earnings may be used as another means of developing innovative programs. One impediment to innovation is the concentration of all funding discretion with the highest authority. This change adds one more element of entrepreneurship to the entire system. When all of the aspects of programs are geared to accomplishment, whether it is individual outcomes or resources, the energy going to creativity only increases.

Encourage Supervisors to Examine Their Practices. I strongly encouraged everyone in the organizations to review their own practices and determine whether or not they are promoting personal responsibility or hindering it. I remind them that whenever they take on a parental role, they are actually hindering the development of personal responsibility. Each time an employee brings a problem to them, they should try to ask the employee what solutions they would suggest rather than automatically lending a sympathetic ear or, even worse, immediately telling them what they should do. They also needed to remember that when delegating they retain the responsibility but are using a sense of trust. This means that while one can delegate the responsibility for something to be done, it does not let them off the hook. Thus, they would want to make every effort to be certain that the individual being delegated understands what needs to be done and what the consequences are if it is not. This may appear somewhat simplistic but often we confuse delegation with relegation. The supervisor retains an interest in the outcome and cannot simply shift the burden over to a subordinate if something goes wrong. With this in mind, managers and supervisors should take their delegation more seriously and truly allow the person to get it done. So often what happens is the supervisor delegates and when it does not get done they do it. This diminishes the importance of the trusting relationship and ultimately makes the supervisor very ineffective. Much less gets done when only one person takes responsibility. I also remind leadership to focus on its own communication behaviors and to set the tone for an environment of personal responsibility. Again, this means taking the responsibility that is truly theirs and not being so quick to state that they messed up when they did not. Rather, discuss what happened and how it may be avoided in the future. (I find discussion of blame and fault rather useless most of the time it is much more useful to use error for learning and growth.)

Agency Staff

Agency staff is key to the transformation of any system to one of outcome-based methods is to transform the agency from bureaucratic overseer to facilitator and cheerleader. Agency personnel should view this as a wonderful opportunity to enhance their work. Removing the need for rule enforcement, stemming from deficiency identification alters the task environment for agency personnel in a way that returns the basic altruistic motivators that they probably possessed when they entered the field. Rather than having to be equally slaves to bureaucratic constraints, the agency, from directors to the program officers, can turn their efforts to being problem solvers and witness actual accomplishment for the community/citizen/consumers.

Developing Strategies for Facilitation. As soon as possible, the agency should plan for outcome accomplishment instead of rule enforcement. By calling upon the staff themselves to develop these plans, the overall concept of personal creativity and transformation is carried forth throughout the system. Every effort must be made to break down the fears of job loss or threats to prestige as this transformation takes place. Agency staff must be encouraged to embrace the focus on outcomes. To be honest, this may not always happen since so many have been immersed in the bureaucratic mentality for so long. If all attempts to convert the agency staff member to the transformational model fail, then they must be encouraged to move on. This means early retirement or transfer to another agency should be encouraged. However, under no circumstances should anyone be removed or demoted as a punitive measure simply because they refuse to join the effort. This will only insert a potential saboteur into the system. There is every reason to believe that over time as the excitement of accomplishment spreads that even the most resistant will join. It may require patience and persistence, though.

In Collaboration with all levels of Management Develop Data Needs. This is the complement of the second recommendation for management. However, in addition to the data requirement system, agency staff should be anticipating how they may employ this data to encourage creativity and goal accomplishment. The responsibility is to help the entire system move away from the concept of data collection as a means of control. Instead, it should be used as a way to generate enthusiasm. This enthusiasm should be pushed outwards to providers and communities. One area of responsibility for state agencies that goes largely overlooked is the need to develop the public forum as well as citizen contribution to human service efforts. The sooner the communities are attracted to these programs and incorporated into the process of problem solving, the sooner the system is transformed from the state providing services to clients to the community addressing its own needs. Something as simple as using data appropriately can go far to generating this kind of energy.

Develop Resource Data Base. Through a supportive process, agency personnel should begin collecting information regarding resources available throughout the system. This will include identifying individuals with special skills that may be needed by others, facilities, equipment, and programs. Rather than emphasizing only the competitive nature of entrepreneurship, the agency can actually use this resource base as a means to encourage cooperation. Competition is actually overstated as it relates to entrepreneurship. The truly long-term successful organizations are those which have identified their strengths and cooperated with those which may alleviate their weaknesses. This may be especially the case in non-profit organizations in the world of human services. There should be no pretensions that no one suffers from so-called healthy competition. If a consumer is denied the opportunity to pursue an interest or enter a program that adds to their quality of life simply because one organization does not wish to give an edge to another, then everyone loses. The agency can add to its role as facilitator by identifying resources and referring any provider to another when a need arises. This truly shifts the emphasis to outcomes instead of organizational survival.

Seek Additional Training Funds. The agency can play a key role in implementing this outcome-based system by using their influence to secure funds for training of staff and management. The most important attribute that the Oregon DD Bureau contributes is the ample amount of funds for training. They have correctly understood that their greatest asset is in the management and staff. Investing resources into that asset can only yield high returns. These funds are not necessarily exclusively public. The agency should feel free to use their own development personnel to seek private contributions through corporations, foundations, and local efforts. This is a tremendous opportunity to become creative in a manner that facilitates the process and helps to solve another problem. It fits into the larger scheme of things since this transformation will necessarily require considerable training and development of staff. After all, the change involves a paradigm shift. This is not something that can be accomplished without considerable training and effort.

The Community Level

Community, of course, may be defined in many ways. With respect to this endeavor, all such meanings apply from the world community to the neighborhood. The community in question relies heavily on what outcome is being sought. Countering global warming is a world community issue. Trade relations require the cooperation of the international community. Health care may be both a national and a local concern. Just the same, it is necessary to describe some steps that will improve the overall success of communities in general. For the most part, it is reasonable to assume that issues should be addressed at the local level. Assuming that the basic construct of all things is appropriately seen in terms of fractals, it makes sense to seek out solutions at the local level, which in turn, brings about change at the global. In this regard, there are two key strategies which will initiate implementation of a Transformational system. First, changes made in organizations will stimulate the needed changes at all levels. Since we are an organizational species, it only makes sense to confront our many challenges by altering the way in which we organize. The second type of change will involve how we define problems. If organizations are to operate in an outcome centered manner, focusing on the pursuit of a set of values, then communities must be about the business of defining what the values are to be and how they are observed with respect to change. This brings us to an important concept that is gaining momentum in many sectors, sustainability index measurements.

While it is neither practical nor particularly appropriate to detail all the elements of sustainability indexes, it is necessary to describe in broad terms what they are and how they may be used. *Sustainable Community Indicators are a means for communities, individuals and organizations to state clearly what matter to them in the long run, and to measure actual progress toward sustainability as opposed to isolated social, economic, or environmental goals.* [3] It should be relatively easy to see how this fits into our new paradigm. If organizations and governments are to function based on values and outcomes, it is vital to be able to clearly define what they are. The use of sustainability indicators is the vehicle needed to accomplish this. There are a number of examples of this type of work available through a variety of sources, including:

- Sustainable measures: These measures are derived from a variety of economic, environmental and social sciences methodologies. Net energy analysis, ecological modeling, social indicators, ecological economic and other interdisciplinary ap-

proaches developed to measure various aspects of sustainable development.
- Ecological footprint: This is an innovation that is barely ten years old; it enables us to quantify our relationship with nature by computing the acres needed to support consumption. This effort is part of a worldwide movement to study Earth's total ecological capacity and humanity's long term prospects and quality of life. [4]
- Performance measurement: Largely found in the non-profit sector, performance measurement focuses on outcomes rather than process. Outcome measurement shifts the focus from activities to results, from how a program operates to the good it accomplishes. Information on the extent to which program participation is having the intended outcomes is powerful and useful feedback. [5]
- Indicators of sustainability and quality of life: Indicators to measure local sustainability or quality of life are now widely used throughout the United Kingdom. The purpose is to (1) identify to what extent and in what ways measurement influences decision-making and positive action towards sustainability; (2) increase understanding of why indicators are influential in some contexts and not in others; (3) identify a set of guiding principles for making measurement more influential in local government. [6]

There is a groundswell of these kinds of projects around the world. They involve a recognition that it is essential to identify, measure, and report on all endeavors in such a manner that are both sustainable and improve the quality of life. These should not be seen as some fringe effort by environmental groups or leftist political movements either. They are widely recognized as important efforts to change how we go about the business of development, governance, and planning. Alan Greenspan acknowledges the need for this work in a speech he gave to the Federal Reserve Systems' Community Affairs Research Conference:

> [I]t is important to establish formal procedures for program assessment. At the start of a program, the nature of the problem should be identified, as well as the presumptions of the various causes of that problem. With a clearer understanding of the issues, policymakers and community leaders are better able to devise a strategy for overcoming the problem. Finally, a well-constructed program must include a projection of its benefits to serve as a benchmark for later evaluation. [7]

These remarks attest to the fact that these efforts are already considered mainstream. There is no need to describe in detail how they are carried out since that is well documented. In order for any transformational strategies to succeed these kinds of projects are crucial. Any public leader is well-advised to seek out a model that works best for her/his community in order to develop the necessary outcomes and values to drive the needed reforms.

Summary and Conclusion

When this study began, I anticipated identifying some successful outcome-based programs and then adjusting them to existing systems. However, that did not turn out to be the case. Instead, I found many models but little success. This caused me to turn focus on analyzing what was obstructing the success of what makes so much sense. The use of outcome-based methods remains a key element of moving to a public entrepreneurship model. What I underestimated was the extent of the challenge. After considerable research and interviewing, I concluded that public administration had reached a point of profound importance. The time had actually come to discard the Rational paradigm and replace it with something that would allow us to move ahead. Perhaps some would suggest that this is a bit of overkill. However, the evidence is rather substantial that it is not. The level of frustration and cynicism being expressed by citizens, providers, clients, and bureaucrats themselves is intense enough that any reasonable person would assume something very fundamental is wrong.

Once I was convinced that such a dramatic transformation was necessary, I shifted the emphasis of this study a bit. Initially, the task was to design an outcome-based system and self monitoring mechanism. Realizing that even the best system would not survive because of the paradigmatic incongruence, I moved to describing the nature of this tension. The overview of outcome-based models gives enough to work with, that ultimately each organization or community should be able to develop their own system. This is particularly desirable since the models are situation specific as far as effectiveness is concerned. The strengths and weaknesses of these models also contribute to the ability to develop appropriate localized methods. The steps toward establishing a system are more than adequately formulated by others so there is really no need for me to add to them. The pivotal discovery was through observation of the experiences of other states. It became clear that rebureaucratization was the likely result unless something else was done.

In the beginning, the general concept of the need for a shift in paradigm was presented. This demonstrated more the nature and extent of the incongruence than anything else. The fact remained that something very essential was interfering with success. After all, common sense would seem to dictate that outcome-based programs would be an improvement over bureaucratic, process centered programs. Through this discussion, I trust that I made the case that the greater need was to shift paradigms in order to move to this more sensible strategy. I then moved to the discussion of the paradigm challenge in much more detail. First, the focus was on the nature of the Rational Model from its fundamental base and how this ran contrary to the desire to focus on outcomes. Then the challenges that the Rational Model has undergone over the years were described to demonstrate that the paradigm has not been without its difficulties. Using two of the more significant challenges, quantum mechanics and relativity, I argued that even some of the basic elements of the model were questioned. The paradigm survived though by making some basic adjustments to allow for these factors. The conviction of the general population that the Rational Model is real remained intact, however. This is crucial to understanding how it has become so powerful in our social expectations, particularly in our commitment to the bureaucratic ethos (despite our denials.)

Then I elected to be so bold as to propose an alternative model. This is drawn from an increasingly popular concept called Chaos Theory. Basically, chaos theory has evolved within the fields of physics, biology, and ecology. Its fundamental tenets are that order comes forth from chaos and not as its opposite. All systems contain elements of turbulence. Through this turbulence all systems drive toward disequilibrium until bifurcations begin to shake the system itself apart. As the bifurcations accelerate, a chaotic episode ensues resulting in a transformed system. This indicates that systems are designed to evolve not through natural selection but by essential intent. The other prominent aspect of the chaos paradigm is that all systems are composed of fractals, which are basically the smallest units which contain all of the features of the larger system. The lowest fractal units are where the transformation takes place since they contain the turbulent energies.

The Chaos Model was then applied to the area of human organizations to demonstrate how this philosophical base alters the way such systems work. This suggested that the best way to transform the human organization from bureaucratic to outcome-based was to operate under the Chaos paradigm. The change would be from one which discourages creativity to one that thrives on it. It would also place more responsibility for accomplishment at the individual level. It creates an environment that returns humans to the human organizations in that they are permitted to take risk and then to learn from the experience. The focus shifts from deficiency to capacity. The creative forces are expanded since the entire organization, not just those at the top are charged with being problem solvers. By placing the creative process at the lowest fractal level, the forces of turbulence are allowed to pursue transformation with the least amount of disruption.

Finally, drawing from the application of the Chaos Model to human organizations, a set of recommendations is offered. One level of change must occur at the organizational level. These recommendations are collected under three points of contact: individual staff, management, and agency. This is done because under the current conditions, each of these groups has different needs in order to move to the new paradigm. The individual staff need to learn how to be creative risk-takers who take more personal responsibility for accomplishment of tasks and who learn from problems rather than avoiding them. Management needs more flexibility in order to move resources, including personnel, to achieve the greatest level of accomplishment. They also need to be incorporated into the system in a collegial manner. Agencies need to learn to become facilitators and cheerleaders rather than rule enforcers. The other level of change is found in the development of sustainability measures of various kinds. These indicators can then be used to establish desired outcomes and values to be served.

All of these changes are genuinely revolutionary in so many ways. However, that does not mean that they are not achievable. Quite the opposite is true, unless these kinds of essential changes are undertaken, the system will continue to drive itself to a chaotic episode that will be much more disruptive. This is a call for unleashing the creative energy and transformational force that is much more natural for human beings than the artificial boundaries imposed by the Rational Model. Through these kinds of adjustments at the organizational and community level, the proper role of government may be reestablished. Even more importantly, the members of the community may be reconnected because they are tied to both the process and the outcomes being sought.

---

1. Bridges, William, *Transitions: Making Sense of Life's Changes*, 2nd ed,(New York: Addison-Wesley, 2004).
2. Chell, E. (2004) Critical Incident Technique. In, Cassell, Catherine and Symon, Gillian (eds.), *Essential Guide to Qualitative Methods in Organisation Studies.* (London, UK: Sage), 45-60.
3. Communicas, *Strategy, Communications and Brokering for Sustainable Development*, (Louisville: Imagine America, 2003).
4. Hancock, Ann, *Report on the Sonoma County Ecological Footprint Project*, (Sustainable Sonoma County, Sebastopol, CA, 2002).
5. Plantz, Margaret C., Martha Taylor Greenway, and Michael Hendricks, *Outcome Measurement: Showing Results in the Nonprofit Sector,* (Outcome Measurement Resource Network, United Way of America: Alexandria, VA, 2002).
6. Sommer, Florian, *Making Indicators Count: Making Measurement of Quality of Life More Influential in Local Governance*, (Bristol, England: New Economics Foundation, 2002)
7. Greenspan, Alan, "Remarks at the Federal Reserve System's Community Affairs Research Conference," *Sustainable Community Development: What Works, What Doesn't, and Why*, (Washington, D.C.: March 28, 2003).

Index

Accreditation Council (AC), 55
Administration Period, 52
Administrative Management Period, 52
Age of Reason, 25
Aid to Families with Dependent
 Children (AFDC), 50, 71
Annual Performance Review, 148
Babbie, Earl, 59
Bargaining/negotiation/mutual
 cooptation, 123
Barnard, Chester, 52
Baudrillard, Jean, 29
Benefit-assessment, 122
Bronowski, Jacob, 16, 144
Brownlow Committee, 53
bureaucracy,2, 8, 9, 10, 12, 15, 16,
 17,18, 19, 20, 23,31, 34, 37, 49, 50,
 63, 64, 83, 114, 116, 125, 126, 152
Bush Administration, 49
Chaos Theory, 131, 135, 136, 158
Civil War, 98
civitas, 14, 22
Clinton administration,32, 71, 120, 127
commodified, 25
Community Facilities Districts, 123
Consumer and Family Quality
 Measures, 55
Consumer-Centered/Empowerment, 33
Contracted Services, 21
Contracting out, 122
Coproduction, 121
Co-provision, 121
Cowden, Anne, 117, 119
Cutback management, 119
Deer Lodge County, incident in, 64
Deinstitutionalization, 31
Deleuze, Baudrillard, 29
Deleuze, Gilles, 29
Deming, W. Edwards, 32, 58
Denhardt, Janet and Robert B., 34, 116
Downs, Anthony, 10, 79
Drucker, Peter, 80
Durkheim, Emile, 101
Ecological footprint, 155
Emphasis on Quality, 32
Enactment theory, 89
Enterprise zones, 122
Entrepreneurship, 120
Etzioni, Amitai, 108
External mechanisms, 122
Federalist Papers, 99

Feidler, Fred E., 38, 42
Fisher, P.S., 111
Flexible human resources, 121
Ford Motor Co, 18
fractal, 134, 141, 145, 158
Franchise arrangement, 122
Frederickson, H. George, 53
Future Shock, 145
Gaebler, Ted, 80, 116, 120
Gore, Al, 32
Gulick, Luther, 52
Hawthorne Effect, 81
Henry, Nicholas, 51
Homeland Security, Department of, 10,
 117, 118
Human Relations School, 53
Hummel, Ralph, 18
Hurricane Katrina, 9
hyperreality, 28, 29
Index of Sustainable Economic
 Welfare, 127
Indicators of sustainability and quality
 of life, 156
Individual Program Plans (IPP), 62, 82
Individual Service Plans (ISPs), 34
Industrial Age, 18
Industrial era, 49
Innovative budgeting, 121
Interagency Task Force on
 Developmental Disabilities, 31
Intermediate Care Facilities for the
 Mentally Retarded (ICF/MR),36, 44
Internal mechanisms, 121
International Business Machines
 (IBM), 18
Intrapreneuring, 121
Investment approaches, 123
Job Expectation Agreements, 148, 151
Kanter, Rosabeth Moss, 94
Kirlin, John, 117, 119, 124, 129
Kretzmann, John P., 101
Kuhn, Thomas, 14, 26, 143
Landlord Association, 107
language games, 28
Lanterman Developmental Disabilities
 Services Act, 62
Levine, Charles, 110
Likert scale, 102
Lindblom, Charles, 66, 128
Load shedding, 119
MacIntyre, Alasdair, 1

Index

Managed Care, 35
Management (Star of David organization), 151
Management by Objectives, 54
Management Science Period, 53
March, James G., 53
Marketing of public services, 123
McCain-Feingold bill, 118
McKnight, John L., 25, 101, 106
McVeigh, Timothy, 5
Medicaid, 36
Mitroff, Ian, 38, 40
Mitroff, Ian, 40
Montana Freemen, 5
Montana Institute on disAbilities,15, 27
National Aeronautics and Space Administration (NASA), 63
National Performance Review, 32, 49, 120, 127
Neighborhood Living Project, 55, 59, 60, 75, 76, 77, 152
New Public Service, 34, 35, 64
Newton, Isaac, 143
NIMBY, 8
non-government organizations (NGOs),32
Nunn, Senator Sam, 6
O'Brien, John, 24, 27, 80, 86
Obama administration, 1, 108
Oberly, Nicholas, 29
Occupational Safety and Health Administration (OSHA), 65
Osborne, David, 80, 116, 120
Paradigm Systems, Inc, 58
Paradigmatic shift, 144
path dependence, 87
Pay-for-Performance systems, 121
Performance Management Period, 54
Performance measurement, 156
Perrow, Charles, 38
Pfeffer, Jeffery, 92
Pollister, Barbara, 56
POSDCORB, 52
Power from within, 95
Power over, 95
Power with, 95
Private enterprise, 18, 19
Professional Career System Period, 53
Programming, Budgeting, Systems (PPBS), 53
Proposition 13, 60, 67, 71, 108, 110, 115, 119, 139

Proposition 4, 120
Public Cooperatives, 20
public entrepreneurship, 32, 63, 116, 117, 120, 124, 125, 126, 127, 157
Public Health and Human Services, Department of, 57, 64
Public Health and Human Services, Montana Department of (DPHHS),57
Public/Private partnership, 120
Public/Private sector competition, 122
Reagan administration, 108, 112
Rebureaucratization, 83
Reform Period, 52
Regulatory and tax incentives, 123
Rehabilitation Accreditation Commission (CARF), 55
Rehfuss, John, 112
Residential Outcomes System, 59, 76
Retrenchment, 120
Savas, E. S., 112
Scientific Management, 37, 52
Self Monitoring, 150
Senior Executive Service, 54
Simons, Herbert, 53
Small business incubators, 122
Sociological institutionalism, 87
Spencer, Donald, 100
Star of David organization, 142, 143
Strauss, 61, 82
Subsidy arrangement, 123
Sundram, Clarence J., 30
Survey Guides for Individual Service Plans, 55
Sustainable measures, 155
SWOT, 73
Systems and Organizational Culture, 54
Task Environment, 36
Taylor, Frederick W., 52
Term limits, 5
Thompson, James D., 53, 92
Total Quality Management (TQM), 32, 58, 75
turbulence, 132, 134, 135, 137, 138, 139, 140, 144, 145, 146, 158
Urwick, Lyndall, 52
User charges or fees, 122
Valued Outcomes Information System (VOIS), 59
Virtual agreement, 35
Volunteers/Fundraisers/Citizen Bureaucrats, 121

voter initiated fiscal limits, 113
Vouchers, 123
Weber, Max, 16, 49
Weick, K.E., 89
Welfare State, 25
widgetize, 75, 85
Willoughby, W. F., 52
Wilson, Woodrow, 51
Wittgenstein, Luwig, 28
Woolsey, D., 111
Zero-Based Budgeting, 54

Biography

Dr. Edgar received his BA in History/Political Science and Master of Public Administration degrees from the University of Montana, a Master of Divinity degree from the Franciscan School of Theology in Berkeley, CA, and his Doctor of Public Administration from the University of Southern California. He has worked for a variety of agencies including the Department of the Navy, the Veterans Administration, and Dawson Community College in eastern Montana. He operated his own consulting firm for over 20 years, providing services to state agencies and local governments throughout the Northwest. Consulting projects spanned a wide variety of topics from housing studies and plans, and citizen satisfaction surveys to morale interventions and an analysis of administrative strategies.

Dr. Edgar is currently the Director of the Master of Public Administration program and an Assistant Professor at Southern Arkansas University. He lives with his daughter and three of his seven grandchildren in Magnolia.